RETHINKING FEMINIST ETHICS

The question of whether there can be distinctively female ethics is one of the most important and controversial debates in current gender studies, philosophy and psychology. *Rethinking Feminist Ethics: Care, Trust and Empathy* marks a bold intervention in these debates by bridging the ground between women theorists disenchanted with aspects of traditional 'male' ethics and traditional theorists who insist upon the need for some ethical principles. Daryl Koehn provides one of the first critical overviews of a wide range of alternative female/feminist/feminine ethics defended by influential theorists such as Carol Gilligan, Annette Baier, Nel Noddings and Diana Meyers. She shows why these ethics in their current form are not defensible and proposes a radically new alternative.

In the first section, Koehn identifies the major tenets of ethics of care, trust and empathy. She provides a lucid, searching analysis of why female ethics emphasize a relational, rather than individualistic, self and why they favor a more empathic, less rule-based, approach to human interactions. At the heart of the debate over alternative ethics is the question of whether female ethics of care, trust and empathy constitute a realistic, practical alternative to the rule-based ethics of Immanuel Kant, John Stuart Mill and John Rawls. Koehn concludes that they do not. Female ethics are plagued by many of the same problems they impute to 'male' ethics, including a failure to respect other individuals. In particular, female ethics favor the perspective of the caregiver, trustor and empathizer over the viewpoint of those who are on the receiving end of care, trust and empathy. She argues instead for a radically new dialogical ethic that preserves the important insights of female ethics while making them more defensible and practical. Drawing on Plato's dialogue *Crito*, Koehn demonstrates how a principled, dialogical ethic can instil a critical respect for the view of the other without slipping into moral relativism.

Rethinking Feminist Ethics provides a much-needed overview of the debates concerning female ethics and proposes a refreshing new alternative ethic. It will be of interest to all those concerned with ethical issues in gender studies, philosophy, psychology and politics.

Daryl Koehn is Wicklander Chair of Professional Ethics at DePaul University, Chicago. She is the author of *The Ground of Professional Ethics* (Routledge).

RETHINKING FEMINIST ETHICS

Care, trust and empathy

Daryl Koehn

London and New York

First published 1998
by Routledge
11 New Fetter Lane, London EC4P 4EE

Simultaneously published in the USA and Canada
by Routledge
29 West 35th Street, New York, NY 10001

© 1998 Daryl Koehn

Typeset in Times by Routledge
Printed and bound in Great Britain by
Creative Print and Design (Wales) Ebbw Vale

British Library Cataloguing in Publication Data
A catalogue record for this book is available from the British Library

Library of Congress Cataloguing in Publication Data
Rethinking feminist ethics: care, trust and empathy/Daryl Koehn.
Includes bibliographical references and index.
1. Feminist ethics. 2. Caring. 3. Dialogue. I. Title.
BJ1395.K64 1998
97–52282
170′.82–dc21
CIP

ISBN 0–415–18032–5 (hbk)
ISBN 0–415–18033–3 (pbk)

FOR ALL WHO LISTEN WITH
A DIFFERENT EAR

CONTENTS

ACKNOWLEDGMENTS

I am indebted to a number of friends and colleagues for reading and commenting on various drafts of this manuscript. I offer a warm and heartfelt thank you to: Peg Birmingham, Jason Drucker, Elisabeth Hoppe, Karen Kapner Hyman, Sanni Sivula Judy, Beverly Kracher, Pam Maben, Gary Mauschardt, Michael Naas, Astrida Tantillo, Jane Uebelhoer and Tama Weisman. Neil Luebke and Laura Pincus offered useful criticisms on several earlier articles I wrote on care and trust. I also benefited from the criticisms of several readers who read the manuscript I submitted to Routledge. The questions and objections of all these people helped to shape ideas that found their way into this book. Conversations with John Cornell disclosed whole new avenues for thinking about the value and importance of dialogue. Rebecca Roberts McCarthy deserves a special thank you for her help in editing the manuscript.

I am extremely grateful to the University Research Council at DePaul University for helping to fund both the research for this book and the production of the manuscript and for allowing me a year's research leave in 1995–6 to write the book.

Finally, I owe a special debt to the Routledge staff: Lisa Blackwell, Tony Bruce, Emma Davis, Adrian Driscoll, Anna Gerber, Wendy Lees, and Melissa Weatherly. Their good sense and professionalism made it a joy to work with them.

INTRODUCTION

According to Greek legend, the earth mother Demeter had a much beloved daughter Persephone. The young Persephone caught the eye of Hades, ruler of the dark underworld of the dead. Hades persuaded Zeus to decree that Hades could take Persephone as his wife. So one day while Persephone was engrossed staring at a narcissus, Hades came up from below and seized upon her, taking her back to his underworld domain. Demeter was distraught when she could not discover what had happened to her daughter. She sought for news of Persephone until she learned that Zeus had sanctioned Hades' seizure of her daughter. Demeter persuaded Zeus to return her daughter to her. Her request was partially granted. Persephone was permitted to live six months of the year with Demeter while spending the remainder of the year in the underworld.

This myth has become something of a rallying cry for women thinkers who are dissatisfied with the tenets of traditional ethics.[1] Although much of this dissatisfaction is well grounded, I shall argue that the alternative ethics offered by women ethicists are fraught with substantial difficulties of their own. Some of these difficulties become readily apparent in the way in which the Demeter myth has been used. On the one hand, women ethicists interpret the myth as a defense of the human practice of caring for and empathizing with particular individuals. Demeter loves her daughter deeply and is willing to fight to preserve her connection with Persephone. She imaginatively re-creates Persephone's loneliness and is determined that her daughter not slip away into darkness and be forgotten. The tale appears to portray the goodness of caring for particular people and of imaginatively entering into their situation.

So read, the myth stands as an important corrective to the focus of ethics offered by most male philosophers. These "male" ethics have tended to downplay or even deny the value of intimate, particular relations, focussing instead upon relations and actions in accordance with universalizable maxims for action. By contrast, women thinkers, like Carol Gilligan, Nel Noddings, Annette Baier, and Diana Meyers, would have us attend more closely to the dynamics of family relations and friendships. These relations are quite fluid and often both presuppose and require a trust and imaginative engagement for which there are no rules. It is hard to see, therefore, how the traditional strategy of modeling human behavior

1

by specifying systems of rules for human interactions will apply to much of what goes on within families and friendships. Yet there certainly are morally good and bad ways to act within these relations. Indeed, how we treat strangers in the political realm would seem to depend at least partially on whether we have learned from intimates what it means to truly respect, trust and appreciate another human being. It is no accident that, according to the myth, the world at large falls into disarray when Demeter's bond with her daughter is severed. Caring for particular people and caring for the world as a whole are intertwined.

Women theorists also would have us attend to Demeter's plight, a plight suffered by many women. In a world in which men (e.g. Zeus and Hades) have most of the power, including the power to devise theories declaring what counts as a moral action, women's desires and forms of action frequently get ignored. Zeus and Hades do not even consider how Demeter and Persephone may feel about the bargain the two male gods strike. In a sense, the myth re-enacts what is presently the case: it is not so much that Persephone disappears into the dark realm of Hades but that both she and Demeter are *already* in the dark, invisible to the men who are ruling the world.

As Carol Gilligan and Annette Baier have argued, men model those relations with which they are most familiar and comfortable. These relations have tended to be arms'-length relations with colleagues and strangers governed by certain rules and conventions that may work well for a men's club but that do not work at all for relations with children, the very old, or the especially vulnerable. Under the influence of Western scientific methodologies,[2] male psychologists and philosophers have argued for a quasi-mathematical form of ethical reasoning. In these "male" schemes, ethical reasoning qualifies as mature only if it decides ethical dilemmas by employing universal principles and appealing to a hierarchy of rights in which some rights trump others.[3] Ethical reasoning is not distinguished by any effort at consultation with others but rather by a desire to state, defend and apply universal principles. "Ethical reasoning" gets identified with one particular sort of thinking about human actions—namely, a principled, universalistic mode of reasoning. This identification proves problematic for women who, according to many women philosophers and psychiatrists, favor a more consultative form of deliberation. Women treat situations and human character as fluid, paying attention to parties' feelings and struggling to find some resolution of dilemmas acceptable to all parties. From the standpoint of male ethical theories, women's reasoning appears to be ethically undeveloped, and women themselves immature and childlike.[4]

By implication, the desires and thinking of these "immature" women do not need to be taken as seriously as that of principle-using men who are fully ethical and autonomous. Furthermore, to the extent these traditional male ethics are largely self-contained and closed systems, those who subscribe to them have no reason to reassess their position and to seek to uncover any possible strengths of this more inclusive form of reasoning. Consequently, these systems not only relegate women to the position of second-class, ethical citizens but also make it very difficult for women to appeal or contest this judgment of them.[5] Women are thus doubly silenced. In terms of the Greek myth, Demeter and Persephone are first ignored, as if they were dead; and then they are judged by Hades—ruler of the dead—in such a manner as to insure their voices will not be heard in the future.

The Demeter myth is highly suggestive, and the interpretation women philosophers have offered of it is plausible. Nevertheless, we should remember that myths are symbolic narratives, not position papers. Part of the power of myths lies in their ability to reveal the dark side or shadow of various human practices. The Demeter myth is no exception. It discloses a dark, less positive dimension to caring, empathy and trust, a shadow side largely overlooked by many women philosophers who defend these practices. It is my contention that this blind spot leads these theorists to defend female ethics that reproduce the same violence, silencing, and manipulation they discern in the "male" ethics of Immanuel Kant, John Rawls, and John Stuart Mill.

For example, it clearly is possible for people to care too much. A desire to preserve relations with the child may lead a parent to be over-involved in the child's life and to deny the child sufficient scope to exercise her own discretion. Growth and development involve separation as well as connectedness. In many versions of the myth, Persephone *chooses* to remain separate from her mother. Zeus decreed that Persephone could return to Demeter only if she refuses all food. Persephone opts to eat some pomegranate seeds, providing nurturance for herself. We could read the myth as pointing to the importance of breaking ties with an overly-protective parent, ties which are not giving one the "food" one needs. Persephone returns to her mother for part of the year, but is able to do so on her terms. In fact, the whole myth can be read as a metaphor for the process of organic growth. The seed or offspring of the parent (Persephone) must separate from the parent organism (Demeter) and fall into the fertile earth (Hades). The seed lies dormant for a period in the furrow, drawing strength and sustenance from earth (Hades is also known as Pluto, derived from the Greek word for "wealth"). Only after this time is the organism able to bloom forth into the daylight and to lead a healthy, independent existence.

We should also ponder the myth's not so subtle hint that women's "caring" and violence may go hand in hand. Noddings and Gilligan either forget or gloss over the fact that Demeter is so angered by the loss of her daughter that she attempts to kill all living things on the face of the earth in retaliation. Demeter is so convinced of the rightness of her own caring that she will brook no opposition to her will. She is going to rescue her daughter at all costs, even though it is far from clear that Persephone wants to be rescued. To the extent that an ethic of care or empathy provides no incentive to self-reflection, the caregiver may easily slip into a self-righteous anger. Care (trust, empathy, etc.) and manipulation are not necessarily mutually exclusive. What appears to an empathic trustor as a "betrayal" may be a healthy distancing in the eyes of the person who is resistant to the other's care or trust.

This book examines the ethics of care, trust and empathy defended by Carol

Gilligan, Nel Noddings, Annette Baier, Trudy Govier, and Diana Meyers. These so-called "female"/"feminist" ethics articulate many important insights, some of which I will develop at length. However, these ethics are riddled with problems, not the least of which is a marked tendency to reproduce the rigidity and insensitivity to difference that they attribute to "male" impartialist ethics of principle. This book tries to rethink key insights of female ethics in such a way as to make them more defensible. In order to be defensible, female ethics must become more dialogical. That is, these ethics must provide some space in which people who are on the receiving end of care or trust or empathy (i.e. what the caregiver, trustor or empathizer thinks of as such) can contest effectively the caregiver's, trustor's or empathizer's expectations. Providing for such a space turns out to require certain principles. Although these principles take a very different form from those employed in traditional ethics, they are principles nonetheless. The contrast between "principled" male and "consultative" female ethics is not, therefore, as clear-cut as some women philosophers seem to think. A defensible ethic requires elements from both male and female ethics.

Before sketching this rethinking of female ethics in more detail, I need to say a word about my usage of the controversial expression "female ethics." I want as well to outline in more detail what I take to be a number of the key, shared tenets and commitments of women ethicists who argue for a departure from traditional male ethics.[6] Such an overview will help to convey a sense of what exactly is at stake in the currently raging debate over the relative merits of male and female ethics. In addition, since the ethical approach I defend in the latter portion of the book has many affinities with female ethics and aims at incorporating their insights in a more defensible form, I want to be clear early on as to what I take to be the core concerns of female ethics.

A note on usage

For purposes of this analysis, I group the various ethics being offered by women philosophers under the single rubric "female" ethics. Since these ethics are being portrayed as a diametrically opposed alternative to the "male" ethics prominent in a philosophical tradition dominated by men, they are appropriately described by the opposite of "male"—"female." Some women ethicists have argued for a further distinction. They contend we should distinguish between "feminine" (or female) and "feminist" ethics.[7] "Feminine" ethics describe and celebrate the form of reasoning many modern women employ, often focussing on the way women speak and behave in their marriages, their friendships and their relations with their children. Since some of these *status quo* relations are unjust, feminine ethics may perpetuate inadvertently prejudicial societal norms regarding what is "feminine." Feminists fear ethics of care and trust will assign women to an all too "familiar ghetto rather than a liberated space."[8] What is needed, therefore, are more explicitly liberationist ethics by women for women. Like feminine ethics, these "feminist" ethics reject traditional male reasoning; but, unlike feminine ethics, they take their bearings from an overarching commitment to freeing women from unhealthy relations, detrimental stereotypes and debilitating norms of a patriarchal society.[9]

The feminists' point is well taken. Many of the criticisms advanced by self-described feminists such as Claudia Card, Linda Bell and Sarah Hoagland are quite cogent; and I develop and refine some of their concerns in subsequent chapters. However, I think that ultimately it is not possible to draw a hard and fast distinction between "feminine" and "feminist" ethics. A "feminine" ethicist such as Nel Noddings clearly has as one of her aims the liberation of women from stultifying strictures of traditional ethics advanced by men. Furthermore, the differences between the feminine and feminist ethicists are less significant than the large number of similarities. Many of the serious reservations and objections I want to raise apply to so-called "feminine" and "feminist" ethics alike. Therefore, for purposes of this analysis, I shall treat both under the rubric of "female" ethics.

Central tenets and concerns of female ethics

That said, I turn now to what I take to be the key tenets or features of female ethics. I take a "female ethicist" to be any theorist who subscribes to all or most of these tenets. Women who adopt a more traditional approach to ethics thus would not qualify as female ethicists. Conversely, male philosophers or theorists who make these claims *in principle* could qualify as female ethicists. However, precisely because most men have not had the experience of finding their experiences excluded from philosophical discussions and of having their voices silenced, they have not been led, as women have, to argue for the claims discussed below. Nor have they been inclined to bring the experiences of women to the foreground of their arguments. So, *as a matter of fact*, there are few, if any, men doing female ethics in the sense in which I am employing this term.[10]

Feature 1: the relational self

The female ethicist takes the self to be relational, rather than discretely individualistic.[11] Some female ethics go so far as to claim that the self *is* a relation.[12] While this last claim is somewhat extreme, female ethics in general stress the fact of human interdependence. Despite Hobbes' assertion to the contrary, human beings do not spring up like mushrooms.[13] The fiction of a totally self-contained agent may be useful for some legal and political purposes. If we are not careful, however, we will come to think it a weakness to be unable to live a totally self-sufficient life devoid of emotional attachments. We will forget that human beings must be born and then nurtured if they are to survive and that there is often strength in interdependence. As we age, we depend upon family and friends to help us execute various plans and to aid us when we fall ill. Even during our prime, we must trust in others' good will (or at least in the absence of malice) if we are to thrive. Human beings are thoroughly embedded in a host of involuntary, as well as voluntary, supportive social relations through which we define ourselves.

Feature 2: benevolent concern for the vulnerable

Given that the self is thoroughly relational, relations between the parent–child (particularly the caring mother and her child) or among friends are appropriate paradigms for thinking about the character of ethically good behavior of human selves. Granted, there are difficulties with these paradigms. The relation between parent and child is not an equal one and may prove misleading as a model for human relations in general. Furthermore, not every woman is a mother. She is, however, a daughter. So perhaps it would be better, as some have argued, to examine what it means to be a good daughter.[14] These skirmishes aside, female ethicists agree that intimate relations constitute an important part of human life. They serve as better models for thinking about what is involved in the good life, more so than contractual relations between voluntarily consenting strangers. The legalistic contractual thinking, so favored in traditional analyses, may alienate persons, rather than draw them together.[15] The legalistic approach also ignores the large portion of the population who either have not yet reached adulthood or who have become mentally or physically incapacitated. Male ethics, stressing individual freedom and arms'-length relations with others, usually impose minimal duties of benevolence upon agents. Female ethics, by contrast, argue for something like a duty to care for and to empathize with these vulnerable members of our community.[16]

Feature 3: the publicness of the private

It should be clear from Features 1 and 2 that female ethics treat the so-called "private" realm of familial and household relations as being of public significance. Persons who learn to trust and care within the realm of the home bring these virtues with them into public life as well. Conversely, failures in nurturance often lead to violence inside and outside the home. An angry son may become a bellicose man in a position of power who has little capacity to feel for and to respect other people.[17] No community can afford to be indifferent to this violence. Yet the ethical tradition has been insufficiently attentive to child nurturance and education. Philosophers have become fixated on the problem of defining the idea of a right, defending the existence of particular rights, grounding these rights and identifying the correlative duties. Since rights must be enforceable; and since the law is the preferred enforcement mechanism, the rights-based approach to ethics has tended to reduce all ethical issues to quasi-legal ones. Since legal obligations are often of only the most minimal sort, this reduction impoverishes our ethical world.[18]

Female ethicists regard our ethical obligations as more extensive and perhaps demanding than our legal ones. Our children do not have a *right* to our love, given that love does not seem to be an activity or emotion that can be produced upon command. On the other hand, we think good parents are those who love their children and are willing to devote years of their lives to rearing good children.[19] Friendship, too, seems misconceived in terms of rights and duties.[20] When my sick friend thanks me for visiting her in the hospital, it seems perverse to respond: "Yes, I did so out of my sense of duty to be benevolent." It could be argued that my friend's thank you is spontaneous gratitude for an equally generous gesture on my part originating in a free love for my particular friend, not in some perception of a duty I might have felt toward any sick human being. The language of care and love seems more appropriate when discussing our relations with intimates who are often needy and vulnerable.

Feature 4: the importance and value of difference

Female ethicists are wary of rights- or duty-based ethics (e.g. those offered by Kant, Rawls, Nozick) for a second reason as well. These ethics tend to try to deduce maxims of action from a set of logically consistent principles and to specify a hierarchy of rights in which some rights "trump" other rights. The belief in the system's objectivity often precludes listening well to persons with different perspectives. "Male" ethics often presuppose or posit a completely impartial "rational" or "prudent" person who is alleged to be representative of all members of the political community.[21] Anyone who fails to agree may be dismissed as "irrational" or "immature" in ethical development. Female ethics, by contrast, take respect for and attentiveness to possible difference, instead of formal consistency, to be a hallmark of ethical maturity. Female ethics see no particular virtue in consistency, given that an agent could be a perfectly consistent racist. Respect for difference, however, *is* ethically important. Without respect for difference, we paradoxically tend to lose any sense of the personal *individuality* that makes each of us so special and which the male ethicist would have us respect. Marilyn Friedman makes the point quite nicely:

> Indeed, there is an apparent irony in the notion of personhood which underlies some philosophers' conceptions of the universalized moral duties owed to all persons. The rational nature which Kant, for example, takes to give each person dignity and to make each of absolute value and, therefore, irreplaceable, is no more than an abstract rational nature in virtue of which we are all alike. But if we are all alike in this respect, it is hard to understand why we would be irreplaceable. Our common rational nature would seem to make us indistinguishable and, therefore, mutually interchangeable. Specific identity would be a matter of indifference, so far as absolute value is concerned. Yet it would seem that only in *virtue* of our distinctive particularity could we each be truly irreplaceable.[22]

Seyla Benhabib takes the point still further. If we do not have discrete individuals, then we cannot, she argues, logically speak of persons as being "interchangeable." Male ethics treats as moral only those choices and policies that

7

we would endorse were we to change positions with other people affected by these choices. But such interchangeability presupposes identifiable, discrete individuals who can exchange positions. If we cease to think of persons as distinguished by their various histories and interests, there are no discrete persons to adopt one another's point of view.[23]

Feature 5: emphasis on imaginative discourse

Male ethics stress deductive reasoning as the hallmark of ethical reasoning. These ethics would have us derive our duties from the Kantian categorical imperative, from a state of nature, or from some other original position. While female ethicists do argue for their ethic, they highlight the importance that imagination plays in our ability to relate to our fellow human beings and in our characterization of the various practical problems and choices we daily confront.[24] In particular, imagination plays a large role in the female ethics' virtues of care, trust, and empathy, all virtues (or quasi-virtues) largely overlooked by previous ethics. Female ethicists think that we should not assume away difference by positing a *typical* community member. For female ethicists, the ethical and political problem is largely one of achieving sufficient imaginative insight into the perspectives of persons with experiences and commitments different from our own to be able to undertake joint actions and to form mutually beneficial relations.[25] By repressing difference, male ethics assume away the ethical problem.

Female ethics are sometimes described as "discursive ethics."[26] This characterization is apt. Women theorists suspect ethics derived from some theoretically objective, impartial point of view and emphasize instead the importance of talking with particular persons who have a history and who are facing some highly contextual dilemma or choice.[27] We are to listen to their stories and attempt to negotiate with them to arrive, if at all possible, at a course all affected parties find acceptable. Making sure that conditions for discourse are such that conversants are equal participants becomes every bit as important, if not more so, than spelling out the allegedly objective form ethical reasoning must assume in order to be ethical.[28]

Feature 6: making a difference by changing the world

Having themselves suffered the experience of having their ethical concerns ignored or dismissed as "irrational," female ethicists are very attuned to power dynamics within communities.[29] We are always already living in some historically conditioned community in which people have vested interests in trying to preserve their positions, status, and income. To assume a clean slate—a state of nature prior to society or some original position in which people are divorced from an outlook thoroughly influenced by class, gender, wealth, and a host of other factors—risks ignoring the very real practical difficulties faced by women, the poor, persons of color, recent immigrants, etc. Any ethic worthy of our trust

8

ought to at least try to grapple with the problem of power differentials within the community whom it addresses.[30] An ethic cannot lead to the good life unless it speaks to persons' lived lives; female ethics attempt to be more realistic by beginning with the "situated" character of agents' lives.[31]

Since we are historical creatures who live in a history made by human beings, it follows that we can change the world in which we live out our lives. Our world, then, should not be viewed as a static given. We make the world in which we act, sense and love through our actions. Like the existentialists before them, female ethicists assign a tremendous power to reform. If our actions make the world, then we can act to change the very conditions under which we love, laugh, trust, work. We can bring a caring and trusting world into existence through acts of caring and trusting.[32]

The distinctiveness of female ethics

These are serious claims. Indeed, I suspect that precisely because these claims are quite important, others have begun to busy themselves with denying that those who advance female ethics have anything unique to say. Everything worth saying has already been covered, we are told, by male theorists. After all, existential ethics celebrate the creative power of human action. Aristotelian virtue ethics focus on human development, embedding human beings squarely within the communal or "relational" realm. What is more, virtue ethics question the possibility of an impartial spectator who is able to represent all persons. For a thinker like Aristotle, the perspectives of the vicious and virtuous human beings are in critical ways incommensurable and therein lies the ethical problem.[33] The philosopher Mill champions the value of human individuality in various works.[34] Kant understands full well that any social contract theory already must presuppose the social relations it is meant to ground.[35] He thus anticipates the female ethics' critique of contract theory by 150 years. Furthermore, the Kantian duty of benevolence binds us to look after the vulnerable to the extent that it is feasible and wise to do so. Professional ethics, too, direct our attention to the more marginal members of society. Indeed, these ethics (e.g. medical, legal, ministerial) have been thought to derive their distinctive character from their insistence upon putting the sick, spiritually troubled, or accused at the moral center of the professional–client relation.[36] Professional ethics have already been very far down the path now being traveled by female ethics.

Some portions of the critique unquestionably have been anticipated by others. Still, while certain strands of female ethics do appear in other thinkers, no other ethic weaves together all of the strands I have identified as being characteristic of female ethics. Moreover, female ethics derive much of their significance and poignancy from women theorists insisting upon placing *the experience and reasoning of women as related in their own voices* at the forefront of their analysis.[37] While this reasoning does not become ethically sound simply by virtue of coming out of a woman's mouth, any ethic making pronouncements about how *all* human beings should reason and act would do well to consider objections actual human beings might raise to these injunctions. Suppressing, ignoring or devaluing the opinions of half of the human race seems unjust and foolhardy as well as logically inconsistent.

Female ethics try to correct this deficiency, in part, by listening to women. As Virginia Held puts it, no other ethics "have paid remotely adequate attention to the experience of women."[38] It is true that other theorists have written on empathy and care and on the unwise neglect of these activities. Willard Gaylin, Milton Mayeroff, and Robert Goodin all have done early, important work on care and empathy and on duties owed to the vulnerable in our society.[39] They do not, however, speak directly to the extent or politics of the exclusion of women's experience and voices. Women theorists' focus on women's experience and on the dynamics of exclusion warrants calling their ethics "female."[40]

Female ethics differ from other ethics in their methodology as well. Instead of laying out grand systems in the manner of a Kant, Mill, or Aristotle, they reflect upon women's practices and try to derive guidelines for action from the character or essence of a single activity or virtue (e.g. care or trust or empathy). In this respect, these ethics are akin to specific professional ethics (e.g. medical or legal ethics) that derive norms from the character of the particular end pursued (e.g. health or legal justice). For some female ethicists (Baier; Noddings), trust or care by itself grounds what they seem to think of as a stand alone ethic. Others (Gilligan; Meyers; Held) conceive of their female ethic of care or empathy as a separate but equal supplement to rights- or duty-based ethics.[41] In both cases, though, female ethicists tend to treat the activity in question as intrinsically good, even though it may not provide for the complete good. This approach is sufficiently distinctive to warrant close scrutiny: can an entire ethic be grounded in a single interpersonal activity of caring, trusting or empathizing or even some combination thereof? What guarantees that care or trust will not prove manipulative or pathological? Are these activities self-regulative in some way? If not, could they be reconceived in some more defensible fashion?

The project

While philosophers and psychologists have quarreled over the empirical question of whether women actually do reason differently than men about moral matters, thinkers have devoted less attention to the logically prior question: even if women do have a different way of reasoning, is it truly ethical? Some groups (e.g. the Ku Klux Klan) might have a distinctive mode of reasoning, but distinctiveness *per se* does not make a form of reasoning morally sound. Before we build an entire research industry around female ethics, we need to step back and try to assess the extent to which these female ethics are defensible. Since my aim here is to critically assess female ethics with a view to rendering them still more defensible, I want to state at the outset which claims of female ethics I find cogent and persuasive and will be trying to salvage and which claims seem indefensible. I begin with the claims I accept.

1   I concur with female ethicists' contention that human beings are not autochthonous creatures. If the idea of a self sprung from the earth is indeed *the* modern view of the self, then the modern understanding is defective. Infants are not self-nurturing, and no human being acquires language except through inter-action with other human beings. The very fact that we are living, language users suggests that we are already in relation with our fellow human beings. Therefore, the attempt by Hobbes and others to specify ground rules (including linguistic ones) to be used to build up trusting relations among human beings is miscon-ceived. The attempt to build these relations from the ground up will presuppose the very relations of trust and care or, more generally, the sociability the rules supposedly make possible.

Moreover, there does appear to be a logical difficulty in conceiving of the self as an interested individual who has no interests in particular, has no history, and has no body.[42] If people are totally interchangeable, then it becomes impossible to differentiate them as individuals—i.e. different selves. In a related vein, we might well ask whether it even makes sense to speak, as some traditional theorists do, of individuals who have no particular interests apart from an interest in being treated fairly. Normally we think of an interest as a distinguishing feature: my friend Joe is interested in jazz, while Susan has an interest in dance. While the Kantian and Rawlsian attempt to derive ethical norms from the abstract idea of a universally shared interest is ingenious, it is hard to see how any norms so derived could apply to *individuals*. Since a generic interest by definition is shared by all persons, the individual has once again disappeared from the picture.[43] Since I accept that there are individuals with distinctive and distinguishing interests, I will be offering an ethic that preserves and respects individuality.

2   I concur that traditional theories' separation of the public and private realms is morally suspect. Stating and defending an absolute distinction between the two has proven notoriously difficult (e.g. are corporations really "private" given that they are legal fictions of states?). Furthermore, the same person inhabits both realms irrespective of how we draw the distinction. It is doubtful whether we can separate the behavior of the father or mother in the home from their roles as doctors or citizens. "Private" choices have a way of leaking into "public" ones.[44] Such considerations show how tenuous the public/private distinction is. Precisely because the idea of two distinct realms is contestable, there is all the more reason to solicit different persons' points of view and to do so in a way that does not slot persons in advance into one realm or the other. Female ethicists correctly note that women historically have been assigned roles limiting them to what has been dismissed as the "private" sphere. If the public sphere determines persons' roles, then there is some danger that women will be kept in their place by assigning them a place that they, by definition, cannot effectively challenge.[45] The very possibility of such a danger would seem to make it incumbent upon ethicists to try to hear the voices that have been silenced. One important way of doing so is to admit the contestability of the public/private distinction and throw it open for discussion to anyone who cares to comment upon it. To the extent that female

ethics attempt to initiate and sustain such a conversation,[46] their effort merits our support. The ethic I will be defending supports this effort and allows us to revisit and recast the public/private distinction.

3   No doubt there are many objections one might raise concerning the traditional ethical approach of positing a necessary principle and then trying to formally deduce an equally necessary system of further rules or procedures for deciding any and all ethical crises. For example, this approach inevitably makes some determination as to what sort of actions lie within the moral domain (e.g. only actions done from duty) and who qualifies as a moral subject (e.g. only those persons who possess enough conscience that they are able to act from duty). Persons who do not assent to these characterizations may find that the ethical system in question gives them no chance to protest because their response (or their person) has already been determined to lie outside of the moral domain. Their objections may be sound; the theorist may be wrong about his principles. At a minimum, an ethical theory should create a space in which critics can register objections. Without such a space, the theory will be violent in the sense that agents will be subjected to determinations they think are unjust and will have no way to challenge these determinations. The theorist, too, will be at risk. For, in the absence of such a space, he has no way of learning about his mistakes because his own theory has foreclosed potentially interesting lines of reasoning.

In addition, the traditional approach relies upon descriptions of actions and situations it provides. Principles are applied to situations the theorist characterizes. But why should we accept this theorist's characterization as correct or as just? For example, a Kantian might characterize a party's broken promise as an unwarranted breach of trust. However, the "offending" party may see her action as justified.[47] She may think either that she has, in fact, honored the promise or that there was no trust left to betray. Given that it is usually precisely this description of an action that is the subject of dispute, the description cannot legitimately be presupposed.[48] By calling our attention to the problem of perspective implicit in any description of a situation, female ethics rightly warn us against "ethical" approaches that, in effect, assume away the ethical issue—how to hear and then adjudicate among competing descriptions of a situation.

While I accept the legitimacy of the above three concerns, I think each of these points needs to be further elaborated and refined. I do *not* accept the way in which female ethics to date have attempted to solve these concerns for several reasons.

1   It is highly questionable whether we can save the individuality of the self by adopting female ethics' idea of the self as completely relational. The problem here is not simply the oft-voiced feminist concern that such a view of the self destroys individuality by locking women into pathological relations created and sustained by patriarchal societies. Even if these relations were not pathological, they would still be problematic for a number of reasons. One reason is logical. If every self is

in a relation of a certain sort (trusting, caring, empathizing), then all selves once again become interchangeable and thus lose individual identity. We might try to avoid this logical difficulty by defining these relations as ones capable of respecting other people in all their concreteness, individuality and historical particularity. This maneuver, though, leaves the relation generic—i.e. "a relation that respects individuality." This generic quality is not especially surprising since some generic dimension to the self will be unavoidable, given that we are thinking about the self and our thought always deals in abstraction. What is still more worrisome is the way in which this maneuver simply sidesteps the difficult issue of perspective. From whose perspective is the act of caring "respectful"? The caregiver's? Or the cared-for's? As we shall see, practices of caring, trusting and empathizing have many pathological forms. What passes as respect in the caregiver's or trustee's eyes may look like an evil projection to the trusting or cared-for party. We need an ethic that preserves the idea of a respectful and responsive self but that does not construe the self as so constructed by relations that an agent lacks any freedom to contest other people's practices and assumptions.

A related worry is our relations are not as transparent as female ethicists seem to think. Female ethics tend to forget that every encounter with another is mediated by those images we bring to the encounter. For example, two women may have very different images of who qualifies as a caring mother. If what we mean by being a "mother" is debatable—and there is no reason to think it is not—then we are not entitled to treat the mother–child relation as if it were an uncontroversial, ethically exemplary relation. Shifting our focus to the mother–daughter relation does not solve the problem because who or what a daughter is remains debatable as well.

2   Nor do I accept the idea that we should deal with the problem of the relation between the public and private realms by treating the act of ministering to one another's needs as a public function.[49] Desires and needs are not easily separated from one another in the case of human beings. People can be manipulated into having certain oppressive needs—e.g. a need to be very thin. As Stanley Rosen has argued, the creation of arts to meet our needs continually results in the creation of new "needs."[50] Human beings came to need meat as part of their diet only after they had invented the arts of hunting and cooking. Furthermore, talk of meeting another's needs is psychologically naive to the extent it overlooks human beings' tendency to imitate one another. Frequently what we claim to need is something *we desire for no other reason than because someone else desires it.*[51] If so, then our needs already always lie in the public sphere. And, unless these mimetic dynamics are kept in mind, our caring for and empathizing with others will be subject to a pathological mirroring. This mirroring may lead to an escalation of desire instead of the fulfillment of our "needs."

Even if we could restrict "needs" to those fundamental, felt compulsions that either are constitutive of a person's individuality (e.g. the need for self-expression; the need for privacy) or are conditions for life itself (e.g. the need for food or shelter), we will encounter some difficulties. We surely cannot be bound to meet the needs of all persons. A serial killer might have a "need" to kill others in order to express his sense of his own power and to keep this power. But it does not follow that we should collectively pander to this need. In more general terms, the ethical problem is not simply one of injecting policies or attitudes of care, trust, etc., into the public realm. Rather the problem is to figure out precisely how simultaneously to honor the concrete otherness of persons *and* to rule out behaviors that interfere with our ability to sustain a shared, communal life. Our ethic should lead us to care for justice and the rule of law as well as for our needy and vulnerable friends and acquaintances.

3   Finally, although we should be sensitive to the ways in which our principles lead us to foreclose possibilities, we also must recognize the peculiar and important power of principles to set liberating limits. Principles enunciating absolute prohibitions can open up, as well as close, possibilities. For example, the language of absolute, inalienable rights has been instrumental in allowing persons to oppose tyrannical governments or persons and in placing limits on what agents legitimately may do out of loyalty to their ethnic group or race.[52] Gilligan herself appeals to an ideal of respect, which she treats as an absolute principle, claiming that it must be honored at all times.[53]

Furthermore, while it is true that our commitment to some principle may lead to a premature formulation of a problem or characterization of a situation, getting rid of principles does not solve the problem of contestable descriptions. Just as the traditional ethicist will describe a situation in such a way as to enable him to apply his principle or rule, so will the care ethicist or trust ethicist inevitably characterize certain situations as ones calling for care, trust or empathy. When and whether a situation will be seen as involving trust will depend upon the female ethicist's definition of trust. So female ethics are every bit as prone to premature formulations of situations as traditional ethics. If we are to guarantee persons the opportunity to challenge these formulations, we may need something akin to an absolute principle granting them the privilege (or right?) to question the framework or system of discourse in which the other is operating. An ethic employing explicit regulative principles of discourse may be better than one that subjects those on the receiving end of care or empathy to a host of non-explicit rules or expectations built into the caregiver's or empathizer's view of their own practices.

The structure of the argument

The first half of the book (Chapters 1 through 3) examines three forms of female ethics: ethics of care, empathy, and trust. Chapter 1 elaborates the care ethics offered by Carol Gilligan and Nel Noddings. The primary focus of this chapter is on the work of these two women, although the chapter occasionally draws on later work done by women theorists who see themselves as further elaborating and extending the care ethic. Chapter 2 considers Diana Meyers' ethic of empathy; Chapter 3 examines the trust ethics defended by Annette Baier and Trudy Govier. While each ethic has its own peculiar strengths, they share a number of worrisome defects. First, there is nothing self-regulating in care, empathy or trust insofar as these practices are conceived of as strictly interpersonal activities. Apart from some rather vague claim that it is good to be in relation with others, there are few or no regulative principles in these ethics. The lack of principles is troubling because, as we shall see, the practices of caring, trusting and empathizing frequently are manipulative and harmful to both the active party and the person who is being cared for, trusted in, or empathized with. While some versions of these ethics do grant that there are certain people who may not merit our trust or care, these ethics allow this determination of worthiness to be made solely by the trustor, caregiver, or empathizer. As a result, these ethics not merely encourage but actually tacitly sanction a dangerous self-righteousness. They mislead as well because they make it seem as though if we are just open enough to others we can grasp exactly what they are thinking. No such mind-meld is possible, however. We always mediate what others are saying through some conception we have of the issue under discussion. To the extent these ethics fail to address this problem of mediation, they prove every bit as rigid and exclusionary as traditional ethics.

In addition to lacking any checks on self-righteous projections or abusive relations, these ethics lack any vision of human good capable of organizing our lives into a meaningful whole. The injunction to care for (or trust in, etc.) other persons ignores the fact that the form of care matters a good deal. It hardly seems ethically good for my doctor to refuse to heal me because she wants to care for me by writing my will. What provides focus in this type of case is some particular good around which the relation is organized. Female ethics have evacuated various practices (e.g. the professions and arts) of their moral content in their zeal to have persons engage in generic practices of caring and empathizing that are defined entirely in terms of purely formal operations.[54]

This lack of any organizing good is troubling in a second way. It undermines female ethics' ability to make sense of virtues like integrity and to resolve practical dilemmas. How are we to make sense of integrity, much less maintain it, if the self is nothing more than the product of random trusting encounters with others or if the self is totally constituted by prevailing social relations of nurturance, trust, etc.? If we are morally bound to empathically apprentice ourselves to every person we encounter, how can we ever get around to achieving our own goals and to executing our plans? Moreover, for whom are we to care and with whom are we to empathize when confronted with competing objects for our attention? What justifies our choice?

These issues arise because female ethics have glossed over the question of limits. They envision a world in which persons are maximally nurturing and understanding and in which, as a result, each person has a chance to achieve self-fulfillment. But insofar as these ethics are lacking in an end or goal (*telos*), it is hard to see exactly what can possibly be meant by self-fulfillment. Moreover, requiring that we be infinitely open to and nurturing of our fellow human beings would seem to threaten the rule of law as well. If caring conflicts with the law's demands, is the agent entitled to make a private determination that she may flaunt the law?[55] It is doubtful whether any rule of law could withstand such determinations. Are we to do away with the laws that define the political sphere? If so, what is to regulate relations among total strangers and check outbreaks of violence?

The second half of the book argues for what I call a "dialogical ethic" that preserves the crucial insights of female ethics while avoiding many of the problems noted above. This ethic begins with the insight that everyone of us is prone to error. That does not mean that all actions, characters or choices are equally good (or bad). Nor does it means that we are incapable of distinguishing good courses of action from bad ones. On the contrary, to speak of an error or mistake is to imply, first, that we are capable of using the truth to identify problems in our positions and those of other people; and second, that our speech can be more or less truthful. If we can speak the truth about what is truly good for us; and if we do not desire to harm ourselves, then we are in a position to knowledgeably identify, desire and pursue genuinely good courses of actions. Since conversing with other people who may possess relevant insights into living well is one important way open to us for correcting our errors, it follows that conversation or dialogue with others is practically desirable and an essential part of living well.

Care must be taken, though, to specify what is meant by a "conversation." I argue that not every exchange of sound or even speech qualifies as such. Conversation requires that one or more of the parties to the spoken exchange is persuadable by what is said in the exchange. In order for persuasion to be a possibility, participants must commit to certain principles, principles that are not derived transcendentally but that are articulated and consented to in the course of conversation itself. These principles are absolute. So, on the one hand, the dialogical ethic is able to avoid the charge of moral relativism to which female ethics are always susceptible because they seem to glorify in trying on, and even submitting to, different perspectives simply because these perspectives are different. On the other hand, this absoluteness is in the service of preserving dialogue between particular individuals whose interests and points of view may not be known prior to the dialogue itself. The dialogical ethic, therefore, does not assume a god's eye point of view so often present in accounts that appeal to what all persons of "reason" would think or accept. Neither does it attempt to derive a whole system of practical precepts or rights and to then allege that everyone is obligated to honor these rights. Rather the dialogical ethic is able to appropriately resolve practical difficulties or disputes through a conversation that is both highly specific to the participants involved and also generic by virtue of complying with the principles of the ethic.

The dialogical ethic refines the insights of female ethics in several ways. It maintains the openness to particular individuals rightly prized by those women defending ethics of care, trust and empathy. Unlike some traditional ethics, this ethic imposes no advance restrictions on the types of questions and concerns people may express in their interaction with each other. It makes no attempt to derive moral precepts by appealing to some representative prudent or rational person. In these ways, then, the dialogical ethic is akin to female ethics. However, it differs from them in providing for a *critical* openness. Conversants are allowed to bring their truths to the table but they are not obligated to "apprentice themselves" to the other party's perspective. Using the example of the conversation between Socrates and Crito, I show in detail how the same principles that conversants accept in order to make genuine conversation possible equally oblige them to test the truth of what is being claimed and to evaluate its implications for living well. The ethic gives a focus to interactions and relations—a focus on living well—without requiring all conversants to begin with the same definition of the good life.

The dialogical ethic also acknowledges the fundamental relatedness of human beings. It makes an individual's welfare dependent on having conversations with other people from whom he or she potentially may learn things of great practical importance. But this dependence should not be confused with some female ethics' claim that the self is either nothing but a relation or nothing other than a social construction. These two views deprive the self of the freedom to oppose manipulative or violent societal structures. The dialogical ethic reserves to the individual a *viable* right or privilege of withdrawing from abusive interactions or exchanges with little or no persuasive potential. As I noted earlier, not all verbal exchanges are conversations. If and when it becomes apparent to a participant through attempts at dialogue that the other participant is unpersuadable, then the first party is entitled to leave the relation. The dialogical ethic is sensitive to power dynamics and the likelihood that attempts to dominate others will sometimes masquerade as "conversations." By ensuring a viable right of exit, the ethic avoids locking women and others into abusive relations.

Third, the dialogical ethic extends female ethics by placing the contestability of our various claims at its center. To the extent female ethics emphasize the need to listen to the possibly unique position of every individual with whom we interact, these ethics must contend with the possibility that one of these persons will raise a crucial objection to our position, an objection we may have overlooked. Female ethics, therefore, are implicitly committed to what the dialogical ethic makes explicit—namely, that we should not lose sight of the possibility that we have erred, perhaps seriously. We may be mistaken not only about the particulars of some case but also about the character of care, empathy, trust; about who qualifies as a mother or daughter; about what it means to be liberated or free. Keeping this possibility before us provides a strong motivation not only for listening to another person but also for actively seeking out, playing with and critically testing different perspectives. In other words, caring for our critical conversations with other people gives us a reason to care for, to trust in, and to imaginatively travel with them. In this sense, the dialogical ethic I am proposing does not so much displace or replace female ethics as reorient them toward the need for critical conversation. This need is fundamental because such conversation enables us to assess the status of other "needs."

This reorientation results in an ethic far more political than most female ethics. I shall argue that the principles making conversation possible simultaneously necessitate a radical rethinking of what is meant by the rule of law. In particular, to be morally legitimate, the laws we pass and support must protect individuals by guaranteeing them a viable opportunity to contest the laws and a viable option to leave the community if and when persuasion of those in power proves impossible. Caring for individuals and respecting them thus turns out to be considerably more onerous than female ethics have acknowledged. We have to do more as citizens than simply apprentice ourselves to, or play with, other people's point of view. Unless we revise female ethics to take into account tensions between individuals and the law, female ethics unwittingly will reinforce a possibly unjust legal system.

Finally, the dialogical ethic preserves female ethics' insights while making them more practical. Since female ethics treat human relations formally and make no appeal to any kind of organizing good, they are lacking in synthetic power. They do a good job of identifying problems with other approaches and of specifying conditions processes must meet in order to qualify as mutually reciprocal. They provide far less help when it comes to making a good choice between competing objects of care or trust. Lacking an organizing good, they have no way to focus and order various concerns or to create consensus among people who initially differ over what should be done.[56] After we are "open" to other people's concerns, then what? We may still disagree, so female ethics leave us adrift in the ethical waters without a rudder or a wind. By contrast, those who adopt the principles of a dialogical ethic are able to build consensus and to arrive at a good resolution of the problem or crisis they are confronting. The dialogical approach offered here is thus not simply a theory of discourse. It truly is a practical ethic capable of providing for non-arbitrary, mutually acceptable resolutions of problems.

In all of these ways, then, dialogical ethic both builds upon and strengthens female ethics' claims. However, insofar as the ethic appeals to principles, it bears a certain resemblance to "male" ethics. Does the dialogical ethic qualify as "female" then or not? I am inclined to reply along the following lines: while "female ethics" is a convenient rubric for grouping certain concerns of women ethicists—including many of my own worries—no philosopher of whatever gender should lose sight of the fact that the rubric is just that—a rhetorical category. The dialogical ethic I defend is "female" and "feminist" insofar as it insists upon giving women the opportunity to voice their own concerns, upon attending to the concerns of women writing about ethical matters, and upon identifying various oppressive strands within ethics of trust, empathy and care. But not all thoughts or ethics will fall neatly within either the "male" or "female" category. Nor should we forget that sometimes the contrary (read: "female" ethics) of an error (read: "male" ethics) is not the truth but another error. In the final analysis, I am less concerned as to how the dialogical approach is labeled and more concerned whether other people will find it persuasive. This book is my attempt to engage both men and women in a conversation seeking to find a thoughtful and critical, yet open, way of being an individual in a community of individuals. If we are to hear those among us who speak in a different voice, we need a different ear. We require a discerning way of listening capable not only of attending to the plurality of perspectives in our human community but also of assessing their truth and relevance to the good life.

1

AN ETHIC OF CARE

The world is full of care, much like unto a bubble; Women and care,
and care and women, and women and care and trouble.
(Nathaniel Ward, quoting a lady-in-waiting at
the Court of the Queen of Bohemia)

It is tempting to begin a book on female ethics by hearkening back to the first
female ethicist. This temptation must be resisted. Who qualifies as a precursor
depends upon how one conceives of the event or activity in question and upon
what one takes to be the crucial or relevant issues. In this sense, Borges is quite
correct:

> The word "precursor" is indispensable in the vocabulary of criticism, but
> one should try to purify it from every connotation of polemic or rivalry.
> The fact is that each writer creates "precursors." A writer's work modi-
> fies our conception of the past, as it will modify the future.[1]

It thus would be misleading to pretend that any one woman thinker has origi-
nated female ethics. Gilligan's work *In A Different Voice* unquestionably helped
to crystallize many women's frustrations with traditional ethics. But the frustrations clearly were already there. Indeed, her work and that of Nel Noddings[2]
gained such quick prominence, in part, because women found they readily understood these two women's critiques. Women readers made Gilligan and Noddings
into "precursors." Noddings' and Gilligan's ethic of care is not, therefore, a
necessary starting point for a critique of female ethics. Their care ethic is, nevertheless, a useful starting point because Gilligan and Noddings are so intent upon
distinguishing the care ethic from traditional modes of ethical analyses that they
tend to overstate their claims and to overlook difficulties with their own
approach. Since this book aims to put important insights of female ethics on surer
ground, this overstatement is useful for separating the dross from those insights
that are pure gold.

Since my analysis is focussed on the question of whether female ethics are themselves ethically good, this chapter on the care ethic addresses four interrelated

questions: What are the central tenets of an ethic of care? What precisely is meant by "care"? What exactly is the basis for the assertion that we *should* care for each other? Are these claims sustainable? This last question, in turn, has four inter-related elements: (1) Are those acts which we are told we should do actually possible? (2) Are the recommended acts and attitudes consistent with female ethics' own insistence upon hearing the distinctive voices of individuals? (3) Are the recommended acts and attitudes consistent with justice understood roughly as that virtue or practice that enables potentially violent individuals with differing views of what is good to share a life together as members of a community? and (4) Does the framework have any power to resolve practical difficulties, dilemmas or crises in a non-arbitrary manner? I shall show that an ethic of care, in its present form, fails all of these tests.

Tenets of care ethics

Both Gilligan and Noddings contrast their ethical stance of care with that of principled, male ethics of justice (e.g. Immanuel Kant's; Lawrence Kohlberg's).[3] Justice ethics seek to discover and then apply universal rules or laws of justice to situations. Often this application requires that some rule "trump" other rules or points of view. To take one of Gilligan's examples: a traditional male ethicist might argue that a pharmacist's right to make a profit from inventory he owns "trumps" a sick person's claim to a drug she needs to stay alive but cannot afford.[4] The care ethicist, by contrast, resists applying universal rules in a hierarchical fashion.[5] She thinks the justice approach falsifies moral dilemmas by abstracting those features of the situation to which the rules are most easily applied.[6] By contrast, her caring "moves to concretization where [the agent's] feelings can be modified by the introduction of facts, the feelings of others, and personal histories."[7] So, while Kant condemns suicide as immoral because it violates the demands of universal reason; and while he dismisses the effect of suicide on others and the particular situation of the victim as irrelevant, the care ethicist wants to hear the personal tales of the victim and of those affected by the act. Before she judges the suicidal act, she wants to learn of their feelings and their thinking as part of perceiving the act in all its conceptual and emotional fullness. Her "moral judgment is more contextual, more immersed in the details of relationships and narratives."[8]

The care ethic places great weight on the importance of listening. An agent single-handedly can apply Kantian or Rawlsian rules of justice or perform utilitarian calculations to determine what act or rule will maximize pleasure.[9] He need not consult with others in the applications of these principles. Precisely because these male ethics are non-consultative, Gilligan and Noddings argue that the concerns and reasoning of others tend to be overlooked or shunted to the side. The principles are applied in a manner disrespectful of individuals because the distinctive and individualizing concerns of other parties never enter into the agent's deliberations. Traditional ethics thus fail their own ethical standard of respecting the individual. The care ethic, by contrast, requires us to become "engrossed" in one another.[10] We must "move" toward the other at least to the extent of trying to really hear what other people are saying. We need not endorse the other's motives or projects. But we do need to still our inner voices and objections enough to "receive" the other in his or her otherness.[11] The truly caring, ethical agent lets the conversation with the other supply the relevant categories for judgment. She does not come into the conversation with a fully formed set of categories or rules for judgment which she then applies. She has a high tolerance for ambiguity.[12] The caring person even may act in a fashion that appears to more rule-bound people to violate the principles of justice.[13]

True caring involves "receiving" the other person in the manner just described and then seeking to preserve a connection with him or her. Beyond that, we cannot say much more concrete about caring, for every act of caring is unique.[14] What is universal about caring is not its form but rather the demand upon each of us to be caring. We remember having been cared for when we were young; this warm, pleasant memory leads us to long for goodness and motivates us to care for others. According to the care ethicist, the desire to act well is rooted in the desire to return to this state.[15] This state is only possible if we care for others because it is caring that engenders caring. On this view, we create the world in which we live through our actions. Only if our actions are motivated by an ideal of caring can we live once again in the world we loved as a child.

In a sense, the care ethic is quite selfish. Agents care in order to live in a world they find desirable. There is no requirement in this ethic that agents be self-sacrificing.[16] On the contrary, the agent is bound to find her own voice and to speak for herself. As Gilligan puts it, the ethical woman stops letting her boyfriends or her parents speak for her. She learns to speak for herself and to exhibit a "caring with autonomy."[17] Only when she does so is she fully a member of the world created through people speaking their concerns. The ethical agent listens well to others but takes time to speak for herself, too. She must do so because her perceptions are unique, born of her roles, her experiences, her history, etc. Unlike the Kantian who purports to know that all rational beings are alike and, therefore, must will the same course of action, the care ethicist takes seriously the idea of individualism. She insists both upon speaking her own concerns and upon hearing others speak their feelings and ideas because, strictly speaking, only the individual can properly express his or her own concerns. She suspects any analysis of compassion or caring which talks about party "A" acknowledging "B" through the force of some shared capacity. This type of analysis treats individuals as if they were interchangeable people whom we can know and talk *about* without ever having to talk *with* them.[18]

The care ethic has an existential dimension lacking in male ethics. In the care ethic, the moral world is not already "there," fully formed in its rationality.[19] If the world is to be good, the caregiver must make it so through her acts in accordance with her personal ideal of herself as a caring person. Since no one can specify necessary and sufficient conditions for an act to be caring, the caregiver is finally thrown back upon herself to assess the goodness of her acts.[20] Positive response from the cared-for may be a sign she has been behaving well; but the cared-for party may be deceived or may respond negatively to a genuinely caring act for some private reason. As caregivers, we must live with the anxious question: have we done everything our ideal of caring demands of us? All we can do in response is to receive other people as best we can and see if we find we can live with ourselves under the circumstances.

We are not bound to love everyone. However, we are required, on this view, to care for those who come within our purview. The hungry man or animal who shows up on our doorstep has a call upon our resources and attention.[21] It may be that we have no food to give. Still, we are bound by our commitment to our world-creating ideal to care for these creatures as best we can. In the case of a person, such caring might involve explaining that we have no food. Or we may refer the hungry man or woman to the farmer down the road who raises potatoes. We cannot say what exactly constitutes a caring response. All we can say is that, if we do not receive another person (or animal) sufficiently so as to experience anxiety, then we have not cared. This questioning and anxiety, though, are a private matter. No universal, uninvolved, rational spectator of the sort usually presumed in male ethics of justice can legitimately judge us for not caring (or praise us for doing so).

Is it ever legitimate to confront and blame somebody within this ethic? The care ethic does not say that the agent cannot judge. It does maintain, however, that there is "no place for fear, anger, hatred"[22] or any emotion or stance that interferes with receiving someone in all of his or her individuality. Agents are to listen to those they find objectionable. Ethical selves never demonize the other person by seeing him or her as being totally unlike themselves.[23] Instead, the agent's response should be therapeutic.[24] If a stance is unacceptable, the caring person will talk with the other party to find out why she holds this stance. According to the care ethic, it is legitimate for the caregiver to try to persuade the cared-for party to alter her stance. However, he must examine his own beliefs as well. Perhaps he is implicated in whatever dynamic is producing the standoff. He, too, may have to change.

The care ethic's definition of care

Gilligan never offers a definition of care, and Noddings' idea of care as receiving others (or, at least, wanting to receive them) on their terms is not very rigorous. Still, we can tease out some threads from their analyses and refine them into something like a working definition of care. It is clear, for example, that both think ethical caring—i.e. caring we should engage in—goes beyond mere concern for or about a person or thing. In the first place, concern *per se* does not qualify as true care unless it is active.[25] We properly wonder about the genuineness of people's concern if they claim to care for the environment but refuse to recycle their garbage, compost, dispose of hazardous materials properly, or do anything that is currently thought to help protect the environment. The proof of care is in the activity.

Yet ethical care is more than active concern for an object. A teacher might be actively concerned to manipulate one of her students into sleeping with her. Or some group may take an active interest in seeing that all convicted rapists receive stiff penalties. The group cares that the convicts remain in prison for many years. Yet, their zeal for their cause may make them insensitive to the feelings and rights of the convicts and may lead, at the extreme, to possible miscarriages of justice. The active concern must be of a certain type. What type is this?

Care, as conceived of by Gilligan and Noddings, is less a matter of being concerned that something will happen and more a matter of being attentive to another's well-being and of being willing to act to promote it. Thus care is best conceived as an active, interpersonal, mutual reciprocity. On this view, the Chief Executive Officer (CEO) can care for his employees but not, strictly speaking, for the corporation because the corporation is merely a legal fiction incapable of reciprocity. Only people can respond to each other's needs and concerns. While it might be argued that caring includes everything that maintains or repairs our world and environment,[26] the care ethic of Noddings and Gilligan treats caring as most manifest when we strive to meet the needs of our fellow human beings. Humans can and do individuate themselves to a high degree. Since this individuation can be properly appreciated only by listening to their individual voices discussing their particular needs, *interpersonal* caring stretches all of our listening skills to the maximum. The wife who is so attuned to her dying husband's needs that she can tell from a mere gesture that he needs his pillow adjusted and who plumps the pillow exhibits care in the strong interpersonal sense of that term.

Of course, nurses, too, provide comfort for their patients. The care ethicist, however, deprecates this sort of professional attention. The concern of a doctor, lawyer, or cleric is quasi-impersonal, extending to all patients, litigants, or penitents as such. (Receiving pay for caring may also be a problem insofar as the agent may not be acting out of a desire to be in a caring relation but rather to earn a living.) Professionals' concern is mediated by their professed commitment to the end occupying the moral center of their practice (health in the case of medicine; salvation in the case of the ministry). This kind of caring is principled insofar as it takes its bearings from a known commitment to a particular, narrow end. Care ethicists suspect these commitments to principles. Noddings goes so far as to claim that caring is opposed to fixed rules or principles of any sort[27] and that professions should not be analyzed in terms of any formal requirements arising from the practice of a particular activity but rather in terms of caring itself.[28] Professional commitments, antedating the encounter with particular individuals, can distort our relations and prevent us from appreciating the "total person."[29] Persons with whom we are interacting may get reduced to a "representative type" and thereby lose the very uniqueness responsible for making them the individuals they are.

In general, the more principled the attention paid to another human being, the

less it qualifies as genuine caring in the eyes of the care ethicist.[30] Principled attention frequently degenerates into "tending," a kind of "domestic labour
performed on people."[31] Thus, if a person visits his friend in the hospital because
he has calculated that the general happiness will be maximized by this action, his
act displays a strange coldness in a situation in which warmth and spontaneity are
desirable.[32] A wife does not want her husband to make love to her because he
thinks it is his duty: Thursday night, bowling for him; Friday night, sex for her.
These cases trouble the care ethicist because the agent neatly packages the relation and confines it to certain (allegedly) known dimensions. The agent decides
the case by subsuming it under some principle or some role-responsibility instead
of allowing the relevant terms of judgment to spontaneously evolve out of interaction with the party in question.[33] When we think this way, we fail to put
ourselves into play. For the care ethicist, true caring—or at least caring in the
highest and most interesting sense—is an affective stance in which both the caregiver and cared-for put themselves at risk as part of a process of committing to the
forging of a shared self.[34] This is the kind of caring one sees in intimate, loving
relations. So, not surprisingly, intimate relations are paradigmatic for both
Noddings and Gilligan.

While each caring relation is unique, we can identify certain types of relations
that presumably would not qualify as truly caring ones. For example, neither
Gilligan nor Noddings would think that obsessive lovers who stalk or harass their
"love objects" really care for these others. These "lovers" never bother to explore
with the "beloved" what he or she truly values or what a healthy relation with this
person would look like. This kind of concern is fanaticism, fetishism, or a quest for
self-validation; but not ethical caring. At the other extreme of uncaring are those
who are completely indifferent to other people. Indifference may be just as brutal
as cruelty as Simon Gray's character Beth explains in this diatribe against her
husband:

> You know the most insulting thing, that you let me go on and on being
> unfaithful without altering your manner or your behavior one—one—
> you don't care about me, or my being in love with someone else, or my
> betraying you, good God! . . . . But you do wish I hadn't actually
> *mentioned* it, because then we could have gone on, at least *you* could,
> pretending that everything was all right . . . you probably still think it *is*
> all right—and—and—you've—you've—all those times we've made love,
> sometimes the very same evening Ned and I—and—and yet you took
> me—in your usual considerate fashion, just as you take your third of a
> bottle of wine with dinner or your carefully measured brandy and your
> cigar after it, *and* enjoyed it all the more because I felt guilt, God help
> me *guilty* and so tried harder for your sake—and you *admit* that, no, not
> admit it, simply state it as if on the difference made by an extra voice or
> something in your bloody Wagner—don't you see, don't you see that
> makes you a freak![35]

Sympathetic relations would presumably be problematic as well.[36] Sympathy could be defined as the acknowledgment by the sympathizer of someone else's presumed unwelcome feelings (e.g. gut-wrenching grief over the loss of a loved one),[37] coupled with the sympathizer's simultaneous awareness that these feelings are the other person's and not necessarily the sympathizer's own.[38] My sympathy will be uncaring if I project what I think my friend ought to be feeling without bothering to converse with her and to enter imaginatively into her situation as she describes it. If my friend's husband beats her daily, she may feel little grief when he dies and may be irritated at my projection that she is feeling unwelcome distress. Moreover, sympathy always introduces a distance between the sympathizer and the object of her sympathy. This distance from the other's presumably unwelcome plight can easily slip into condescension. The pitying self may fail to try to create a shared self in which parties are mutually vulnerable to each other. Sympathizers may even delight in their escape from the distress plaguing another. Or, worse still, sympathizers may begin to desire the existence of vulnerable people in order that they may gratify their own feelings of largesse:

[P]ity would be no more
If we did not make somebody Poor;
And Mercy no more could be
If all were as happy as we.[39]

For these reasons, the female ethicist insists that, while sympathy may be a spectator sport, ethical caring never is.[40] We must "feel with" the other.[41] There must be an affective component to our caring for another, a feeling of engagement arising in part because the caregiver knows the stakes are high.[42] Our very selves are at stake when we care because we are working at creating a shared self, invented as we proceed. Caregiver and cared-for alike do not know until they get there what this "there" is like. Nor do they get to remain "there" for long. The self keeps evolving through a process of attending to what the other takes to be his or her needs and then rethinking its own self-image. The caring self is far more dynamic than in those "male" ethics which view the self as a static locus of rational agency bound by duties grounded in the idea of rational agency as such.[43]

To summarize: for the care ethicist, ethical acts are caring ones of a certain sort. They are those acts in which the caregiver actively concerns herself with attending to the individually expressed needs, feelings and interests of the cared-for and strives to create a shared self with people who are similarly committed to a secure world in which beings are nurtured and given an opportunity to realize fully their individuality.

Problems with the care ethic

While I think that there are many problems with the form the care ethic seems to be assuming in the literature, I do not accept the claim that the care ethic has nothing to say about ethics because it is, at best, merely a psychological theory of ego development. More is at stake in this critique than simply a psychological theory of ego development.[44] In very general terms, an ethic is a reflection upon the conditions for shared and satisfying human living in a community in which human beings have differing perspectives on what qualifies as a good and satisfying life.[45] Ethics—be they Kantian, communitarian, liberal, utilitarian, or virtue ethics—may disagree on matters such as what is meant by "satisfying"; who qualifies as a relevant member of the community; whether these differing perspectives are commensurate with each other; whether some perspectives are more defining of the self than others; whether any of these perspectives are objective, etc. But such disagreement merely confirms my claim that, to be persuasive, every ethic must concern itself with how and whether differences in opinions and outlook can be and should be accommodated within a community. Gilligan's and Noddings' analysis of caring does have ethical significance insofar as the analysis speaks directly to this concern.

In particular, the care ethic contends that we will not be able to identify the conditions under which individuals can co-exist satisfyingly within a community if we fail to create a space in which we can hear from individuals in their own voices. If we simply impute positions to them; or if our methodology leads us to dismiss certain kinds of concern as morally irrelevant, impermissible, or immature, then whatever ethical scheme we devise will fail to be satisfactory. We cannot have identified conditions of satisfying living for all members of the relevant community because our mode of proceeding has prevented some members' concern from being present to us. If all people thought exactly alike, there would not be a problem. But the ethical problem is that people do not think alike. Hence, we see Gilligan going out of her way to interview a variety of men and women to hear from them about their concerns in their own respective voices.

Second, the care ethic calls our attention to the fluidity of our descriptions of ethical dilemmas. There is no value-neutral description of a dilemma. What some will see as involving an issue of property rights, others will see as an issue of relations. Furthermore, when confronted with some description of a dilemma or options, an agent may reject this description because she thinks the dilemma is too contrived or because she believes there are other options available to her. Since it is hard to see how we could possibly anticipate every objection every human being might raise to a particular description of an action, a legitimate ethic cannot justifiably appeal to, or employ, descriptions of actions as though these descriptions were uncontestable. We might try to specify in advance what qualifies as a reasonable description of an action, but what counts as "reasonable" is, in principle, contestable as well. The care ethic tries to cope with this ethical problem by suggesting that we allow the terms of our judgment of an action to evolve through our concerned interactions with those who are affected by the action whose rightness or goodness we are trying to assess.

The problem, then, with an ethic of care is not that it is totally lacking in ethical content. The claims Gilligan and Noddings make are ethical ones and their worries regarding traditional or standard ethical approaches are legitimate. The problem lies rather with the way in which the care ethic tries to resolve these difficulties. In the following pages, I shall argue that: (1) care ethics in their present form have, at best, limited regulative force, in part because they require agents to do what may be impossible; (2) care ethics overlook various pathological forms of care that do not respect the individuality of other parties and fall prey themselves to the presumption that they can speak for others; and (3) these ethics show insufficient concern for the human autonomy or self-definition that produces individuality.

The limited regulative power of care ethics

Problem 1: not every ethical act need be a caring one

The care ethic takes caring to be the ethical activity *par excellence*. It alleges that we desire to be good and to act well because we desire to be in sharing relation with other people. This formulation is not a particularly happy one because it makes it sound as if caring by an agent is ethically good simply because the agent desires to care. However, it is obvious that having a desire *per se* is not ethically good. Insofar as desire is taken to be the moving cause of an act, it will be trivially true that people who care have a desire to care, just as people who steal have a desire to steal. The goodness or badness of the act cannot lie in the mere fact of desire but must instead reside in the description of the act that the agent desires to perform. The care ethicist must show, therefore, that being in a sharing, mutually defining relation with others is good.

Care ethicists offer two arguments in support of this claim. First, they argue that all people are always dependent upon each other. Human thriving depends upon others' assistance. To the extent we humans want to thrive, we logically must desire interdependence.[46] Second, they contend that the desire to be in relation motivates us to act well. A desire to act well is good because, if good actions are good and if the necessary conditions for producing good actions or states of affairs are themselves good, then the desire to act well must be good since it is a necessary condition for a good action. The desire to be in relation equally must be good because it is a necessary (and thus good) condition for the desire to act well.

How are we to understand the first claim? Taken as a description of human affairs it seems unproblematic. Human beings *are* dependent upon others for the success of their activities or, more generally, for their thriving understood as attaining freely chosen goals. At a minimum, we rely upon other people not to interfere with our actions. More positively, we frequently need their support and help in order to start and complete projects dear to our hearts. In what way, though, is this fact of interdependence regulative of action? Both Gilligan and Noddings combine this claim with other suppressed premises to draw regulative conclusions. As far as I can tell, they employ a version of the following syllogism:

1   Human beings desire to thrive and are entitled to thrive.
2   Human beings are dependent on others for their thriving.
3   A human being, therefore, will often desire the help of other human beings in order to thrive.
4   Women are human beings.
5   Therefore, women, like all other human beings, may consider their own desire to thrive and look to others for help even if society tells them, that as women, they must be self-sacrificing.
6   The only way there can be a world in which people receive the help of others is for people to be caring.
7   Therefore, people who desire to be cared for and to thrive (and we all do so by 1–5) must also strive to be caring.

Insofar as this argument is advanced as part of raising women's consciousness, and insofar as the premises are true, it seems unproblematic. As Bill Puka has argued, Gilligan can be read as urging women to acquire a voice in which they express their own needs as well as cater to the needs of others.[47] Steps 1–5 very well may work to counter a societal expectation that a woman be a helping figure. It is hard to see, though, how this argument could help any agent, male or female, decide the whole host of issues people historically have found troubling—e.g. should they turn in their own son who is selling crack? Should they fight in a war they deem to be unjust? Addressing these issues would seem to require an ethic with a wider scope, an ethic that looks beyond the question of what liberates women to issues of justice and human rights.

To meet this objection, Noddings is driven to widen the care ethic's applicability by making the desire to care *the* motivating force behind all ethical action (see Steps 6 and 7 above).[48] This attempt fails on several scores. The desire to be in a needs-meeting relation is simply posited as *the* basis for the desire to act well.[49] This claim ignores other candidates—e.g. the love of the good or of the just; a desire to be the beloved of God. In addition, the claim is completely unverifiable because the care ethicist never specifies in any detail what constitutes a good act. If we do not know what qualifies as a good action, we cannot examine good actions to see whether they are in fact always necessarily motivated by a desire to care.

Noddings and Gilligan do give some examples of good acts, almost all of which seem to be acts of nurturance. The desire to care appears to be identical with a desire to alleviate human suffering and pain and to meet the material needs of all concerned parties, including the caring agent herself. Feeding another human being or animal, refraining from inflicting pain, or stopping another's suffering are all good acts.[50] Perhaps, though, suffering has its own important lessons to teach the sufferer and those who witness it. Some such belief presumably underlies our respect for Jesus' death on the cross. No one advocates taking him off the cross and putting him to death as we might an injured cat whom we wanted to put out of its misery. A similar point could be made about hunger.

Hunger is not always bad. Someone on a hunger strike may choose to forgo food in order to achieve a good he deems more important.

Noddings' and Gilligan's versions of the care ethic assume a Maslowian hierarchy of needs in which physical needs are the most pressing.[51] The truth of such an assumption is far from obvious. Others have stressed the primacy of psychological needs.[52] Indeed, Gilligan herself sometimes talks as though every human being has a fundamental need for, and even right to, autonomy and self-respect.[53] We also should remember that, in some cases, refusing to meet others' needs may be the right course of action. For example, in Plato's *Republic*, Socrates and his interlocutors defer eating and having sex in favor of thinking about the nature of justice. That discussion, in turn, leads to the conclusion that the best life is not simply one of meeting animal needs. They discover that a person may not always know what he really needs. If so, then "receiving him on his own terms" may simply reinforce his mistaken belief that he fully understands himself. The care ethicist forgets that what someone assumes to be needs may be little more than the demands of insatiable desire. Alternatively, the individual may be pretending to have needs in order to get attention or to manipulate others.[54] Given these not unlikely possibilities, the ethical issue does not appear to be one of meeting another's needs but of helping others to see their desire for what it is and to limit it. The care ethicist either must discuss the structure of desire or must argue that it is irrelevant to ethics. Gilligan and Noddings do neither. As a result, their central claims—that we desire above all to care (and be cared-for) and that this desire is intrinsically good—are not persuasive.

Finally, even if we were to accept that all ethical acts are, in some sense, nurturing ones, we would still confront a problem of judgment. Determining whether someone is needy is not always straightforward. An excessively maternalistic commitment to nurturing people may lead the caregiver to impute needs to people that they do not have and to take steps that curtail their freedom.[55] If freedom is a prerequisite for the choices that define us as the individuals we are, the care ethic's nurturing stance may often prove to be inconsistent with the respect for the individual it purports to prize. I will return to this problem of projection shortly.

Problem 2: little guidance in particular cases

Another problem concerns the care ethic's ability to actually provide for a nonarbitrary resolution of practical conflicts or crises. If an ethic does indeed aim at specifying the conditions under which we can live a shared and satisfying life among other human beings, then an ethic should offer some guidance to agents who are confronted with a problem calling for action on their part and who want to make a choice they will find satisfying (as rational beings, as pleasure-maximizers, etc.). The care ethic cannot provide much help in thinking about concrete cases, largely because it supplies no principle or end for orienting or guiding our deliberations. Consider the following case:

An advertising executive approaches her corporate manager with a request to be allowed to work out of her home during her pregnancy and for a year following birth of her twins. During the same period, another employee asks the corporate manager for release time to pursue a MBA. The corporation does not have a policy in place authorizing extended pregnancy leave or release time for professional development. But the manager has been empowered to work with his employees to make them both more productive and happier within the workplace. How should the manager respond to these two requests?

We know the care ethic values being responsive to the individual and particular needs of others. Consequently, *ceteris paribus*, the care ethicist presumably would approve of both the corporation's empowerment policy and any steps the manager adopts to empower himself and his employees. However, it is not clear that the manager should grant the woman's request. In this case, there is at least one other employee who desires release time. The care ethic understands caring as a two-party process. Rarely, though, do our actions affect only one person. Caring for an elderly parent may come at the expense of one's children. In this case, giving the woman a leave may make it impossible for another employee to get further education. Clearly, some principles or guidelines are needed to think about balancing multiple parties' claims. Simply telling agents to listen to others' concerns receptively is not terribly helpful. The ethical challenge is not simply the *analytic* problem of merely identifying and listening to various parties' claims. At some point, one has to figure out how to *synthesize* a plan of action that is appropriately responsive to various legitimate concerns of these different parties. The care ethic does not provide any way to arrive at this synthesis. It escalates our level of anxiety about doing the right thing and doing enough and then simply leaves us in this neurotic state.

Let me be clear. I am not claiming that the woman's request *must* be given equal weight as the man's. While a Kantian might take such a position and then insist upon granting or denying requests on an all or nothing basis, I am willing to concede that a case might be made for weighing some parties' claims more heavily than others in some circumstances. My point is rather that, when there are competing claims which cannot both be honored, there is a need for a weighing process that culminates in a judgment. This weighing process cannot proceed without taking its bearings from some principle or some way of being in the world that is substantive enough to help the agent or agents arrive at a reasonable, satisfactory solution.

The care ethic, unlike Kantian or virtue ethics, does not provide for these guidelines. There are some indications that, if forced to choose between the two leave requests, a care ethicist like Gilligan or Noddings would give precedence to nurturing a child over obtaining an MBA. For, as we have seen, they take interpersonal caring as exemplary. However, this precedence must be argued for, not simply asserted. A compelling countercase certainly could be made for granting the MBA request. Traditionally, education has been thought to play a pivotal role in enriching people's lives. Indeed, two-person caring may even presuppose caring for higher education and culture. Without well-educated fellow citizens, bringing children into the world may be a cruel act. Caring for children surely includes providing a secure community in which they can thrive. Two-person unprincipled caring seems to be a much too narrow and too vague framework for thinking through either issues of justice or those involving the meaning and value of caring.

The current care framework is not merely too constricted. It also is difficult to relate to professional ethics, business ethics, and other well-established modes of thinking about practical problems. These other ethics unquestionably face difficulties of their own. However, before we can decide whether we should embrace a care ethic, we need an argument showing that it is superior to these other ways of thinking. It certainly is not obvious that it is better. To see why not, consider another case:

> A project manager works in the operations area of a bank. One of his corporate customers wants his area to do some special processing of their securities. The operations area could do this work but not without implementing a host of special procedures. Should the project manager accept this piece of business?

According to the care ethic, truly ethical agents reach out toward the person who is asking for help and struggle to individualize their response. Applying a rule is not permitted since doing so tends to rigidify the situation and distance the ethical person from the cared-for party. Yet this analysis is unduly rigid in its own demands. Surely the banker ought not to be so responsive that he jeopardizes the bank's welfare, the jobs of all of the bank's employees, and the deposits and loans of all the bank's customers. However, the "caring" act threatens all of these parties' welfare. Processing tailored to suit a particular customer's needs frequently entails substantial operational risks. Workers may not be accustomed to dealing with processes in which they do not engage routinely. Mistakes in delivering securities can be quite expensive. Furthermore, the sheer expense of setting up and monitoring an alternative form of processing may more than offset revenues earned. For all of these reasons, the project manager quite reasonably may hesitate to take on a number of customers, all of whom desire some customized product.

The banker would be foolish not to consider these risk and expense factors. The care ethicist fails to consider the reasonable limitations the various ends of professions place upon an agent's response. Once again the difficulty can be traced back to the care ethicist's preference for *interpersonal* caring. While it seems sound to insist that the agent show his respect for another person's individuality by listening to his or her special concerns, the agent cannot be bound always to accede to, or perhaps even to negotiate with, another's demands. In some cases, people act manipulatively. In business, for example, a customer may not state his real reason for wanting to do a particular deal or to buy a certain product. In other cases, customer expectations may simply be inconsistent with the businessperson's obligation to keep a company productive and profitable over the long term. If this point is granted, then the ethicist has effectively conceded that something like a professional ethic is going to "trump" a care ethic. What then exactly is the additional value the care ethic brings to the analysis of business or other spheres of human activity?

We are told that caring for an end, cause, idea or thing is merely an analogue to caring for another person.[56] However, the cases I have been discussing suggest that perhaps it is care for people that is the derivative notion. Certainly a case could be made for the primacy of caring for ends. Given a choice between a non-communicative physician who is able to heal and a "caring" incompetent, most people would choose the former. The doctor's end of healing "trumps" caring in the sense that the act of healing gives shape to the doctor–patient interaction, providing it both with its focus and its limits. The doctor who tries to "care" for the patient by sexually massaging her has acted unethically because, while palpitation is healing, sexual massage is not.

It may be objected, "The doctor who gives a sexual massage is not truly caring for his patient." That may be so, but what limits the physician's intimacy with his patient is clearly the professional end of healing, not caring *per se*. Caring as conceived by Noddings and Gilligan always drives parties in the direction of greater intimacy.[57] I would also note that, once caring is treated as primary, the specific end of a practice is made to play second fiddle. In a funny way, the end of medicine becomes preserving relations, not healing people. But the doctor who does no more than keep the patient in relation with him or her is practicing a kind of fraud on the patient who is there to be healed. While the "male" model may err on the side of advocating cold, distant treatment of clients, patients, and customers, the "female" model mistakenly treats corporations, professions, and other institutions as though they existed simply in order to constitute and maintain relations among different parties.[58] Although female ethicists repeatedly emphasize the need to attend to the special obligations people have, they entirely neglect the role-based obligations of professionals and officials and focus almost exclusively on special relations among family members or friends. They forget that bank managers, doctors, and attorneys each have a primary, specific end of promoting a good of certain parties—the corporate shareholder, patient, and client respectively. It is this end that provides professionals with practical focus.[59]

This end is not necessarily incompatible with caring. As I have argued elsewhere at length, a form of caring for the individual as such is built into, but also qualified by, the particular end in question.[60] The care ethic's mistake lies in ignoring the history and the rationale behind well-worked-out ethics of various practices. It opts in favor of requiring people to care. This demand is practically naive not only because it overlooks the role played by the specific ends of particular practices but also because it ignores the various ways in which caring may depend upon arrangements supported by these other ethics it has cavalierly dismissed. Think of the psychiatrist who desires to attend the wedding of his daughter, a child for whom he cares deeply. On the day of the wedding, one of his patients has a major crisis. Few people would deny that the patient, as well as the daughter, has a claim on the psychiatrist's time and attention. Given that the psychiatrist has taken a public oath to come for the benefit of the sick—an oath designed to elicit and sustain the patient's trust—the patient legitimately expects medical assistance now that he is sick.[61] In this case, the conflict is not one intrinsic to caring itself (i.e. it is not like Noddings' problem of how a caring person can lovingly look after both dogs and cats at the same time and in the same house). The conflict instead is a fairly typical one arising because an agent has two sorts of commitments—personal and professional. The patient's claim to the doctor's attention is grounded in a promise, a promise supported by an institutional apparatus designed to make trust possible. The conflict can be resolved not by virtue of the psychiatrist's caring "more" but by an appeal to this institutional support structure. The psychiatrist can go to the daughter's wedding because he can call upon fellow psychiatrists who have publicly promised to provide just this sort of support. It is the more impersonal professional ethic that makes the personal caring possible.

Problem 3: political naiveté of the care ethic

There is a third practical problem with care ethics. How are the regulative principles of care (such as they are—e.g. "receive the other as a total person") to be related to the rule of law, another very important regulative principle in communities generally deemed ethically legitimate? The law regulates relations among strangers, some of whom are violent. What insights does the care ethic offer for dealing with such people?

Gilligan herself does not say much that is helpful on this topic. She simply "exhorts us to recognize difference, to engage in dialogue, and to validate women's thought."[62] This response has struck many women as far too glib. A number of female ethicists, especially some of the more explicitly feminist ones, have attempted to go beyond Gilligan's and Noddings' early versions of care ethics and to extend their insights to ethics of rights and justice. Diana Meyers, for example, interprets care ethics as requiring that the legal system make more of an appeal to equity. She would change the scope of current rights talk. Precisely because law is formulated to deal with groups or classes of people, it is not as attentively supple as it should be to the individual needs and desires of people living in the community. Our jurors and judges should recognize this problem with the law's generality and attend unsentimentally and objectively to real differences in the situations of people subject to the law.[63] In addition, lawmakers should incorporate the concerns of those who have no voice and whose interests have consequently been overlooked. Our representatives should realize that vulnerable people like the handicapped, children, and elderly need protection and care. Laws should be redrafted with a view to honoring practices of interdependence instead of always emphasizing individuals' claims against each other. Held, for example, argues:

> Instead of importing into the household principles derived from the marketplace, perhaps we should import to the wider society the relations suitable for mothering persons and children. This approach suggests that just as relations between persons within the family should be based on concern and caring rather than contracts, so various relations in the wider society should be characterized by more care and concern.[64]

No doubt a case could be made for more equity in the law. And, if marketplace principles are indeed resulting in policies that are keeping large classes of people in our community from thriving, then Held's idea is one ethicists will have to take seriously. However, whether either of the above proposals will result in better laws and government is questionable. It is not clear what the connection is, if any, between care as ministering to needs and particular forms of government. A totalitarian regime might be able to meet a person's needs as well as, and maybe even better than, a democracy. (NB: The mortality rate in the former USSR has been steadily rising as the regimes have become less totalitarian and more democratic.) Is there any necessary connection between "care" and democratic values? If there is none, we may want to think twice before we restructure government to meet personal needs better.

It also should be noted that neither proposal grapples with the possibility that the law will not merely overlook some group but actually may legitimate its oppression. Calling for the law to be applied more equitably has little force if the people whose situations are not being respected have limited access to the legal system and media and hence possess no way to publicize their position. In this case, caring paradoxically may legitimate a structure that represses the very voices of individuals we should be attending to as caring individuals. Held's "caring" strategy of having legislators speak for the disenfranchised has its dangers as well. Why should everyone who is bound by the law be subjected to Held's vision of suitable mothering relations? Moreover, the introduction of care concepts into justice talk may simply result in care issues being rephrased in terms of rights and rigid rules, the very language female ethicists have found too unwieldy for dealing with the nuances of human relations.[65] If the justice and care perspectives are to be combined (and it seems they must be, if a care ethic is to have any impact on our public life), we need a more radical rethinking of whether and how democratic law can be made more caring and responsive to individuals (see Chapter 4).

In addition, if the care ethic is to be practicable, it needs to address the problem of violent individuals. We might argue, as Plato, Kant, and to a lesser degree Aristotle do, that the political problem of organizing a state in which all members can thrive and be fully free arises largely because people do not "receive" each other. That is, they do not see value in what the other does and is. For example, if Plato is right, people without certain training and a sense of honor never come to value the life of philosophers.[66] Lacking such an understanding of the worth of other people's practices, they act to destroy the lives of others and themselves as well. The care ethic simply sidesteps this issue. By requiring us to act so as to usher in a nonviolent world, the care ethic completely avoids the issue of the psychological cause(s) of violence. In doing so, it jeopardizes its practicality and regulative force because it is unclear whether a nonviolent world is even possible. By focussing on the case in which one agent (the mother) is by definition predisposed to see the child as worthy of attention and nurturance, the ethic glosses over the political conundrum: what sanctions or punishments, if any, may a community legitimately impose upon people whose behavior it finds unacceptable and perhaps even threatening?

The care ethic recommends that we should work with these people. We are told to reach out to them and to examine ourselves to make sure that we are truly caring. While there is good reason to engage in self-scrutiny (see Problem 5), might there not be some limits to this scrutiny and to the alleged obligation never to place our fellow citizens beyond the pale? For example, Aristotle argues for absolute prohibitions against murder and theft. These acts are always intolerable everywhere for two reasons. First, they make individual human thriving or fulfillment impossible. I cannot be thriving if I am dead. Similarly, in order to accomplish my plans and projects, I need some sort of property rights which I can reliably invoke. Second, such acts are inconsistent with the reasoning of the well-ordered person (who can help build and rule a thriving state). For example, it makes little sense to claim that I can steal another's property and make it "my own" when the notion of ownership depends on a system of law and rights which the thief's act is undermining. The existence of these absolutes helps explain why we allow a violent self-defense when someone is trying to murder or steal from a person. The care ethic (or at least Noddings' and Gilligan's version of it) has difficulties handling this case of self-defense because it grounds the morality of all actions in a natural impulse to care and to remain in relation.[67] Yet it is precisely caring which seems out of place here. While there may be problems with this Aristotelian argument for absolutes, care ethics must offer their own version of whether, when, and why acts of self-defense or even theft and murder are morally permissible. The care ethic fails to do this.

The political naiveté of the care ethic equally is manifest in its curiously cramped discussion of human relations. While Noddings asserts that a woman might sacrifice principle to save a child, this assertion ignores the fact that women do not always oppose principles to caring. Think, for example, of the mother who discovers that her teenage son has been molesting children and who turns him in to the authorities. The mother grieves for her son. She would like to see him saved. Yet she may care equally for these violated children, for the other potential victims of her son, and for these victims' grieving and angry parents. It would seem that true caring must somehow encompass these other parties in its purview as well. If it does not do so, it is little more than nepotism. What enlarges the scope of our concern in cases involving violence or bigotry appears to be some absolute principle that we should not wrong *anyone*.[68] In other words, in deciding how best to care, we must look to an end of our interaction with other members of the community, an end that includes communal justice understood roughly as rendering each member his or her due. The care ethicists' contrast between care and those principles that we typically associate with justice is sustainable largely because the examples they cite are two-person and involve people who are already in some actual, voluntary intimate relation (boyfriend–girlfriend; mother–foetus). These friendships often are founded on caring or love; legal justice may be out of place in these friendships. The moment we complicate the picture with third-party and involuntary relations with strangers who may prove violent, the contrast is considerably less clear and defensible.

Gilligan does concede that we need an ethics of justice as well as of care. One ought not supplant the other. Rather they should work in tandem to enable us to arrive at an ethically good stance.[69] This response, though, misses my point. The two points of view may pull in opposite directions, and how then are we to adjudicate this tension? From which stance—the care or justice perspective—do we make the requisite judgment? Furthermore, this response ignores the question of what force or factor enlarges the scope of caregiving. To the extent that the claims of justice are responsible for this enlargement, the care ethic is not the co-equal of the justice ethic. While the care ethic might be reconceived in a way which gives it equal stature with an ethic of justice (see Chapter 4), it has not been so conceived to date.

It is tempting to think (as Noddings does) that our memory of having been cared for ourselves will do the work of enlarging our sphere of concern.[70] However, this move to ground ethics in the individual's psychology paradoxically provides even less reason to hope for an enlarged sensibility. In the first place, we do not know exactly what the cared-for will remember. If he recalls being cared for by a white woman, he may associate caring with certain racial traits and become suspicious of those who are of a different race. So a memory of having been cared for in the past may undermine, rather than foster, an attitude of active concern for other people. Furthermore, given the large number of abused children and spouses within our society, many people are not going to have the requisite scope-enlarging memories. On the contrary, they may be the very parties most likely to abuse others. Somehow we collectively must evolve a way of living with abusers and their victims. As long as the care ethic can provide no satisfying answer to this problem, the charge of political naiveté still stands.

Finally, we ought not forget that the political has an impersonal dimension completely overlooked by the care ethic. On the one hand, there are power structures in which individuals tend to operate unwittingly. On the other hand, the political realm has an arbitrariness to it that we have to accept for the sake of orderly living. To take Kurt Riezler's example: it does not matter whether we all drive on the left or right side of the road. What does matter is that we give up the right to make our own private determinations and empower some authority to make that decision and to enforce it. If an anarchistic American decides that he wants to start driving on the left side of the road, the response most consistent with human thriving surely is not to become "engrossed" in this person but rather to enforce the law and get him off the streets before he kills someone.

Pathologies of caring

Problem 4: caring cannot be specified in purely formal terms

Since the care ethicist takes every act of care to be unique and thinks that the end result of a caring interaction will vary depending upon who is involved and what their circumstances are, she is driven to characterize the caring act in purely formal terms of engagement.[71] Take the case of the mother–child relation so favored by care ethicists. Through mutual responsiveness, the two struggle to form a new self, a shared self.[72] Noddings goes so far as to claim that the mother and child are not *in* a relation. They *are* the relation.[73] A caring act is one which recognizes this fact.

This characterization of an ethically good action is woefully inadequate. Caring for the child is not an infinitely open or endless activity. The responsible mother does not endorse every whim of her child. *Pace* Noddings, the mother sees that there is some value to discipline and to requiring children to do things they may find repugnant.[74] Developing greater physical co-ordination and mastery of many arts require that children practice movements and do exercises they may not initially desire to do. She cares for her child by taking steps to have their relation evolve *in a certain way*. In very rough terms, she wants her child to acquire those traits that enable her not merely to get by in the world but to thrive in it. Nurturing has an end. It is this end which gives it its value, a point that gets overlooked in talk about honoring others' activities and becoming engrossed in their perspectives.[75] A purely formal definition of care does not capture the goal of nurturing, and consequently misses what is ethically good about the mother–child relation.

Furthermore, a relation does not qualify as ethically good *even by the care ethicists' own standards* just because it forges a shared, mutually responsive self. It matters crucially what sort of shared self is being forged. We can imagine a sadist and a masochist creating a high-risk shared self in which each party's needs and interests are attended to meticulously by the other person. This relation would seem to pass all the tests for a caring relation stated above and yet might be rife with self-deception and possibilities for manipulation—i.e. be disrespectful of the people whom we are supposed to be receiving in their totality. To take a historical example: Bonnie and Clyde would seem to have met all the criteria for being caring. They certainly were mutually responsive. The relation opened up new vistas, albeit vistas for criminal activity. It was a "snug fit," so much so that each self got redefined as a relational self.[76] It is no accident that we always refer to them as a pair. Nevertheless, it is hard to see how a shared criminal self or a relation founded on a desperate mutual fear of being alone qualifies as good, given that these relations are often manipulative. Recall that the care ethicist criticizes traditional, male ethics on the ground that they may legitimate relations of unequal power in which one party does not permit the other to be fully present in his or her otherness. The same charge applies to ethics of care.[77]

The difficulty, then, is that being in a relation *per se* is not ethically good. Indeed, Noddings' requirement that we *never* place the other beyond our care risks condemning people to an unhappy life of enduring disrespect.[78] Consider the care ethicists' response to the following sort of scenario:

A woman works as a cash management consultant. She must routinely meet with a male treasurer at a different company. Recently this man has begun to make sexual innuendoes every time they meet. Although the woman tells him that sexual jokes and references are not germane to their business and that these comments leave her feeling uncomfortable, he continues with his comments.

Regardless of whether the man's behavior constitutes sexual harassment in the legal sense of the term, the care ethicist would object to the man's behavior. The woman has her own values and is entitled, in the care ethicists' view, to continue with her own projects. She should not have to quit her job to avoid constant embarrassment and frustration. On the other hand, the care ethic prohibits confrontation or any action that leaves the person ostracized or removed from the human circle of caring. The woman should "move" toward the man and try to embrace his concerns, seeing them through his eyes, and should attribute the best possible motive consonant with reality to the cared-for.[79] The "one-caring considers always the possibility that the one-appearing-to-do evil is actually in a deteriorated state, that he is acting under intolerable pressure or in error."[80] In this sense, Sarah Hoagland is right to accuse the care ethic of therapizing all relations.[81] For the care ethic seems to obligate the consultant to explore with the man why he thinks it appropriate to attempt fixedly to transform a business encounter into an intimate one.

Unlike those feminists who categorically condemn this therapeutic approach (and who thus fail to live by their ethical principle of considering the nuances of the individual case!), I am willing to concede that the therapeutic response may have merit in some contexts. Speech often does discover ways of illuminating others' behavior for them without leaving them outside the realm of human concern. Consider Jesus' encounter with the Pharisees who ask him whether they should follow the Law of Moses and stone a woman caught in adultery.[82] Jesus' answer—"Let him who is without sin throw the first stone"—radically transforms the situation. It acknowledges the Pharisees' concern with enforcing their communal law. Jesus never says that adultery is not a sin or even that adulteresses should not be stoned. On the contrary, he discovers through the encounter itself another possibility *implicit in the law*. If everyone is bound by the law, then the Pharisees need to look within and consider whether they have thought of themselves as bound by this law they would enforce. In effect, he forces them to deliver judgment upon themselves. Unwilling to die for their sins, they drop their stones and slip away.

One of the strengths of the care ethic is its desire to move us beyond an often mechanical and vindictive enforcement of rules toward a thinking that includes all parties affected by our actions within its purview. However, it must also be acknowledged that the therapeutic response is of little value if and when others are unwilling to participate in this thinking. Jesus' speech works only because members of his audience still possess a sense of shame and are willing to consider the possibility that they, as well as the adulteress, have sinned. If the obnoxious treasurer lacks such a sense of shame and simply is unwilling to hear what the woman says, speech is unlikely to transform him. In fact, adopting the therapeutic, relational response may serve to increase intimacy, which is exactly the outcome the woman is trying to avoid.

As I noted in the prior section, the law exists in part to rein in those whose behavior (including their speech) signals that they are unwilling to participate in a communal discussion of the right way to behave. Some people simply want to have their own way and are willing to violate other people's rights to privacy, property, and even life in order to prevail. We have seen that the care ethicist insufficiently values the important ways in which the law and mechanisms of institutional enforcement supplement caring. Here I would echo the oft-expressed concern about the potential danger to the self posed by care ethics' insistence that people keep on "working at the relation."[83] Surely we know enough about battered women syndrome to be wary of this sort of demand.[84] Being in a relation capable of fostering thriving may be valuable (I hedge because we haven't been told by the care ethicist exactly what "thriving" is). But staying in a relation because each of us supposedly is a relational self can be pathological and can interfere with our ability to discover and develop our own voice. So once again the care ethic appears to impose demands that are not consistent with its own understanding of care as a practice respectful of the individuality of the caregiver as well as of the cared-for.

Problem 5: inadequate self-suspicion in this ethic

The previous problem centered on the risk the care ethic poses to the caregiver. The care ethic puts the cared-for at risk as well. Given the well-known phenomena of bad faith and projection, the ethic should have some feature or factor capable of engendering self-suspicion in the caregiver regarding her own motives. There is, however, no Socratic daimon nor any warning regarding pride and hubris in this ethic. Nor is there any standard external to the two parties to which the cared-for can appeal in the event he or she feels misunderstood or abused by the caregiver. The care ethic bases itself upon only the subjective desires, whims, needs of the cared-for and caregiver; and the caregiver's feeling that she must receive the other.

The idea of "receiving," as opposed to manipulating, the other is supposed to do the work of countering projections. The problem is that this receipt is never passive. While Noddings does acknowledge that "receiving" another person or thing alternates with a more active state of manipulating and hypothesizing,[85] she overlooks the fact that the receipt of other people or things is itself theory-informed. Numbers and solutions to problems visited the mathematician Ramanujan in his dreams. However, he spent his whole day working with numbers and problems before arriving at the solution to those problems. Solutions did not pop randomly into his brain.

If receipt is not purely passive, then the concern about projection re-emerges in connection with this receiving of the other. There are at least two major problems. First, if there truly are no public criteria for caring (e.g. that certain acts must be done in some cases or done in a certain way),[86] then it is hard to see how the child is to learn how to care and to become ethical. Second, since the care ethic provides no public or more objective standard for care, it leaves the cared-for in a very vulnerable position. This caring is largely unidirectional, modeled on the mother–child relation (more about this analogy under Problem 6). But an adult is not a child. While I certainly would not advocate ignoring children's opinions, the concerns of adults have a better claim to be honored because they are presumed to be more reasoned. What, then, compels the caregiver to honor the concerns of the cared-for adult in the case where the caregiver herself is oppressing the cared-for party? What, for example, protects the disabled adult from the "care" of a caregiver who is so intent upon nurturance that she does not see the way in which she is infantilizing the disabled person?[87] The ethic of care underestimates the danger of oppression and fails to provide the cared-for and caregiver with any viable strategies for identifying and fighting it.

Problem 6: worrisome privileging of the earth mother

Close attention to Gilligan's and Noddings' choice of paradigmatic relations shows that this concern with projection is not misplaced. On one reading, the whole care ethic borders on one large projection because Gilligan and Noddings and other advocates of caring (e.g. Ruddick) take the nurturing "earth mother" as exemplary. No one would deny that we were all children once nor that children reach adulthood only if they get some caring along the way from adults or that the fact of dependence can figure in our moral reasoning.[88] Even a traditional "male" ethicist like the Kantian Alan Gewirth appeals to interdependence when he argues that we have a duty to be benevolent. It is a contradiction in will, and consequently immoral from the Kantian perspective, to say that we want to complete our own projects but do not want to help anyone else who needs our assistance. It is a contradiction because many of our projects cannot even get off the ground without other people's help. Therefore, wanting to complete our projects entails wanting to help others with theirs.[89]

So interdependence is undeniable. That said, we must beware of slipping into a nostalgia for childish dependence. When Noddings says she cares for her children—and adds "even one of my grown children"[90]— her afterthought certainly suggests that she believes the most important caring occurs with respect to the infant. If so, what will check a caregiver's temptation to infantilize another person so that she can experience the joy of nurturing? Granting the growing child independence may be quite threatening to a woman who has defined herself as a mother who provides security for her dependants.

It is striking in this regard that Gilligan and Noddings both celebrate the goddess Demeter's caring, yet neither deals with what is clearly the "shadow" or the "dark side" of the Demeter-earth mother myth. After her daughter is abducted by Pluto, an enraged Demeter sets out to destroy the earth. Demeter will not accept separation. Her daughter must always be with her if she is to be the Demeter (i.e. the demonstrative mother) she believes herself to be. Demeter's caring has a narcissistic component, and her rage reveals a basic non-acceptance of the inevitability that children will grow up and that the world will intrude into the security of the family circle. It is not accidental that Persephone is abducted while Persephone—the daughter Demeter has tried to create in her own image—is engrossed *with a narcissus*. Both Demeter and Persephone must learn that the family circle is not and cannot be hermetically sealed off from the world. The moral challenge is not simply to care but to love in a world filled with betrayal. A parent who tries to keep her children and herself absolutely immune from betrayal prevents both from moving into a realistic relation with the world.

If, as Noddings suggests, caregivers do indeed desire to act morally because they want to experience the pleasure of being cared for, then we, as caregivers, are always in danger of re-encountering ourselves in our meetings with other people. In one sense, this re-encounter is inevitable because we have no way of meeting each other except through the ideas each of us already has about the world and about another. Still, we have the option of checking our interpretations of what others are saying by asking, "Do you mean this sort of thing?" or "If you say X, would you consent to Y as well?" If our respondent says, "That is not what I mean, not what I mean at all," then we can try again to grasp what she means. I worry that care ethics in their current form discourage this sort of probing. To the extent the caregiver's primary motive for caring is the desire to recapture the warm and fuzzy feeling of infantile life, the caregiver has little reason to stay engaged should the cared-for party reject the caregiver's interpretation. Rejection is not a warm and fuzzy feeling. The caregiver may be tempted to move on or to become angry with the cared-for party who has failed to value the caregiver's concern.

Noddings may be aware of the danger of projection. She acknowledges, for example, that parents sometimes become over-involved with their children.[91] We might plausibly interpret this phenomenon as one of projection: the parent attempts to live through her child the life she wished to have. But what will check such over-involvement given that, in this ethic, there are no objective demands of virtue or reason to require that we treat the person as someone with different, yet possibly legitimate, opinions and outlooks? This problem is particularly acute within the care ethic because it privileges the biological relations of reproduction and nurturance. Others have observed that reproduction itself can be seen as the selfish attempt of the parent to reproduce his or her life in the child.[92] While not all parents are selfish, some are. A narcissistic caring risks reinforcing this selfishness. For thinkers like Aristotle and Kant, the political is distinct from the personal life of the home and reproduction, and it imposes demands of its own. These political demands (e.g. the duty to honor other citizens' rights in the case of Kant, their distinctive essence in the case of Aristotle) work to counter the conservative tendency of tribes and the family circle to protect and endlessly reproduce their "own." The care ethic, by contrast, largely collapses the personal into the political and does so in such a way that the political is not available as a counterweight to narcissistic caring.[93]

Nor is Noddings' appeal to Martin Buber of much help. She uses Buberian language to argue that, in true caring, the cared-for party "fills the firmament" of the one-caring.[94] This metaphor should not give the cared-for party much confidence because it was, of course, Narcissus' image that "filled the firmament" as he bent closer and closer to the water. To have our horizons entirely occupied by the other is no guarantee of ethical behavior. The perceived other may be nothing more than our own reflection. Again, the contrast with another thinker is helpful.

Plato's Socrates counters the possibility that he will hear only what he finds gives him pleasure: (1) by talking to a variety of colleagues instead of becoming "engrossed" in a single "cared-for" party; and (2) by insisting that all parties hold themselves accountable to what argument discloses. I will say more about the type of argument and the meaning of such accountability in Chapter 4. Here I would merely note that the relation Socrates has to his multiple colleagues is mediated by the spoken argument (in Greek, the *logos*) and the desire not to assent to falsehoods that will frustrate desire in the long run. In other words, for Plato, there is no "direct" relation with, or "receiving" of, other people. Any person legitimately may call anyone else on the carpet by recalling a prior argument to which that person assented or by offering a new argument that parties to the conversation find compelling. Gilligan and Noddings, however, make the self ultimately accountable only to itself. In the event of rejection or challenge by someone else, the agent's only responsibility is to look inward and ask himself one question: has he been truly caring? As long as he can answer in the affirmative (using what is perhaps a fatally flawed notion of care), he has no further responsibility. Self encounters itself endlessly in a caring relation bordering on idolatry.

Problem 7: the diminution of responsibility

There is another problem: a perception of one's self as caring may undermine one's ability to act upon one's beliefs. Children who grow up seeing themselves as very connected to their parents may have difficulty resisting authorities whom they believe are acting badly. If they depend upon these familial authority figures for support and for their definition of their self, then contradicting other authority figures may be a scary and difficult course to even contemplate, much less undertake. Some research supports this claim. In her study of students' involvement with the Free Speech Movement, Norma Haan found that a significant number of students who saw themselves in very relational terms did not get involved in this protest, even though they claimed to support the beliefs of those who did actively protest. Seeking for harmony, they were disappointed and frustrated by the "moral complexity of civil disobedience" and "reacted with defensive withdrawal and denial."[95]

The point is not that resistance to authorities is always the right course. We can easily imagine violent or angry students seizing upon occasions to be confrontational irrespective of how their actions would affect their and other parties' ability to live a good life. The concern is rather that the desire to "remain connected" will be used as an excuse for not confronting and resisting people when it may be appropriate to do so. Inaction can be rationalized on the ground that action will alienate people. If the prospect of a loss of harmony results in the self feeling angst, the care ethicist will say the action is bad. However, some cases of political action will involve a great deal of stress and anxiety, especially if they force the agent to rethink some of his or her fundamental commitments. The care ethic provides agents with an excuse to flee from this anxiety. On this score, the care ethic might be said to be anti-developmental or pathological because it does not in any way keep people's feet to the moral fire and require them to work through their concerns and conflict.

The need for greater autonomy

My final set of concerns centers on the care ethic's view of the self as a relation. We need to consider whether this view of the self goes too far in denying an agent the right to some self-drawn boundaries. If I am right that an ethical perspective specifies the conditions under which all people may enjoy a shared and satisfying life within a community, then an ethic cannot require agents to sacrifice themselves for each other. In principle, such an ethic of self-sacrifice might require that everyone in the community die for the sake of each other. Then the ethic would be in the self-contradictory position of attempting to regulate *shared living* by requiring that everyone die. The ethic of care risks becoming no ethic at all because it minimizes the value of selfishness and is too quick to dismiss the traditional concern with autonomy.

Problem 8: the overlooked value of selfishness

Let us backtrack for a moment and ask: how exactly are we to understand the claim that the self is relational? It is obviously true that the human self has permeable boundaries. We develop a personality and acquire character through interaction with others. The very mechanisms for this acquisition of character appear to be developed through social intercourse. Thus, while children apparently possess an innate capacity to develop a sense of shame, infants do not blush. The child needs social intercourse to develop a self capable of being an object unto itself—i.e. to feel ashamed of what he or she has done. This development comes along with the acquisition of language in society and the concomitant ability of the self to name itself to itself—"*I* did this naughty thing."

It is true as well that we are dependent upon others' good will and care in all kinds of ways. We would have died as infants if we had not been fed properly. We routinely rely upon others to look after our interests by maintaining the elevators we ride and the bridges we cross. More importantly, we define ourselves in terms of our overarching concern for other things and people. Van Gogh cared passionately for his art; the devoted teacher's care for her students transforms a job into a lifelong vocation. All of this must be conceded. Nevertheless, there is a difference between claiming that relations are important to self-development and self-esteem and maintaining, as Noddings does, that the *self is nothing but a relation*. This latter claim is incoherent. Many of our relations, e.g. with friends and colleagues, are voluntary. We can and do break these relations. We do so *as individuals* in a relation. No relation ever breaks itself.

The boundaries between people in a relation are usually drawn by these same people. The line unquestionably can be drawn poorly. The care ethicist can be read as railing against the conception of the self as largely independent of others and with a right to his or her own space. To the extent that this conception of the autonomous self ignores the many ways in which we define ourselves in relation to others, we can say that the line is badly drawn. But it does not follow that there is no line between the selves. *A permeable boundary is a boundary nevertheless.* Children know this very well and try in various ways to distance themselves from parents who are too clingy or controlling. Some studies of children's literature, for example, have shown that

> great children's books subvert the conventional structures and ideals of the adult world. Children's favorite stories tend to express ideas and emotions of which grown ups disapprove, to poke fun at parental authorities, and to offer honest, clear-eyed appraisals of social pretense.[96]

Children draw the line, distinguishing themselves from others, and so should adults. We should reject the attempt to define caring as "not being willing at any difficult moment to say 'Well it's your problem'."[97] Sometimes other people's problems are *theirs* to be worked out. Indifference may be exactly the right strategy with a friend who is in love with her neuroses and unwilling to address them.

In the remainder of this section, I want to sketch an argument that ethical caring is not identical with unconditional love. The self is sufficiently distinct from the relation as to be entitled to specify some conditions which her voluntary relations should meet. In the event these conditions are not met, she is entitled to break off these relations. I am not here trying to provide an exhaustive list of necessary and sufficient conditions for a healthy, ethically caring relation. While I will later make the case for the need for some general regulative ethical principles, I accept female ethics' claim that specifics of relations always must be worked out by the involved parties. At this juncture, I will settle for offering a few general observations about relations with a view to making plausible my claim that we are individually entitled to impose some conditions upon our relations, even though the precise meaning and form of these conditions may vary in different situations. I will focus on the case of friendships, as opposed to the more distant citizen–citizen, professional–client, or businessperson–customer relations because friendships are generally thought to be the more caring.

It seems reasonable to expect our friends to be willing to challenge our self-conception or actions. While it may not be pleasant to accept criticism, one of the ways in which we develop is by asking ourselves hard questions: am I really worthy of this friendship? Have I perhaps let my friend down? Often fights with friends or lovers are the most intense precisely because here the self is potentially most in play. Indeed, we may feel most alive at these moments. For those who are willing to engage in soul-searching, friends can become their most cherished possessions. Our friends care enough for the shared self we are jointly inventing and exploring to insist that we do some hard work on ourselves. Fights sometimes serve to force the issue.

For this reason, it is a mistake to treat all caring as if it were a gooey, therapeutic overture in which the caregiver always maintains her cool and never threatens to break off the relation. It would be truer to ethical caring to admit the possibility of warnings and breaches. For example, if one of my "friends" insists upon being a sycophant, ratifying everything I say and do, irrespective of the wisdom of my speech and actions, then it might very well be a good thing for me to threaten to terminate the friendship unless she becomes a bit more critical. There are many cases in which we mistake our own self-interests. If our friends are unwilling to point out such cases, on whom can we rely to help us avoid unhappiness?

Similarly, it is reasonable to expect that in a truly caring relation each person will have, and be willing to defend, an idea of what the friendship should be. True, genuine friends do not insist dogmatically upon their own respective views of the friendship. But, if one person is doing all the thinking and the other person is nodding along and murmuring, "Whatever you think," then the relation is not going to develop either party's capacity for appropriate self-definition, a capacity which would seem a necessary prerequisite for acquiring a voice of one's own.[98] It may very well be the work of love to embrace another's behavior and to make adjustments to one's own.[99] There must be limits, though, to these adjustments if the caregiver is to retain any integrity of her own. Contrary to the popular song, it is not ethically permissible for you to "bend me, shape me anyway you want to" because "as long as you love me, it's all right."

Moreover, as we saw in the case of child nurturance, whether the caring is ethically good will depend not merely upon the relation being self-defining but also upon what kind of self is defined. While it may be possible to define an ethic in terms unique to care itself, this project will require considerably more fleshing out of the concept of care and attention to problems of the sort posed above. One helpful direction would be to take seriously the idea that a caring relation puts each party's self into play in a radical way and imposes a certain responsibility on these parties to do their part to think and to argue for a shared self *worth fashioning*. Both parties would be equals insofar as they are held accountable for contributing to such a self—i.e. insofar as each party avoids sycophancy and intellectual laziness. On this view, relations among adults would provide the standard by which to judge other relations—e.g. the parent–child relation. Although the child is not the parent's intellectual equal, it still may be a good practice for the parent to treat the child as though one day the child will be his or her equal. Such a practical precept would help to check any parental tendency to maintain the child in infancy forever, never permitting the child to challenge the parental point of view. I will return to this line of reasoning in Chapter 4. At this point, I would just note that an alternative vision of care conceived along this line of reasoning would seem to be more compatible with appropriately defining the self and retaining self-esteem than the care ethic's idea of simply being responsive to each other.

Problem 9: too easy dismissal of autonomy

Given the emphasis on embracing and moving toward other people, it is not surprising that the care ethicist finds an inherent conflict between acting autonomously and being caring. Gilligan worries about people using appeals to autonomy to opt out of relations, while Noddings explicitly considers various senses of autonomy and rejects all of them as too individualistic.[100] Noddings correctly notes that autonomy may be understood either as an ideal or as a defining trait of human beings as such. Both approaches, though, presuppose that an individual is autonomous if and only if the agent's actions are in some sense his or her own and not someone else's. Hence, for Kant, an agent acts autonomously only when he wills a non-contradictory act to which he can assent unproblematically as a rational being. However, for the care ethicist, a woman's action is truly her own if and only if her action honors her relational self. This view poses a problem: if the self is a relation, then every action of the self is actually an act of the relation and therefore the act cannot be said to belong to a single person. Rather it must belong to the relation. For this reason, autonomy in the traditional sense of individual responsibility and self-accountability is impossible. Care ethics would have us realize as much and freely choose interdependence.[101]

This rejection of traditional autonomy is too facile and may destroy women's power in three ways: (1) by requiring too much sacrifice from the women; (2) by stereotyping women; and (3) by forgetting that individual striving makes inter-personal caring possible. With respect to the first point: the idea of the relational self may slide easily into the idea that women should sacrifice themselves to provide care for others. We already have seen how the care ethic sometimes sounds as though it would oblige women to stay in abusive relations. Indeed, logically the woman cannot break these relations because she *is* the relation. This view reinforces cultural expectations that women always are to be available for men.[102] As Marilyn Frye puts it, "Male parasitism means that males *must have access* to women; it is the Patriarchal Imperative."[103] The care ethic sounds suspi-ciously like the flip side. The "Matriarchal Imperative" becomes women *must give access to men in order for women to be their true relational selves.*[104]

The care ethic thus tends to undermine any sense of female power and freedom at the same time as it celebrates the fulfillment and strength allegedly achieved through caring. Certain kinds of caring are fulfilling—namely, those that are freely and prudently chosen by women who have some sense of themselves as making a choice. If, however, women are completely economically dependent upon others or lack any meaningful freedom of choice, then they may find little fulfillment in caring. The torturer's victim cares what the torturer's next move will be. The victim even may make a good faith effort to enter into the thinking of the victimizer. (Think, for example, of the woman's efforts in John Fowles' novel *The Collector* to understand and to reach out to her tormentor as a fellow human being.)[105] Yet this caring is not particularly desirable because the victim does not want to be in this situation in the first place and because the relationship ignores the victim's good. And an *ethic* of care, concerned with specifying conditions for all members of the community to lead *satisfying* lives, cannot consistently endorse such caring.

The care ethic is also suspect because it ignores the erotic longings of the indi-vidual. All human longings are subsumed under the supposedly overriding desire to return to the caring, safe arms of mother.[106] This desire is an imputed one. If individuals were given the chance to describe their own longings, we would find, I submit, that a fair number of women (and men) desire to stretch themselves intellectually as well as emotionally and to pursue a variety of dreams. An artist may desire passionately to complete a sculpture in a new style. Or a scientist may devote herself to understanding how comets move or how a disease is genetically transmitted.[107] I suspect that the care ethicist ignores or deprecates these passions because they originate in the dream life of the individual and ultimately require action from that individual alone. Furthermore, they may interfere with a person's focus on relationships.[108] These dream imperatives may pit the artist or scientist against others who deny the value of the visions or who have other plans for the artist's life (consider the poignant conflict between George Seurat and his lover in Stephen Sondheim's *Sunday in the Park with George*)[109].

The care ethic is conspicuously silent about the role of our self-generated dreams in our ethical life. It makes it seem as though women have no desires in the world except to be in caring relations with children and with men. Yet we all have seen the passive aggression of women who nobly sacrifice themselves, becoming so-called "enablers" of others. People may try to live their lives through others. But when children have left the nest; or when the spouse or significant other has died or taken a new lover, the resentment often surfaces in the form of lament: "I have given to you so much. Why don't you visit (write, talk, etc.) me more often? How could you abandon me?"[110] The care ethic forgets that, in the final analysis, we each have to live our own lives, carving out a character and discovering a vocation for ourselves. In this respect, no one can give another person his or her life. There is a core independence we each have by virtue of the responsibility to choose our lives (and our relations!). To the extent ethics of care ignore and minimize this responsibility, they destroy female power in the name of saving it.

This last observation brings me to the second way in which the care ethic destroys women's power—by perpetuating crippling stereotypes of women. As we have seen, the care ethic privileges the earth mother figure, the Greek goddess Demeter, and ignores the many other goddesses who represent alternative modes of satisfaction. For example, both Noddings and Gilligan lavish praise on Demeter for her care for her daughter. They treat the earth mother as exemplary in other, more subtle ways as well. Gilligan, for example, analyzes at length women's reasoning as they make abortion decisions. She justifies this choice of scenario on the ground that it is here that women make choice about their identities. For her part, Noddings repeatedly alludes to her nurturing relations with her students, children, animals, and plants. Why, though, must Demeter, rather than Athena, Artemis, or Hera, be the central figure in an ethic which purports to capture women's concerns? Might not a woman's efforts to fulfill herself in her profession (an "Athena" concern) be just as important to some women as the decision to become a mother? By privileging the earth mother archetype, these ethics run the risk of stereotyping women (and men), the very evil they impute to male theorists like Kant and Kohlberg. It begins to look as though women who choose not to have children, who choose to love other women, or who choose to focus their energy on their teaching or painting are unethical and perhaps less "female" than all the earth mothers of the world. Furthermore, celebrating "mother care" sends a message that mother care is the best form of childrearing, even though this view is one we have come to believe only toward the end of this century. Perhaps it would be better for mother and child alike if children were raised by a network of other caregivers. Such an arrangement almost certainly would relieve the enormous burden that the ideal of 100 per cent mother care places on poor or single women for whom the Demeter myth is anything but empowering.[111]

Third, the care ethic forgets that, if it were not for individual "male" striving to excel at things like raising crops or building structures, there would be no food or shelter with which to meet others' needs. As I read these ethics, I find myself wondering who is going to supply resources for meeting our animal needs if everyone spends his or her life "receiving" and "caring for" others. The care ethic presumes a society in which either: (1) there are unlimited resources;[112] or (2) there is a class of unethical, non-caring beings who spend their day on farming, constructing buildings, inventing products, etc. The first vision is totally unrealistic and distracts us from the hard questions regarding what limits we should recognize; the second appears unjust. For if the ethical life presupposes these non-caring activities, then it can hardly dismiss them as ethically irrelevant! Moreover, if these other activities are the means to the caring life; and if, as we saw under Problem 1, the means to a good life are themselves good; then we have a whole host of uncaring activities that must be said to be good. Caring and living well therefore cannot be coextensive; and the care ethic must be said to fail to render these other activities their due. In addition, ostracizing the very people whose contributions make caring possible will undermine women's (and men's) efforts to promote another's good and, in this sense, will impede their ability to act well.

Conclusion

Drawing upon the above analysis, we can begin to sketch the outline of a more defensible ethic, a version that incorporates key insights from the care ethic while avoiding the above problems. Two insights are especially ethically significant. As I noted in the Introduction, an ethics/politics (I do not separate the two for reasons elaborated in the second half of this book) identifies the conditions under which it becomes possible for potentially violent people with varying understandings of the good to live a fulfilling, satisfying life together in a community. Care ethics' stress on including and listening to all people is ethically relevant because, if human beings think that their interests are being ignored, they have little incentive to remain in the community or to try to contribute to its functioning well. A defensible ethic will be sensitive to the likelihood that vulnerable and marginalized members of the community will frequently have little or no voice in the political process. We cannot legitimately claim to have furthered the public good if we have not even heard the concerns of a large portion of the public. The problem of inclusion is as much an ethical concern as traditional ethics' preoccupation with the problem of balancing competing claims.[113]

Care ethics are also right to stress the need to hear people express their concerns in their own voice. The care ethic demands that we let individuals speak of their concerns and needs in the terms they think appropriate and warns against the traditional tendency to make advance pronouncements regarding the form or content these interests must exhibit. Since it is certainly possible that any particular theorist's understanding of the interests, concerns and needs of others is mistaken, listening to these other people would seem to be the best way of insuring that they are rendered *their* due as opposed to being granted or given what some theorist mistakenly thinks they should receive. A practice of listening will be less alienating and will better serve to promote a shared, satisfying life for all members of the community.

Problems arise, though, when we consider how exactly persons' interests are to be taken into account. There are at least four major areas of concern. First, a defensible ethic of care should not impose its own definition of care. As we have seen, in their present form the care ethics strategy of attempting to unilaterally define what qualifies as care can result in caregivers who are overly maternalistic, highly narcissistic, and possibly manipulative and who have a vision that is too ahistorical and dangerously exclusive. If we are justified in drawing any conclusion from the analysis of this chapter, it is that the understanding each of us has about care is contestable. Consequently, caring relations need to be reconceived in a manner that creates and preserves a space in which parties to the relation can challenge the goodness of each other's caring.

Second, while it seems promising to think of ethically good caring as a process that creates a mutually responsive, shared self, we need to consider whether this self is worth creating. Two evil selves could be highly responsive to one another. Furthermore, the resulting shared self ought not to be such a tight fit that the individual is completely subsumed into the relation. Such a subsuming destroys the individual self that underpins many of our ethical notions (e.g. respect, justice, integrity) every bit as surely as does traditional theories' emphasis on generic human qualities. Again, the ethic needs to establish some limits on what the individual can be required to do in the name of the relation. For example, it would seem that the individual should not have to endorse another's view if that view seems mistaken. Nor should one party to the relation have the power to coerce another's consent. Both scenarios seem antithetical to human thriving because they preclude or truncate the process of discovering where both parties' true interests lie. A defensible ethic will establish limits allowing for such discovery. However, since these limits may prove as contestable as the idea of caring, they will have to be set by a process respectful of individuals' freedom and particularity. This process cannot consist simply in deriving formal universal and transcendental limits of respect for individual freedom and particularity because invoking universal, transcendental limits simply shifts the problem of contestability from the substance of the debate to the issue of the limits on the debate.

Third, a defensible ethic will need to find some reason or motive capable of inducing the agent to widen the scope of her concern and attention beyond the sphere of intimates. It is not sufficient to say that the caring person "receives" all who come within her purview. For her purview may be quite limited. Driven by an instinct to protect those who are her "own," those she has nurtured in the past, the caregiver may deny or overlook the interests and concerns of people who are affected, perhaps adversely, by her caring. Gilligan may sense that there is a problem here because, although she criticizes the appeal to principles and rights, she herself repeatedly appeals to an absolute right of the self to respect.[114] She and other care ethicists fail to specify, however, what motivates the caring person to care for this universal right. Instead, they settle for a "self . . . [who] is not engaged in internal conflict . . . and [who] is not attempting to correct its flaws by abstracting from itself and seeking to achieve the stance of an idealized observer."[115] While there are problems with the idea of a totally impartial spectator who can serve as a standard for moral behavior because he knows all of his moral prejudices and defects and how to correct for every one of them, there are equally difficulties with an overly complacent or even despotic self who is perfectly satisfied with her parochial "caring" stance toward others. The cared-for who has no principles to invoke—no rights to assert—against such a caregiver is in a precarious position indeed.

A defensible female ethic will need some form of principles in order to force the enlargement of our purview. Principles will also play an important role in checking the violence of those who do not want to form a shared self with us. Principles and rights have traditionally provided the basis for both condemning and prosecuting violent individuals. It is hard to see how an interpersonal, therapeutic approach will address the problem of violence without some appeal to principles. Moreover, insofar as we all share some similarities (e.g. race, sex, class, history) and some problems, it is hard to see how we can avoid caring for principles as part of caring for persons. Surely we would wonder about the person who, in one breath, claimed to care for her African-American or lesbian partner and in the next breath disavowed any interest whatsoever in civil rights or the rights of gays. Caring for causes and rights would seem to be an integral part of caring for people. Definitionally restricting care to two-person relations forecloses the issue that needs to be examined—namely, what exactly is the relation between caring for principles and caring for persons and is there a single concept of caring that incorporates both?

This last example points to a fourth issue. For a person to be ethically good, the agent must care about what it is that should be cared for.[116] Without this second-level reflective concern, the caregiver may understand care far too narrowly and commit injustices in the name of caring for others. Given that there may be other objects of our care besides people and their needs (e.g. goods, principles, causes, the rule of law), then we especially need to care for what we ought to care about because doing so is the only way we can hope to identify and evaluate these various candidates for our care.

A defensible ethic will preserve the care ethic's emphasis upon inclusion and upon hearing people voice their own concerns but it will also address the above issues. Some of the problems I have been discussing have been diagnosed by other women philosophers who have tried to save female ethics by offering their own alternative ethics of empathy and trust. Do either of these alternative ethics qualify as the more defensible ethic we are seeking? Why or why not?

2

AN ETHIC OF BROAD EMPATHY

Everyone has his own way of being betrayed, as he has his own way
of catching cold.

(Marcel Proust)

Diana Meyers offers an ethic that both extends and modifies the claims of care
ethicists. Like Gilligan and Noddings, Meyers thinks women have a distinctive
and ethically sound contribution to make to moral discourse. In particular, she
defends the practice of empathy understood as the practice of trying to meet
other people on their own terms. Empathy is necessary, she contends, if we are
truly to respect difference among people, the difference responsible for individuating each of us. She resembles care ethicists in being suspicious of claims to
impartiality and offers a sustained critique of it. And she shares the existentialism
of other female ethics, believing that we can make the world a better place
through our practices and choices.

   Her ethic differs, though, from ethics of care in being more explicitly feminist.
Meyers celebrates the writings of women thinkers who try to "re-figure"
women's identity and to liberate it from the strictures of male, Freudian
thinking.[1] It is precisely these radical-sounding claims of theorists such as Jessica
Benjamin and Luce Irigaray—claims that upset our "ingrained thought
patterns"[2]—that need to be evaluated empathically, and this Meyers attempts to
do. Her ethic should be considered part of the second wave of female ethics
because it both acknowledges and addresses three of the key problems with the
ethic of care identified in Chapter 1.

   First, Meyers understands that interpersonal activities such as caring, trusting
and empathizing must operate within certain limits to qualify as ethically good.
We need to consider in some detail the constraints she imposes on what is to
count as ethical "empathic" thought. Second, Meyers considers how empathic
thought can play a role in our current institutional framework of rights and
justice. While some institutions unquestionably embody prejudices inimical to
human thriving, we nevertheless need some institutions. No one is proposing
eliminating the rule of law with its attendant structure of rights to which we
appeal in litigating disputes and in punishing violators. Meyers takes empathic

thinking out of the family circle and tries to evaluate its role in the wider public sphere in which non-intimates interact. Third, Meyers explicitly deals with the problem of perspective. As we saw in the prior chapter, female ethics have tended (unwittingly) to privilege the perspective of the caregiver, perhaps at the expense of the cared-for parties. Meyers argues for a multifaceted perspective in which we empathize with various "figurings" (her word), including figures that we might initially find offensive. In this way, our empathy will serve, she believes, as a salutary check on our tendency to favor our own preferred outlook.

While Meyers' notion of a heterogeneous perspective/"dissident speech"[3] is intriguing, it remains to be seen how coherent and practicable the idea of empathy actually is. This chapter lays out Meyers' position in some detail and then examines a number of problems with it. I close with some thoughts on what this more feminist ethic of empathy teaches us about the features an ethic must have if it is to be defensible.

Tenets of an ethic of empathy

Meyers develops her argument in favor of a form of overlooked moral reflection—what she calls "empathic" thinking—through a sustained attack on impartial reasoning in ethics. Having identified some major difficulties with impartial reasoning, she develops a notion of empathy intended to serve as a solution to these difficulties. I will follow Meyers' approach and present first her view of the problem and then her solution.

Meyers begins her critique of traditional ethics by analyzing their reliance on impartial reasoning. Impartial reasoning typically begins by defining a deliberator who is taken to be a representative person or agent and then proceeds deductively.[4] The reasoning locates a series of universal needs to which this rational deliberator finds himself compelled to assent. These needs are identified by asking some variant of the question, "Would I want to live in a society in which this need was not met or this interest was not acknowledged?" If the answer is no, then the need (interest, benefit, freedom, etc.) must be a basic one. Needs identified as basic to all people (or rational agents) provide the justifying rationale for rights to non-interference, to positive benefits or to some combination thereof.[5]

From Meyers' perspective, traditional male ethics' conception of the rational deliberator is a "thin" one. That is, the deliberator or representative person is stripped of all features that might prevent the deliberator from considering only those traits, virtues, and conditions necessary for action to be possible. This traditional form of ethics aims at securing the necessary preconditions for all people to fulfill their potentials and to pursue their projects. It does not try to specify what these projects should be but settles for articulating conditions for action as such. An agent's liberty lies in making choices, individual and unique ones. Therefore, traditional ethics tend to justify a series of rights necessary for self-fulfillment and go no further.

Meyers thinks this concept of the agent is too thin to do justice to the richness

of moral reflection. Precisely because the concept focusses on minimal preconditions for any action, impartial reasoning tends to settle for leaving people alone,
giving them space to perform their actions.[6] Yet sometimes the moral response
requires that we empathically move toward the other person, as in the case of a
friend experiencing an emotional crisis during a child custody battle.[7] Most of us
are disturbed by the example of the doctor who has just diagnosed his patient as
having multiple sclerosis and who then urges her "to buy a wheelchair and sit in it
for an hour a day to 'practice' for when [she] would be totally disabled."[8] The
patient is given space to deal with her pending disability, yet the doctor's response
seems like immoral abandonment.

In addition, the model of impartial reasoning can be used to justify evil actions.
On this model, actions are morally right if and only if the description of the action
(past or proposed) does not involve the agent in a logical contradiction. To see
the problem with this impartialist test for morality, consider Meyers' example of
an engineering professor who cracks sexist jokes in his class.[9] As a college student,
he himself may have been the brunt of nerd jokes. If so, he may reason that his
female students could use some "toughening up" before entering the corporate
world. Therefore, he encounters no logical problem when he tests his action
under the description: "University professors should perform actions which
prepare their students for the routine hazing of the corporate world." He is
perfectly willing to be hazed himself and sees no contradiction in assenting to this
maxim. Therefore, when some of his female students complain that these jokes
are making them feel insecure about their abilities to do engineering and ask him
to refrain from such comments, he simply brushes off their complaints as
improper sensitivity.

The problem here is that "impartial reasoning" need not be all that impartial. In
fact, it frequently is curiously self-validating. The rational deliberator presupposed
by traditional (e.g. Kantian) ethics can justify just about any action, depending
upon the maxim he or she employs to describe the act. Utilitarian reasoning is
subject to a similar indictment. Weighing the various costs and benefits depends
upon identifying parties affected by one's actions and upon describing these
effects. If we think of some groups as less than human, we may not bother to
consider them in our analysis. They do not qualify as part of the community whose
overall happiness the utilitarian wants to maximize. As a result, the utilitarian may
blithely endorse actions which exploit or tyrannize such groups. Furthermore, by
weighing some benefits more heavily than others or by neglecting certain costs, we
can once again ensure that our "impartial reasoning" will yield the course of
action we have preferred from the beginning. As John Le Carré's character George
Smiley observes, the danger is that we will proceed with "one argument predi-
cating another, until the only logic [is] the fiction, and the fiction [is] a web
enmeshing everyone who [tries] to sweep it away."[10] For these reasons, Meyers
does not trust impartial reasoning to combat people's initial prejudices.

Finally, universal reason fails to adequately address the problem of institution-
alized self-perception and what Meyers calls "the dilemma of difference."[11]

Universalists typically reject social arrangements that fail to equally protect all agents' liberty rights and hence their possibility for self-fulfillment. Therefore, we find universalists arguing for salaries for housewives commensurate with the value of their social contribution. Meyers contends this argument ignores the housewives' culturally-ingrained self-perception. If they were to receive salaries, they probably would deposit these checks into their husbands' checking accounts.[12] If they get divorced, these wives are not going to be any more independent and self-fulfilled than they were before the universalist "remedy" was adopted. Unless and until the position of oppressed people is understood more fully, allegedly moral solutions to problems of oppression are likely to perpetuate the *status quo*. We need some way to challenge the very framing of moral problems and judgments, some way that takes into account people's self-perceptions.[13]

An analogous problem emerges in connection with actions designed to make some allowances for differences in people's positions. Let us return to Meyers' example of the engineering professor. Using impartial reasoning, the professor might very well remind himself of his commitment to equal opportunity and decide that for historical reasons his female students are vulnerable in ways other students are not. This new line of reasoning *does* accord moral significance to gender. Our rationally deliberating professor acknowledges that justice may require taking into account differences in people's positions and psychic make-up. However, the professor's impartial reasoning may still end up stigmatizing gender difference while trying to accommodate it. The engineer may muse:

> Isn't it curious that these women mind being treated in a way that I don't mind at all? In effect, they're making demands on me that I don't make on them—seems they need *extra* consideration. Sure starts to look like they're not simply different—looks like maybe they're, well, just a tad inferior.[14]

Alternatively, the professor may reason: "I'll cut the jokes from my lectures on the condition that [the female students] undergo desensitization training and learn to cope with the rough and tumble of everyday masculine humor."[15] His reasoning is now impartial in the sense that the professor does not divide the world into two sorts of gendered people. The women are treated as immature, child-like people who can, with help, "be brought up to par." But this response, too, denies difference by requiring the women to assimilate to the men.[16]

In models of impartial reasoning, the deliberator's mode of reasoning is paradigmatic. Hence, when it comes time to address issues in which difference figures prominently, traditional male ethics end up devaluing difference. They can accommodate difference as in the engineering case but only by treating it as a temporary phenomenon or undesirable deviation from the baseline that should be rectified as soon as possible. An ethic of empathy, by contrast, celebrates difference because it has the capacity to challenge us and to enlarge our view of the world, people's needs, human talents. However, for us to reap these benefits, we must adopt a way of thinking which appreciates difference as such.

I come now to Meyers' solution to the problem of difference. According to Meyers, our universalism must be tempered by "broad empathy." For Meyers, empathy is not merely a matter of appreciating the personality or situation of another. A torturer may observe his victim minutely and may even listen attentively with a view to discovering what features of the world most please and pain his victim. If, however, he then uses this information to inflict the most painful treatment upon his victim, he cannot be said to have appreciated the other in an ethical fashion.[17] This sort of case leads Meyers to insist that empathy differs from mere appreciation. Empathy is the manifestation of concern for the other where concern means roughly "being willing in principle to act in such a way that this other agent will thrive."

Such concern should not be confused with sympathy.[18] While sympathy may sometimes be an appropriate response, it is also problematic because it often means that the agent is feeling sorry for someone else. Insofar as I operate from a position of superiority and pity my friend, I am not entering into her feelings and cannot be said to be thinking empathically. In other cases, an agent may experience a feeling of sympathy quite independently of what others are feeling. The death of a great artist may sadden me, irrespective of what the artist's relatives feel. Since sympathy often operates independently of others' concerns, it cannot be relied upon to provide any real insight into their life experiences.

Empathy, by contrast, requires us to experience someone else's feelings and thoughts *because* we have attended to this party's feelings and thoughts.[19] The empathizer grasps the value of an experience for the party with whom the empathizer empathizes. By attempting to understand what an action, opportunity, or benefit means to this other party on her own terms, we open ourselves to substantial shifts in the way in which we have thus far thought about these matters. Empathy allows someone else's experience and perspective to become a part of our moral baseline and therefore can function to help us overcome prejudices and misconceptions.

Empathy not only allows us to enrich our moral discourse but also to assess our own efficacy as moral agents.[20] If justice involves appropriately distributing benefits and harms among different people, empathy must be judged a precondition for measuring our success in acting justly. If an empathic conversation with another shows us that what we thought was a benefit is in fact a harm, then we had better rethink our claim to be just. Empathy also functions as the source of our wider feelings. We cannot tell whether another person is feeling shame or should feel shame if we have not had at least a vicarious experience of a wide range of personal feelings.

Finally, we need empathy to give us a sense of individuals. Since individuals are unique agents whose outlooks reflect experiences, modes of thought, education, and training that sometimes lie beyond our ken, we must approach individuals empathically if we are to have any hope of appreciating their point of view.

Traditional ethics' propensity to see people merely as representative types diminishes them, reducing them to caricatures. Such reduction calls into question our claim to be acting justly when we adjudicate competing claims and lay down laws regulating the behavior of members of the community. It would indeed be ironic if our mode of thought prevented us from discerning the *individuals* who are affected by the way in which we distribute burdens and benefits in our community.[21]

Empathy, however, is not without its own dangers. It discloses possibilities for feeling. These possibilities may be for good or for ill.[22] In this sense, empathy is morally neutral. If it is to be a morally good force, we must never lose our independence of judgment and critical facility for assessing any disclosed possibilities. We must not sympathetically fuse with the party whom we are trying to better appreciate.[23] Such fusion might very well limit our capacity to appreciate someone else's point of view, particularly if the other party in question is herself narrow-minded.

To guard against these dangers, it is necessary that we practice what Meyers calls *broad empathy*. In this form of empathy, one party does not concentrate on actually feeling another person's feelings. These feelings might not be that clear. Or the other party may not know his own feelings or may be operating in bad faith. Instead, we should try to imaginatively reconstruct what another individual might feel under the circumstances in question. This effort of reconstructive imagination has numerous virtues. First, if the imagination proceeds by observing another person closely and by asking questions regarding his point of view, the effort draws us away from our own perspective. We travel in another's world.[24] This travel enables us to check our tendency to project our viewpoint and prejudices upon others. Second, if we truly discipline ourselves to perform this reconstruction with a degree of meticulousness, we prevent ourselves from lapsing into what might be termed "cheap empathy." It is more than a little annoying to have a stranger tell us that he or she knows exactly how we feel. Third, the sheer effort of imagination distances us from our own feelings. Our empathy is mediated by images that, in turn, suggest further possibilities.[25] These images help to thwart any tendency, on the one hand, to unwittingly conceive of the other in our own image and, on the other hand, to sympathetically fuse with him or her.

In all of these ways, then, empathy makes it possible for us to act with both "analytic discernment and attentive receptivity."[26] Yet precisely because our prejudices are so subtle, pervasive, and ingrained, a further check is necessary. We should be willing to entertain tropes and images that may strike us initially as quite radical and maybe even repellent. Images employed by those who dissent from the *status quo* can shake us up and alert us to previously unsuspected possibilities for action, suffering, and feeling. Benjamin, for example, describes relations between men and women as a form of "rational violence."[27] Since we usually think of rationality and violence as intrinsically opposed phenomena, her pairing of the two catches our attention. It may be cynical to claim that elements of violence exist in every relation between a man and a woman and that these are rationalized as each party attempts to maintain his or her identity against the other. But, if we have made a good faith effort to live in Benjamin's world, Meyers believes we will forever thereafter be alert to signs of such rationalization in relationships.

Problems with an ethic of empathy

Models of impartial reason highlight reason's deductive capacity to arrive at clear, consistent positions. Yet, as Meyers correctly notes, clear-headed bigotry is no particular virtue. Reason has non-deductive functions as well—e.g. to imaginatively construct alternative options for action, to try on tropes, to generate new ways of thinking. These other functions are critical to our thinking about moral issues. In the last half of this book, I will explore how these alternative functions of reason would operate in a more defensible ethic. At this juncture, however, I want to delve more deeply into the exact mechanics of empathic thought. These mechanics are less straightforward than Meyers thinks. Once again it is not clear that the proposed female ethic is possible or practicable. Even if we grant that empathy is possible, some additional constraints are necessary if empathic thought is to be consistent with respect for individuals, with responsibility and with justice.

Problem 1: logical difficulties with this ethic's view of self

Meyers accuses traditional ethicists of appealing to the idea of an abstract universal spectator who derives his moral judgments from a few principles. This understanding of moral situations is allegedly "too thin." But the same charge could be leveled at Meyers' account of empathy. She ignores the subtlety of the dynamics of human interactions. We are told that in order to thrive agents need to apprentice themselves to others' world views.[28] This requirement that we "will" ourselves to be empathic in our relations misunderstands human interactions. If a person is able to be in any relation, then he or she must *already* be minimally empathic. At the very least, the party with whom we are interacting must be able to clue into what we take to be acceptable behavior under the circumstances. Any kind of ongoing relation will be impossible with people who are lacking in this rudimentary skill. The psychiatrist Karl Jaspars insisted that schizophrenics are beyond human empathy precisely because they appear unable to read these social clues or to provide their listeners with a context for interpreting what they are saying.[29] But if every relation already involves empathy in this sense of a rudimentary ability to read clues concerning social acceptability of actions and attitudes, then it is unclear either that empathy is something that has to be summoned up as part of our reception of the other or that there are only two classes of relations—the supremely empathic ones versus the unempathic ones. It seems more likely that there is a range of empathic relations.

Let us assume, however, that empathic relations are a special class of willed relations. A second set of problems now arises: with whom are we empathizing? Meyers has a postmodern view of a fragmentary, constantly evolving self entirely lacking in any core (apart perhaps from a desire to thrive—more on this desire shortly). If there is a self at time one (S1) and another self at time two (S2), with which of these infinite number of selves are we empathizing at any given time? "A" self may say contradictory things or say one thing and do the opposite. To which self have we "apprenticed" ourselves? Moreover, if, as Meyers contends, the reader or the listener is continually evolving as a result of empathically interpreting various speakers, authors and agents, then who exactly is the empathizing self who is supposed to be following the career of other people?[30] Meyers' model of empathy presupposes a core self who persists over time yet she continually celebrates a postmodern, fractured self.

The logical problem is even more complex than the above comments indicate. If the empathizing self is at all thoughtful, she will be continually revising her assessment of the party with whom she is empathizing. As a result, it will be hard for an agent to know whether the other party has changed; or whether she simply did not initially empathize adequately with the other party and consequently failed until this later moment to understand him; or whether she understands him even now, given that her current appraisal may undergo a change in the next minute. In fact, since there never is unmediated access to the other, empathizing cannot mean simply receiving the other on her terms. Whatever we take to be "her" terms will still be *our version of what those terms are*. Although Meyers follows in the steps of care ethicists in treating empathy as a strictly interpersonal activity, I would argue that for empathy to be at all plausible, we will need to appeal to a practice of self-empathy. For if we (our core reflective selves?) do not make an effort to think our way into our own changing perspective and to reflect on the shifts in our understanding, we will tend to mistake alterations in our consciousness for changes in the other party. While these alterations will be changes in the other *as we know him*, they may not correspond to real changes in him. A reflective, self-empathy will be necessary if we are to preserve the distinction between our ideas and the genuine being of other individuals, a distinction that is implicit in the claim that empathy respects difference.

Even if we assume a reflective empathizing self, empathy will still be tricky. As empathizers, we face the problem of not knowing exactly what it is we want. For this reason, any empathy we extend to ourselves must necessarily be incomplete. Conversely, the empathy we offer to and receive from someone else will always be fragmentary. We may think we are understanding the other person on her terms; however, we inevitably single out some trait or statement on which to focus our interpretive energy. We may marshal all of our understanding to grasp some particular feature only to find out that the party on the other end does not think this trait is especially important or revelatory of her character or being. Patients, for example, frequently ask their analysts why the analyst has chosen to comment on one thing rather than another.[31] We should be wary then of any claim that we can fully respect the differences among us by simply willing ourselves to empathize with one another.

Furthermore, the empathizer needs the help of the person she is trying to understand. All interpretation requires a set of contextual clues. These clues provide the requisite hints as to what the person is talking about.[32] Meyers can confidently speak of empathizing with a variety of writers only because these writers have been at some pains to provide an interpretive context (e.g. by citing examples; by stating what they are *not* saying; by placing their own point of view within some tradition or genre). If the other person is not able or not willing to provide any sort of clues, no amount of willing ourselves to think our way into the other's point of view is going to succeed. Empathy is not a one-way street. Treating it as such oversimplifies the dynamics of and difficulties with interpretation. It also puts all of the responsibility for creating a respectful environment upon the empathizer, a problem to which I will return below (see Problem 6).

Problem 2: limits to openness

Meyers wants to combine empathy with other worthy characteristics and traits, including integrity and autonomy.[33] It is unclear, however, how an agent can be infinitely responsive to others and still maintain anything like the self-direction and self-control implicit in the notion of autonomy as an achievable ideal state. If we have no guiding principle apart from "be open to others," any decision we reach on a particular issue will simply be the result of accident and contingencies. Whom did we happen to encounter whose thinking influenced us prior to making this decision? Would our decision have been the exact opposite if we had empathized with party X instead of party Y before making our choice as to how to treat Z? It is hard to see how an agent can make any decision that could truly be said to be his or her choice. True, the agent does contribute to the formulation of the problem by choosing (or failing to choose) to engage in imaginatively reconstructing the feelings and thoughts of affected parties. But this line of response simply begs the question because this choice, too, is the product of the series of random encounters with other selves.

Integrity, too, becomes a problem if we adopt this point of view. Meyers argues that a person who is a chameleon lacks a fundamental and desirable integrity.[34] Yet the empathic character is bound to be a chameleon because she has no guiding principle apart from a self-imposed (if there is a self—see Problem 1) command to be broadly empathic with others. In principle, different circumstances and different situations could result in wildly different decisions over the course of a single day. Integrity entails a certain consistency of self. While consistency *per se* is not an unqualified virtue, Meyers' decision to treat it as unimportant means that she forfeits any basis for saying that the empathic human being has integrity.

Our openness to others needs to be limited for a second reason as well. We simply cannot be open to every tic of another person's character. Nor is it obvious that we have to be in order to act well. Perhaps if we concentrate upon those behaviors and traits most relevant to living well, we will know what we need to know in order to treat the other ethically. Parents, for example, need not empathize with their children on every score in order to act as good parents. If they monitor their children's actions and character traits and focus on developing those traits most conducive to living the good life and on altering those that interfere with this life, then the parents arguably will have shown themselves appropriately responsive.

This argument is not meant to deny that the empathizer will have to be willing to reassess which traits are relevant to the good life in light of objections that might be raised. Certainly there is room for debate on this issue. The utilitarian thinks the good life will be promoted if our actions seek to maximize the pleasure of the greatest number of people. Meyers, by contrast, would emphasize the need to respect human individuality if we are to have a community of thriving people. Nevertheless, assuming we concede Meyers' point (and I am inclined to do so), we still need to know how we are to understand individuality. The problem of what character appreciation entails has just been subsumed into talk of respect for individuality. We are left with the question: how can we ever hope to respect another person if doing so entails noticing and appropriately responding to every single feature of this person?

There are two possible way to salvage the ethic of empathy. First, the empathic ethicist could stress that key character traits tend to go together. Through observation and reflection, we might be able to work out some of the logical connections between these traits and empathy. I think this strategy has merit and, in the next section, I explore some such possible connections among empathy, spontaneity, and elasticity of mind. I am not contending, therefore, that there are no such connections. I am arguing rather that it is incumbent upon the ethicist defending empathy to work them out for two reasons: (1) without such guidance, the agent is totally at a loss as to what it means to appreciate another's individuality; and (2) only if traits come together in perceptible and intelligible "packets" can we ever hope to justly assess another's perspective and avoid getting lost in the infinite number of character quirks. Virtue ethicists like Plato and Aristotle understand this point very well and consequently devote a great deal of their thinking to identifying and exploring the ways in which character traits like justice, courage, temperance, and prudence both presuppose and reinforce one another. Female ethics should consider adopting a similar strategy.

A second line of reasoning would impose limits on openness by appealing to the idea of an end or *telos* to life. Meyers clearly is not advocating that we totally give ourselves over to those whose perspectives we are imagining. Complete fusion with the empathized party is not desirable. Instead, we are to engage in empathy as part of an attempt to live a "thriving life." Meyers never defines exactly what she means by thriving, but in a footnote she writes that

[P]eople want to share a sense of what it is to lead a healthy satisfying life and… they want to lead such a life. They want to love and be loved, to sustain and enjoy friendships, to fulfill their potential, and to make a contribution that society recognizes and rewards.[35]

It is open to Meyers, therefore, to claim that such a desire to thrive will structure an agent's mode of engagement with a party with whom the agent is empathizing. For example, a woman could read empathically a work widely thought to be pornographic yet still not endorse much of what the work expresses. She may find in it a cry for attention or a desire by the writer to gain some measure of control over his or her life through infantilizing or objectifying others. Her attempt at understanding this writer would ultimately involve a judgment on her part. Whether her effort at empathizing produces a shift in her outlook will depend upon whether she thinks the writer's viewpoint contributes to her own loving and being loved, fulfillment of her potential, etc. The empathizer may reason that, if she is infantilized, she will not be treated as a responsible adult capable of making the individual choices required for fulfilling her potential. She very well may conclude that being thought of as an infant by other members of society will prevent her from thriving. Meyers would presumably say that, in this case, the empathizer is entitled to reject this writer's figuration as non-liberating and to move on to other thinkers with the goal of finding figurations that will contribute to her happiness.

Meyers then has at least two lines of defense against the charge that she favors an unlimited openness. Neither strategy, however, will save Meyers' approach. She simply is too facile in her suggestion that we should try on all sorts of figurations. Doing so might harm our characters if, as Wayne Booth has argued, every reader becomes one with the writer insofar as he thinks that writer's thoughts.[36] I do not think the identity is as complete as Booth seems to believe. Every act of understanding also is potentially an act of misunderstanding. Nonetheless, to the extent we understand others at all, there would seem to be an identity of thought that could lead to our acquiring some bad or sloppy habits of thought. Consequently, it is somewhat misleading for Meyers to talk as though our adopting others' tropes is ethically neutral—as though ethics enters into the imaginative act only at the back end when we judge whether the envisioned figuration is liberating or not. If the act of imagination is itself fraught with ethical consequences, we perhaps should self-consciously remind ourselves of this fact and err on the side of maintaining ourselves in a kind of tension. We should not simply "embrace" the other. We should simultaneously push the other away and be a bit selfish. A total giving over of ourselves, even if only for the duration of an empathic reading, may be evil.

Furthermore, before accepting empathy as an ethically appropriate activity, we must hear much more about the notion of thriving. What does it mean to fulfill our individual potential? It could be argued that Jeffrey Dahmer and Ted Bundy fulfilled their potentials as serial killers. Is an individual's potentiality nothing more than the infinitely open-ended set of characters he or she could become through various actions or sufferings? Or does potentiality have close ties to an integrity seen as a thriving wholeness achieved, in part, through reflection on the ways in which character traits come in packages and on the possible dangers of indiscriminate openness? Once again we see the crucial need to work out in some detail the logical connections among traits and the possible ways in which these connections constrain the mode of empathy.

Problem 3: the issue of the scope of deliberations

If moral action does indeed require that an agent empathize with the feelings and thoughts of all people affected by his act, then the challenge of acting in an ethically good manner assumes Herculean proportions. Our acts have many ramifications, many of which are unforeseen and unknown to us in advance. Some may never become known to us. We inevitably will fail to consider the effects of an envisioned act upon some parties. To cope with this problem of scope, Meyers suggests that we should morally specialize in some particular issues. Hitherto we have asked too much of moral thinking. No one person can be an expert on euthanasia, the Bosnian conflict, mechanisms of universal healthcare finance, and prison reform.[37] Those who claim to have "moral" positions on all these topics more likely have rigid, pat principles insufficiently sensitive to the peculiar problems involved in such diverse issues. We, therefore, should be skeptical of such universalism and opt instead for the more modest course of investigating a few issues ourselves and of entrusting moral decision-making and policy formulation to friends and colleagues who share our same moral ideals.[38]

Meyers is undoubtedly right on one point. Those of us who live in the West are inundated by information. We readily sympathize with the humorist Calvin Trillin's decision to "give" his wife Iran for Christmas. She was to follow any and all news developments regarding Iran, while he would concentrate his attention upon other world events. This sly recommendation of a moral division of labor, like most sophisticated humor, has a biting edge stemming from its kernel of truth. Faced with the impossible demand to be thoughtful about every issue, the mind balks and scouts around for ways to subvert the requirement, including bequeathing the task to someone else. However, it seems unlikely that Meyers' strategy of moral specialization will be of much help in solving the numerous practical difficulties in adhering to an imperative of being open to others' perspectives.

There are at least four major difficulties. First, on what basis are we to decide among the various available courses of action after we have empathized with those with whom we are interacting? *Pace* Meyers, the possibility of being pulled in many different directions cannot be said to be an unqualified virtue.[39] We eventually do have to reach a decision. The subjectivity of the empathizer is another worry. Since an agent might imaginatively reconstruct the worldview of someone else quite perniciously and in a manner that the empathized-with party would never accept as *her* point of view, what prevents the empathizer from committing an evil action and then justifying it with the claim that he kept himself open to others? Moreover, even if we empathize fully with those presently affected by our actions, we surely need to operate with an eye to the future. We may set a precedent for actions down the road, actions affecting other groups in a manner far less favorably. Moral specialization does not solve these three problems. We could authorize someone else make a subset of our decisions for us, but she may be insufficiently attentive to precedent and to our own subjective biases. Furthermore, given that there are so many subtleties connected with just a single issue, our designated chooser still may find herself quite torn even if she limits herself to empathizing only with those who speak on her designated issue. So how is she to make a decision?

There is a fourth major problem with trusting others to make select decisions for us. While I may share your ideals today, your ideals may be transformed radically tomorrow by some new thought prompted by your inquiry into your specialty. Indeed, recall that the alleged virtue of empathy lies precisely in its ability to effect major paradigm shifts! Thus, while we might be able to reach some verbal agreement on an ideal described at a very high level, what we mean by these words almost certainly would evolve over time. Unless we share some principles with substantial content and agree to constantly revisit these principles; or unless we both understand our mode of investigation as sharing one or more common formal constraints, our views likely will diverge considerably over time. Simply trusting others to look after our interests looks less and less desirable the more seriously we take the dynamism upon which Meyers insists. If we cannot rely upon moral specialization to solve the problem of scope, then we are left in a curious position indeed. We are enjoined to act in every case in an empathic fashion, yet doing so appears to lie outside the realm of possibility. If "ought" does indeed imply "can," then this ethic of empathy is lacking in normative force.[40]

Problem 4: the finitude of empathy

Closely related to the problem of scope is the problem of finitude. Just as the care ethicist requires that we continually be caring in order to be ethical, so the ethic of empathy would have us perpetually empathize with others in an effort to maintain and respect difference. Such a demand is unrealistic. There are only so many hours in the day. Are we wicked if we sleep in and dream for another hour instead of waking up and making an effort to empathize with our family members?[41] Do we cease to be ethical if we choose to spend some time in the garden planting tulip bulbs or decide to fix the car instead of reading texts and watching the news with a view to empathizing with oppressed groups? Manipulation of things can be dangerous, but it is also true that we can make interesting discoveries about the world and ourselves as we tinker and play with natural and artificial objects. Insofar as respect is owed to the environment as well as to other people, these discoveries are an important part of learning respect completely ignored by an ethic of empathy.

In addition, not all distance from others is bad. Physicians refuse to treat family members because their emotional involvement may compromise their objectivity and lead them to harm their child or spouse. Constant empathy can cause burn-out. No doubt medical professionals would have a richer understanding of families' grief if they attended the funerals of their patients. Such a requirement, though, demands too much. Perhaps going to the occasional funeral would serve to sensitize nurses and doctors to the concerns of patients and their families. Attending every funeral, however, would lead simply to exhaustion. Doctors and nurses might spend their time better by reading journals and honing their technical skills or simply relaxing and playing fetch with the dog. To exalt the empathic encounter over every other action is to produce an ethic every bit as rigid as the male ethics Meyers condemns. What is needed is some way to assess the relative merits of the various frameworks in which we think about our choices (e.g. medical professional ethics versus Kantian autonomy ethics versus care/empathy ethics versus virtue ethics). The ethic of empathy, like that of care, fails to provide any such framework.

Problem 5: the dependence of empathy upon prior character

Just as the care ethicist treats the activity of caring as though it were self-motivating (i.e. the experience of caring and having been cared for is sufficient to make a person want to care) and had no preconditions, so, too, defenders of empathic ethics speak as though the only condition for empathizing is an act of will apprenticing oneself to others. If there are necessary preconditions for this act of will, empathy alone will not suffice to make an agent ethically good. These conditions equally must be met. If the agent is not able to meet the requisite preconditions, requiring the agent to be empathic once again has no normative force. "Ought" implies "can," so when the ability or capacity is absent, the "ought" has no binding power.

Let me be clear about what I am claiming. While an ethic must recommend a course of action lying within an agent's power if it is to qualify as truly ethical discourse (i.e. discourse capable of regulating behavior), I am not contending that this ethic must be capable of persuading everyone to behave in the preferred fashion. Some agents, by virtue of their own past choices or by dint of some natural mental incapacity, may lie beyond the reach of powers of persuasion and beyond the force of the ethical "ought."[42] Yet it remains incumbent upon the ethicist to try to delineate and account for any limits on her ethics' power to persuade. Rendering such an account serves to explain why the ethic may not have any regulative force in some people's behavior. The account also functions as a warning to people who *are* concerned with acting well and who *are* capable of being persuaded by reasons others advance in favor of or against a proposed course of action. These persuadable agents can come to see that they may cease to be agents capable of living the good life if they transgress certain limits. For an ethic of empathy to be persuasive, it needs to follow virtue ethics' lead and explore the constraints that character may place upon people's ability to thrive through the practice of trying on the point of view of other human beings.

Consider the character of William Elliot in Jane Austen's *Persuasion*. William is "rational, discreet, polished," but he never shows "any burst of feeling, any warmth of indignation or delight, at the evil or good of others."[43] On the one hand, this character stands as an indictment of Kantian consistency and rationality. William is consistently principled and never violates the expectations of the best bred members of his society. Yet his very consistency and smoothness make Anne Elliot, the novel's heroine, and the reader uneasy. But, from another point of view, the extremely responsive William constitutes a counterexample to an ethic of empathy. Anne is attracted to a degree of spontaneity totally lacking in William. People who are always taking care to be attentive to others' concerns repel her. She prizes "the frank, the open-hearted, the eager character beyond all others. Warmth and enthusiasm . . . captivate her still." She feels that "she could so much more depend upon the sincerity of those who sometimes looked or said a *careless* (emphasis mine) or a hasty thing, than of those whose presence of mind never varied, whose tongue never slipped."[44]

Austen here suggests that it is not necessarily a virtue to be always considering someone else's point of view. William certainly "travels" to other people's worlds (to use Meyers' metaphor)[45] but he always journeys with a view to fulfilling his own agenda. Anne prefers Captain Frederick Wentworth, who reacts spontaneously and passionately to good or evil. Austen is aware that her character Wentworth's view of what qualifies as good or evil is partial and perhaps deficient. She qualifies her character Anne's dislike of William's steady, rational manner with the caveat, "This, *to Anne*, was a decided imperfection."[46] Every character's perspective, including the heroine's, is limited. Nevertheless, there is some reason to go along with Anne's preference for Wentworth. Insofar as a burst of spontaneous passion takes a person out of a narrow, self-imposed, overly cautious, and calculating mindset, it has the merit of revealing both to the world and to the self something like the "gut" commitments of that person. The passion may be selfish, uncaring, and ill-considered, but it is revealing. In Anne's words, such a person is "frank." When we regard such a person, we find that there is some "there" there that can be relied upon and trusted.

It is no accident, then, that Captain Wentworth, rather than cousin William, eventually wins Anne's heart. Wentworth's feeling character is not completely praiseworthy. He feels betrayed by Anne's decision years earlier to break off their engagement. Even when he begins to suspect that he has judged her too harshly, he finds that he cannot derive benefit from this knowledge of her character: "I could not bring [this knowledge] into play: it was overwhelmed, buried, lost in those earlier feelings, which I had been practicing year after year."[47] Yet, although his resentment at Anne for having broken off an earlier engagement impedes his capacity to empathize, his willingness to passionately reveal himself and to take risks allows him to build the bridge of trust over which he travels back to Anne. Moved by hearing her tell another man that she believes in a man's passion,

Wentworth dashes off a letter to her out of the fullness of his heart, declaring his undying love for her.

Anne unquestionably does a better job of empathizing with Wentworth than he does of entering into her point of view. We should remember, however, that empathy is of little value if there is not much in the way of a thoughtful person on the other end worth empathizing with. Wentworth is a worthy mate for Anne precisely because he is an interesting man focussed on testing himself, on taking risks to advance himself in the naval profession he loves, and on making comparative, thoughtful judgments of people's merits with a view to deciding what his heart and soul truly desire. All of these actions are selfish. And a good thing, too. For they are what make him a full-bodied individual worthy of respect and attention instead of a shell of a man like William who hedges every bet and commits to nothing. A degree of selfish ambition, coupled with honest exploration of our feelings and reactions to others, may be a necessary counterpoint to empathy if we are to avoid losing ourselves in a succession of moments of trying on others' tropes with no particular end in view. Occasionally releasing our feelings is as much a part of self-discovery as empathically re-creating the thinking of our fellow human beings.

Ethical empathy presupposes a second character trait as well—a certain elasticity of mind. Cousin William is perfectly willing to assess the value various behaviors and traits have for those around him. He correctly perceives that Anne does not particularly trust Mrs Clay, a woman with designs on Anne's widowed father. William supports Anne's perspective, in part because he thinks her judgment is sound, in part because he likes and respects Anne, and in part because he has his own reasons for separating Mrs Clay from Anne's father. In this case, William shares Anne's dislike of Mrs Clay and does so for some of the same reasons. William even couches his objections in the language Anne employs. So he meets Meyers' definition of an empathic person. To put the point negatively: William does not resemble Meyers' unempathic, shrewd torturer who closely observes what others like not because these things have value for his victims but because his observations help him tailor his torture to each victim. William *esteems* Anne (somewhat at least), and this esteem is part of why he supports her judgment of Mrs Clay.

Nevertheless, William's esteem for Anne is tainted by his habitual, calculating rationality and tendency to assess how all things, including Anne's virtue, can be used for his own unexamined purposes. Every event and trait is ultimately referred to his desires, whims, goals. He contrasts unfavorably with Mrs Smith, a crippled widow who exhibits great "elasticity of mind."[48] Mrs Smith consistently looks beyond her own troubles. She exhibits a genuine interest in the way the world works, irrespective of how and whether these workings further her goals. Like Wentworth, she has strong feelings. And, like William, she is willing to avail herself of opportunities for improving her lot. These feelings and opportunism, though, are filtered through what Anne takes to be Mrs Smith's defining character trait—a generous and felicitous outlook engendered by her elasticity of mind. Mrs Smith combats her feelings of despondency and her regret over lost opportunities and health by re-engaging herself with the world out of a fascination with the world itself.

Such elasticity would appear to be a prerequisite for an ethically good form of empathy. A solipsist like William may be willing to try on others' tropes and perspectives. Yet, because his overriding mode of engagement with the world makes him, rather than the world, the center of interest, everything he learns is skewed by his focus. No illuminating shift of perspective is likely to occur because the mind in this case has been habituated to operate in a cunning mode. The focus of such a person is inevitably more narrow and less far-reaching and playful than that of someone like Mrs Smith. There is play—elasticity—in her whole mode of engagement. This play increases the odds of a perspectival shift occurring, of the sort Meyers thinks desirable.

In addition to elasticity of mind and a feeling character, ethically good empathy presupposes an ability to see ourselves in our peers, associates, and friends. I do not mean that we are warranted in reducing others to mirror images of ourselves nor that we should be trying to put ourselves, biases and all, into our fellow citizens' shoes. We will overcome our prejudices only if we allow those around us to suggest new ways of thinking about them and our relations with them. But, if these "counterfigurations" are to have any impact upon us, we must have some capacity and willingness to imaginatively conceive of another person as like us. Without this capacity, our empathy is likely to slide into a kind of voyeurism.

G.K. Chesterton's protagonist-detective Father Brown speaks to this distinction between worthy and merely voyeuristic empathy. Father Brown is a priest, not a criminal. Nevertheless, he is able to ferret out criminals because he does not place the criminal beyond the pale of humanity. He can see in a criminal's crime an imaginative genius similar to that of great writers.[49] Father Brown does not identify with or "apprentice" himself to the others he encounters, but neither does he convert them into subhuman demons. The priest nicely captures his humanizing point of view in a little speech (which also clearly applies to the creative process by which Chesterton himself devised his characters and set them into motion):

> There are two ways of renouncing the devil . . . and the difference is perhaps the deepest chasm in modern religion. One is to have a horror of him because he is so far off; and the other to have it because he is so near. And no virtue and vice are so much divided as those two virtues . . . . You may think a crime horrible because you could never commit it. I think it horrible because I could commit it.[50]

Father Brown does not forego judgment. The crimes he solves are, in his estimation, "horrible." How is he able to arrive at this judgment? He can do so because he has educated himself to imagine how the world might look to someone *not that different from himself* who felt it appropriate to commit the particular crime in question. Just imagining this point of view, and thinking these thoughts, brings with it some of the compulsion the criminal himself must have felt in order to commit the crime. Feeling this compulsion then places the act within the realm of ethical possibility for the empathic agent as well. But notice that the empathic agent's response goes beyond merely feeling something of the compulsion under which the criminal suffers. Father Brown simultaneously has a moment of distancing horror. What is the source of this horror? It cannot be the empathy with the criminal because the criminal was not repulsed by his act. If he had been, he would not have chosen to commit it. Father Brown is repelled because murdering a fellow human being is not consistent with the sort of life he desires to live. He grasps the immense responsibility attendant upon his choices and strives to make those decisions that, in Meyers' terms, conduce to human thriving.

My point is two-fold. First, only non-voyeuristic empathy that is infused with the ability to kindredly imagine ourselves committing another's act qualifies as *ethical* because it has the power to affect our choices and our character or "ethos" in a way that mere voyeurism never can. Second, non-voyeuristic empathy is *ethically good* if and only if the empathizing agent simultaneously distances herself from her imaginative reconstruction by considering whether the reconstructed experience of the other person is one that accords with her vision of herself as a thriving person. This distancing process presupposes a core self with the sorts of commitments that lead to living a good life. It is exactly these commitments that are entirely lacking in Meyers' vision of a postmodern self. To the extent they are missing, the ethic of empathy loses much of its appeal.

To summarize: empathy cannot function as the ground of an ethic because ethically good empathy presupposes a commitment to thriving. This commitment must be brought to the empathic moment and thus cannot arise out of it. In addition, ethical empathy cannot be self-grounding because it presupposes character traits such as spontaneity, elasticity of mind, and a refusal to demonize the other. Since ethical empathy presupposes traits like these, empathy logically cannot be the mechanism for developing these traits. An ethic of empathy needs a richer notion of character development and some mechanism apart from empathy for developing our sensibilities and engendering a healthy distance between ourselves and those with whom we empathize.

Problem 6: too much and too little responsibility imputed to empathizing agents

Meyers' empathic ethic continues the tradition begun by Gilligan and Noddings of celebrating the mother who preserves relations through caring. Insofar as this praise is intended as a corrective to an overemphasis on independence and self-definition found in the ethics of many male writers, it is unproblematic. It becomes worrisome, though, when acting empathically is treated as *the* most important ethical practice. Although Meyers positions her ethic as a feminist one capable of liberating women from repressive forms of life, she tends to forget that, in the final analysis, agents have a responsibility to themselves to discover what makes for a truly satisfying life. Since the empathic ethic lacks any notion of self-empathy, the ethic tends in the direction of requiring agents always to be other-directed.

Against this other-directedness, I would juxtapose Alcestis' poignant plea:

> Any woman can be wife and mother; and hundreds have been queens. My husband. My children. To center your life upon these five or six, to be bound and shut in with everything that concerns them . . . each day filled—so filled—with the thousand occupations that help or comfort them, that finally one sinks into the grave loved and honored, but as ignorant as the day one was born.[51]

The ethic of empathy might be described as an existentialistic ethic that has entirely forgotten about angst. Our responsibility is not merely one of creating a safe world in which the differences among all people are respected. Each of us also faces the challenge of coming to grips with our horror of death understood as "the horror of dying with unlived lives in our bodies."[52] As reflective adults, we realize that time is not infinite. Our choices define who we are and carve out one life among many. We are anxious because we wonder whether this life we are choosing is the best one for us and how we are to answer this question. We feel a responsibility to address these issues, a responsibility the empathic ethic glosses over entirely. Celebrating the infinite possibilities with which we could be empathic does not and cannot speak to this question. The infinite possibilities are the problem—the source of angst—not the solution.

The ethic not only minimizes this responsibility to ourselves. It equally minimizes our responsibilities to others. This claim is somewhat paradoxical, given that I have just argued that this ethic is extremely other-oriented. Nevertheless, the charge is, I think, just. Consider what an ethic of empathy requires from a mother who is facing her violent young son. The ethic demands that she imaginatively enter into her son's world and try to appreciate how the world must look to him such that he feels driven to violently attack his friends who will not let him play with their toys. But what happens once she learns that her son knows he could try to persuade his friends to share but he prefers violence? What is the mother to do now?

That she has empathized with him is not sufficient to make her interaction with him good. In assessing her character and the goodness of her actions, we look to see what she does once she has grasped the child's point of view. Some kind of end or goal to human interaction must come into play at this point. If, for example, individuals lead better lives if they generally try to substitute persuasion and discourse for violence, then the mother will have acted well only if she tries to get her son to persuade his friends to share their toys with him and intervenes to stop his violence. Empathy by itself cannot be the basis for an ethic because it asks far too little of the empathizer. It imposes no accountability on the agent to act in a certain way after having empathically entered into the other's world.

In fact, the ethic of empathy risks tying parents' hands when it comes to disciplining their children. I am not in favor of beating children. But surely there are times when parents should intervene confidently and even vehemently to remind their children that there are other people in the world with their own interests. Female ethics' own commitment to respect for individuals certainly implies that the child is not entitled to treat others and the world as things existing only for her pleasure. Learning (perhaps unwillingly) to recognize and accommodate the differences of other people is part of the psychic work in which each of us must engage as part of evolving into a thriving person of empathic integrity. Representing the mother as a sweet, benign, complacent, always supportive figure minimizes the real and important interventionist powers she must exercise in order to develop the child's character. This sweet view encourages misunderstandings like that of the art historian Leo Steinberg. Steinberg complains that Max Ernst's painting *The Blessed Virgin Chastising the Child Jesus Before Three Witnesses* is theologically absurd. Steinberg argues that Ernst should not have painted Mary, halo firmly in place, spanking her young son, whose halo has rolled to the ground, because "Jesus cannot have misbehaved, and Mary cannot chastise unjustly." The female theologian Jorunn Buckley rightly queries how, if Mary had not beaten "the demons of disobedience out of her child," Jesus could "later have graduated to his role as healer"?[53]

This last example suggests that empathy, like caring, has merit as part of a lived life, a life deriving its goodness from the character of its end. Disciplining the child looks like an act of violence if we follow Meyers in taking empathy to be the primary moral activity. However, if the end of life, the challenge confronting each individual, is to discover an integrating meaning for life, then intervening to mold the child's ego in a wholesome direction is entirely appropriate. As Wilder's Alcestis explains: "Love is not the meaning. It is one of the signs that there is a meaning . . . ."[54] It is up to each of us to try to discern what that is and to encourage those we care for in this quest as well.

I said at the beginning of this section that an ethic of empathy imposes both too little and too much responsibility on the empathic agent. I have been discussing the sense in which *too little* responsibility is required of the empathizer. The mother–child example equally illustrates the way in which the ethic imposes *too much* responsibility upon the empathizer. The ethic of empathy puts all of the ethical responsibility on the empathizer to respect the difference of those she encounters. Hence, the mother has a responsibility to feel her way into her violent child's perspective. What, though, about the child's responsibility to his mother and to his friends whom he has been attacking? Let us suppose the mother urges her child to reason with his friends, but the child obdurately insists on hitting his friends. The mother has done her part to encourage the child to abandon violence. But the child is not responding to or respecting her efforts. The ethic of empathy provides us with next to no guidance regarding how to hold other people, including children, responsible for their actions because the ethic fails to look beyond the act of empathy to other people's responses to that empathy. As a result, all responsibility tends to devolve upon the empathizer.

Problem 7: empathy's relation to the rule of law and societal roles

Although Meyers sometimes talks as though empathy is the necessary condition for justice, at other times she treats her empathic ethic as a supplement to traditional rights-based ethics of justice. To her credit, Meyers understands the relevance of political institutions to any defensible ethic. She does not advocate dispensing with the rule of law or with rights because she knows that not all relations are among intimates. The law lays down some important ground rules for relations among all members of the body politic. Meyers thinks the law has a role to play in the good life (which, after all, is lived in large part among non-intimates) *as long as we remember that the language of rights is not always appropriate in every case.* As I noted in the Introduction, friends do not have a right to receive gifts on their birthdays; parents do not have a right to be cared for in their old age. Yet we think these actions are good and, other things being equal, praise people who appropriately fête their friends and look after aging parents. To reduce ethics to the realm of rights does a disservice to our rich ethical life. What is more, since rights tend to establish the minimal responsibilities we owe to one another, introducing rights into every human sphere may undermine those relations that involve more maximal responsibilities. Meyers thinks empathy constitutes an important check on this reductive tendency of rights-based systems of justice.

Meyers also concedes that rights are crucial when we are concerned with the balancing of competing interests but she would have us approach rights in an empathic fashion. Although Meyers does not explicitly couch her position in these terms, she seems to conceive of rights as claims we make to have our voice heard in discussions aiming at adjudicating among interests. Since rights are invoked by *individuals* as a way of trying to get a hearing, it becomes incumbent on us as ethical human beings to try to listen empathically to what is being said by all parties with rights and to fit our various responses to individual needs as best we can. Hence, while free speech is an important right, Meyers suggests we try to feel our way into individuals' right not to be harmed by speech that they find systematically degrading.[55]

Since the ethic of empathy is committed to respecting people's individualism and to mutual recognition, Meyers is unwilling to concede that one right trumps another. Like Gilligan, she is suspicious of such global claims (which are usually based upon some rigid principle). She prefers working toward "microsolutions." For example, we might try banning the publication and/or distribution of pornography on the ground that the resulting benefits to women as a group outweigh the evil of curtailing free speech. However, we would have to monitor the actual effects of this experiment in a particular community quite closely. For the benefits might be less, or the evils greater, than we initially imagined. If so, we would have to rethink and possibly revise our position.[56]

Meyers' stance on rights is consistent, up to a point, with her praise of empathy. It seems plausible that we will be both more likely to render people their due and better able to do so if we try in good faith to enter into their reasoning instead of treating their positions as "straw men." But her appeal to group rights (e.g. of women affected adversely by pornography) is suspect on her own terms. Legal remedies for protecting groups are not particularly sensitive to variations within a group. Class action suits, for example, draw people into litigation who may be opposed to litigation on ethical grounds. We need to ask: who designates these groups? The groups are usually not self-identified. Someone with an axe to grind or some agenda of her own may presume to speak for African-Americans or women in general. If each individual is indeed unique, this approach appears presumptuous and unacceptably non-empathic.

The empathic ethic's attempt to inject empathy into lawmaking and litigation is questionable on a second score as well. The very process of litigation may discourage an empathic attitude. Litigating can harden people's hearts and their positions. It is a scary business to be sued. In their fear, people may lash out or perform ill-conceived acts. If we really want to change the administration of law to make it more respectful of human individuality, a more radical rethinking of the law is in order. In particular, we need to consider what the relation is between the law and the development of those character traits empathy presupposes (e.g. elasticity of mind and a consistent refusal to demonize others). The law has an important role to play not merely in balancing claims (Meyers' focus) but in developing people's character in the first place. The ethic of empathy is worrisome because it is so very conservative. It settles for injecting a bit of empathy into *status quo* legal procedures. To the extent the *status quo* develops traits and outlooks in the citizenry that are actively hostile to the empathic appreciation of difference among individuals, we are entitled to wonder whether Meyers' attempt to combine ethics of justice and of empathy is ethically good.

Third, the rule of law as it exists in modern societies depends upon the existence of certain roles—e.g. the role of judge and lawyer. These roles are defined in relation to the legal profession's specific end of promoting legal justice. By ignoring the specific ends of various practices in favor of interpersonal empathizing, the ethic of empathy threatens these roles and the rule of law, a rule that makes autonomy possible by setting limits on what people in various roles can do. Consider Meyers' argument that we should "apprentice" ourselves to others.[57] If we accept this analogy, it follows that an attorney should apprentice herself to her client. Yet this view radically misunderstands the lawyer's role. Lawyers do care for their clients but in a manner circumscribed by the legal, professional ethic. A defense lawyer, for example, does not so much "try on" the client's perspective as present the strongest possible case for that perspective using available truth. She does not destroy evidence or allow her client to perjure himself even when the client thinks such behavior desirable. She keeps confidences but only insofar as doing so is consistent with the rules of evidence. In short, there are many constraints built into the lawyer's role or, more generally, societal roles. These constraints should not simply be thrown to the wind as part of interpersonal empathizing. They are an integral part of the rule of law of a healthy society, a rule Meyers herself appears committed to defend.[58]

One final concern: this ethic makes it sound as though we will be ethically good agents as long as we take care to respect difference. As in the care ethic, we are largely accountable only to ourselves. Surely, though, there is some basis for Plato's and Arendt's insistence that the individual also hold himself or herself accountable to the law. Yes, sometimes the law is corrupt; and yes, empathizing with marginized individuals may enable us to discover this corruption. But, having discovered the law's corruption, it does not follow that we are entitled to ignore the law. It is worth recalling in this connection Arendt's discussion of the assassins Schwartzbard and Tehlirian. Both shot and killed individuals whom they believed were responsible for instigating pogroms in Russia and Turkey respectively. These men's actions may or may not have been ethically good. To form a proper appreciation of their acts we need to have these men's reasons for action thoroughly vetted before a public that is free to advance its own reasons and considerations in rendering judgment. Arendt rightly praises these two men not for their murders but for their willingness to turn themselves into the legal authorities and to stand trial for their actions.[59] Schwartzbard and Tehlirian thereby remained accountable to the law and the larger public while challenging a particular law they believed had failed to protect them. While an empathizer might conclude that these assassins' actions were justified, she might be wrong in her assessment. Demanding accountability before the law is one way to check biases in the evaluations made by each of us. A jury or panel of judges may err in its judgment but at least these representatives of the community will have made an attempt to carefully examine the reasoning of the accused and to solicit their fellow citizens' insights as a check upon individual biases.

The ethic of empathy does not supply us with even this much of a check on our own perspective. By privatizing all of our judgments and by treating interpersonal empathy and the development of the moral imagination as virtues, the ethic undermines the rule of law and of democratic processes. When empathic imagination is combined with some checks on the human tendency toward hubris, it can play an important role in enabling us to form a well-reasoned, sensitive, nuanced judgment of individuals' action and of the effects of policy on a community composed of heterogeneous groups. But, in the absence of such checks, empathy may encourage the agent to believe that she has a wider and deeper understanding of human motivation than many of her fellow creatures. Empathy divorced from accountability could easily create a self-righteous monster instead of a good human being.[60]

Progress toward a more defensible female ethic

Chapter 1's critique of the care ethic led to the conclusion that a viable ethic would have several important features. It would: (1) be open to the potentially sound insights of others and would refrain from imposing any advance restrictions on what would qualify as an ethical utterance or insight; (2) exhibit a respect for particularity; (3) provide agents with an opportunity to contest what others take to be caring and thus good acts; (4) avoid subsuming the individual into relations; (5) supply some mechanism for enlarging the scope of agents' caring beyond intimates to include strangers; and (6) impose limits on what we owe to others, limits that satisfy us as thinking beings.

Meyers' analysis of empathy further refines these criteria. Meyers rightly realizes that it is not desirable for individuals to be so open and receptive to others as to sympathetically fuse with them. Her empathic ethic maintains respect for particularity (criterion 2) and openness to others' point of view (criterion 1) but introduces some distance between the agent and others and thereby avoids collapsing the individual into the relation (criterion 4). Thus she would not have us actually feel others' feelings but rather enter into their worlds through our imaginative reconstruction of what someone like the person(s) in question might feel under some particular circumstance. Since it is inevitable that our encounters with others will always be mediated by ideas and images we bring to the encounter, Meyers' account is less psychologically naive than that of the care ethics. It recognizes that our respect for others' particularity must be a *mediated* respect—i.e. we must be aware and acknowledge the role our imagination and thinking is playing in all encounters with others.

Meyers also takes a step in the right direction by introducing the idea of the good life into female ethics. While she never defends a vision of the good life, she does argue for empathy as a necessary part of human thriving. The desire to thrive and thriving itself are presumably good. Therefore, if empathizing were to interfere with thriving, we would cease to be obligated to empathize with others. Nothing in the empathic ethic obliges us to perform self-destructive acts. The appeal to the idea of thriving is an advance over care ethics because it provides some basis for limiting our relations with others (criterion 6).

Finally, Meyers deserves credit for trying to integrate empathy into our political practices, including the administration of legal justice. She apparently accepts that rights serve to protect the interests of those who are rights-bearers, including the vulnerable members of our society. In this sense, rights help to prevent us from slipping into a narrow parochialism (criterion 5). However, she puts her own interesting twist on rights. The ethic of empathy treats rights as claims *individuals* possess to getting their *distinctive* voices heard and to entering into a dialogue in which conversants imaginatively reconstruct one another's positions in good faith. Understanding rights in this fashion builds some openness and dynamism into our political discussions. Instead of having one right trump another, she would have us use rights as a way of entering into a rich, ongoing discussion with our fellow citizens. Through conversation, we may be able to arrive at "microsolutions" capable of satisfying both parties. In those cases in which the solutions do not work as well as envisioned, the conversants can return to the drawing board and try again, through discourse, to find a better solution. Once again, given that our claims and solutions are contestable, her attempt to argue for this space for negotiation points us in a helpful direction for thinking about the political dimensions of female ethics (criterion 3).

These advances are considerable. Nevertheless, an ethic of empathy does not speak to many of the problems raised in the prior chapter. On the contrary, the problems plaguing Meyers' analysis are variants of those discussed in Chapter 1. We still confront the same problem of judgment we encountered in the ethic of care. Given that there are many alternative lives we could lead, on what basis do we choose among them? Moral specialization does not address this issue. We might empathize with those who favor the death penalty and then with those who oppose it. But, ultimately, we have to decide whether to execute the inmates currently on death row. It is unclear how empathy helps us resolve any crisis of judgment in a non-arbitrary fashion. In fact, if we empathize with people who live their lives in a rage; and if we, too, begin to feel this anger as a result of our accurate reconstruction of their lives, we might impair our ability to make discriminating judgments and, therefore, to lead a satisfying life. The connection between empathy and judgment would have to be worked out considerably more carefully if we are to take seriously the suggestion that we regulate our lives by means of empathy.

This problem of judgment arises in part because the end of our engagements with others has not been well formulated. It is no good saying that empathic openness enriches our point of view. "Enriches" is often taken to be synonymous with "complicates," but since both of these terms are ethically ambiguous, this elaboration buys us little.[61] While we can empathize with the female ethicists' fear of the too quick formulation, it is an equally serious mistake to celebrate a facility for considering all possible ways of living, be they for good or evil. Since some people may reject the value of empathy, to value empathizing with such parties is a contradiction in terms. It makes more sense to promote being open to select perspectives, especially those that enable us to understand more of the character and conditions of living a good life in a human community. Valuable perspectives reveal both what is true about the human condition and also remind us of any limitations to our understanding of this condition. A perspective showing no self-awareness and displaying few, if any, moments of self-criticism would not necessarily be a perspective to which we should be "open." In a sense, I am advocating that we be a bit selfish in our interactions with others. In particular, we should not lose sight of our ever present need to examine ourselves regarding what it is that truly satisfies us. In short, we need a critical elasticity of mind. Without this end-oriented self-scrutiny built into empathizing with others, we will find ourselves channel-surfing our way through encounters with our fellow human beings. We will be hopping from one narrative to the next, trying it on, discarding it, or (what may be worse) being unwittingly molded and maimed by these narratives. We will empathize ourselves to death without ever noticing that this frantic quest has little practical meaning or value unless and until we locate some "good" or "end" to these interactions.

If this "good" is indeed something like that which truly satisfies us as human beings, then the appropriate object of empathy and care would seem to be less other people and more whatever processes, modes, or methods lead us toward the good. Empathizing with people cannot substitute for the soul-work each of us must do in our waking, and perhaps sleeping, hours. I do not mean that this work need be done by ourselves in isolation. I mean rather that, in our interactions with others, we ought not to lose sight of a selfish end, the end of discovering what is worth knowing. As I shall argue later, there is good reason to doubt whether anyone, even a person bearing the utmost good will toward us, could ever simply give us that answer, no matter how open we are to this guru, no matter how willing we are, in Meyers' word, to "apprentice" ourselves to this master. If so, there is no reason why the demand to empathize with others should "trump" a felt requirement to be reflective.

Lastly, there remains a problem of respect: what exactly does it mean to appreciate the particularity of another person and of the self? Recall that the care ethic provides some minimal focus to our relations with others. We are to enter into mutually responsive relations in which both parties minister to each other's needs as these needs are understood by the person receiving the care. Meyers' ethic of empathy cuts us loose from needs. We simply are to encounter the other person in his or her radical particularity. Must we then notice every wrinkle, hair and quirk of speech before we can be said to have properly appreciated the other person? And, if the particularity of each of us is so radical as to prove ineffable, how can we ever hope to grasp it, much less to judge what important lessons we might learn from entering into the mode through which other people encounter the world? As we have seen in her discussion of rights and the law, Meyers herself is willing to group individuals, thereby implying that a person's perspective may have some generic features. Indeed, when we imaginatively reconstruct others' perspective— e.g. as we read a character's story or listen to testimony of a witness in a trial—we are always making some appeal to what this *sort of person* may think or feel under this sort of circumstance. If so, then Gayatri Spivak is right to insist that "[i]t is not possible, within discourse, to escape essentializing somewhere. The moment of essentialism or essentialization is irreducible."[62] I would add that if we did not "essentialize" (i.e. try to find core groups of traits of a thing or person), it is hard to see how we could ever hold agents responsible for their actions or theories. Laws are always written to apply to classes or types of people. So the legal system needs some essences in order to function at all.[63] Furthermore, if there is no core self, then there is no "he" or "she" who persists through time and who can be questioned about past actions. Given that none of the female ethicists want to throw out the idea of responsibility, this problem of identity needs to be addressed.

Conclusion

In addition to meeting the criteria laid out at the end of Chapter 1, a defensible female ethic must provide for: (1) critical judgment in our appreciation of our fellow human beings; (2) state and argue for some specific end to our engagements with them; and (3) explain how, if at all, we can grasp and appreciate the radical particularity of human beings while still being able to hold people responsible for their actions. All of these problems become especially acute when we follow female ethics' lead and begin to think about the character and value of trust in human relations. Whom do we trust? To what end? Can we ever know enough about people to base our trust upon some calculation of risks and benefits of engaging with them? If not, is trust nothing more than a simpleton's faith and are our politics little more than a crap shoot? How can we trust people without at some point applying some generic standards to them? In appealing to generic standards, do we cease to respect the trusted party's individuality? I now turn to these questions.

3

AN ETHIC OF TRUST

Trust has in it the seed of betrayal.

(James Hillman)

This chapter examines a third strand of female ethics—the emphasis on trust. As early as 1968, Virginia Held argued for the importance of considering trust in our ethics.[1] Apart from discussions of antitrust suits in business, little else was written on the subject of trust until Gilligan's work on care was published. It then immediately became obvious that there were affinities between arguments for care and those for trust. Life among intimates presupposes trust as well as care. Trust might even be said to be a defining mark of intimacy. And, like care, trust does not appear to be rule-based. Human beings often trust in precisely those circumstances whether there are, and perhaps can be, no algorithms for calculating when, how far and whom to trust.[2]

The scope of trust is wide. It permeates not only our households but also our markets. For example, in the bond market, the trader's word is her bond. Some writers have gone so far as to argue that extensive trust forms the basis of healthy economies.[3] Given this pervasiveness of trust; and given that the good life and action itself seem to require that agents trust one another, female ethicists contend that a viable ethic must consider the character of trust and the conditions under which it is fostered.

Two women philosophers in particular—Annette Baier and Trudy Govier—have written extensively on the subject of trust.[4] While the two differ on some points, they are united in their praise of trust as an ethically significant social practice and in their condemnation of male ethicists' neglect of the topic. Here I combine their various points to sketch what I take to be the central tenets of an ethic of trust. Many of their points are quite persuasive. The strengths of their position, however, ought not to blind us to significant problems with their analysis. I begin with the central claims of an ethic of trust and then consider the problems with this approach. The chapter concludes with some thoughts on whether an ethic of trust constitutes an advance over ethics of care and empathy and with some reflections on what the difficulties implicit in an ethic of trust tell us about the criteria a defensible ethic will have to meet.

80

Tenets of an ethic of trust

Trust lies at the heart of many of our social relations.[5] Those advocating an ethic of trust make and interpret this claim in both a descriptive and normative sense. As a description, the claim is incontrovertible. No one would ever grow up to be the thinking individual so highly prized in traditional ethics if it were not for trust. The infant relies upon the parent to provide it with nurturance; the parents rely, in turn, upon doctors to help cure the usual run of childhood infections, upon teachers, journalists and clergy to educate their children, and upon the government and their fellow citizens to protect themselves and their family. We implicitly put our faith in the ability of our language to enable us to communicate and take for granted all of the contextual clues required for empathizing with others. We thus might be said to trust not only in other persons but in our language and social context. Trust is the unperceived ground of many of our perceptions and actions.

While trust is a form of reliance, it goes beyond mere reliance. The citizens of Konigsberg relied upon Kant to take his constitutional walk every morning.[6] We rely upon the sun to rise and the commuter trains to run. In these sorts of cases, we expect nothing more than that some event or action will occur or continue occurring. However, in the case of interpersonal relations, trust is weighted more positively than mere reliance. For while the torturer's victims might expect and *rely* upon the torturer to treat them brutally, they could hardly be said to *trust* the torturer. When we *trust* another person, we expect this trusted person to show us good will. Thus, in good marriages, the partners trust one another to act in their joint interest throughout their lives. Perhaps the reason why we tend to restrict talk of trust to personal relations is that the inanimate objects on which we rely (the sun; our kitchen appliances) have no will. No judgment can be formed, therefore, regarding these objects' likely good will. (Although the more an inanimate computer seems to manifest a will and intelligence of its own, the more trust seems to come into play.)

Govier and Baier treat trust as central to moral thinking precisely because we do depend upon people's good will and because the stakes in doing so are often very high. At this point, the theory takes on normative overtones. Since many of our most cherished endeavors require co-operation, we *should* trust one another and should adopt strategies and institutions capable of promoting trust. According to Baier and Govier, trust is generally to be preferred to distrust. Without trust, co-operation and a thriving life become difficult, if not impossible. We might try to elicit and enforce co-operation through contracts or surveillance. These measures, though, tacitly rely upon trust. We are willing to employ contracts in our business dealings and other relations only because we believe that the legal system and other institutional apparatus can be trusted to interpret and enforce these contracts in a way that will not harm us. We can subject these mechanisms to legal regulation, but then we will need regulators to regulate the regulators.[7] Even if we were to place people under surveillance, we would still have to trust the technicians who maintain and use the surveillance equipment

81

not to betray us.[8] If we are to avoid an endless regress, we simply must trust people to look after our interests. We could not specify and control every relevant circumstance or condition of every interaction even if we wanted to do so. At some point we are driven to trust other persons. As Baier jokes, even Hobbes, a staunch defender of a social contract and a "born twin to fear,"[9] had to trust his mother to feed him.[10]

Baier and Govier think that traditional ethicists and political theorists' neglect of trust arises in part from their focus on voluntary relations among persons who are more or less equals. These male theorists have searched for the norms of well-regulated social living in the

> cool distanced relations between more or less free and equal adult strangers, say, the members of an all-male club with members' rules and rules for dealing with rule breakers and where the form of cooperation was restricted to ensuring that each member could read his *Times* in peace and have no one step on his gouty toes.[11]

As this quote from Baier makes clear, the contractual approach emphasizes relations of non-interference and minimal rules for securing it. This largely male perspective glosses over questions "concerning our proper attitude to our children, to the ill, to our relatives, friends and lovers."[12] In other words, from the female ethicist's perspective, these ethics tend to ignore the hungry infant, the aging father, and the sick patient who need positive help and substantial intervention in their lives. In these cases, the requisite help may be long term and involve a considerable commitment of emotion, energy and time. In many cases, this help (often provided by women) will not be a matter of right. The infirm mother in the nursing home has no right to frequent visits from her daughter. Lacking an enforceable right to be cared for, the young, the old and the vulnerable have no option but to *trust* a helpmate, a parent, or fellow citizen to show them good will.

Furthermore, when there is a substantial difference in two parties' relative political or physical power (e.g. between a parent and child; between men and women), trust functions as an important alternative to "a code of ethics which is designed for those equal in power [and which is therefore] at best nonfunctional and at worst an offensive pretense of equality as a substitute for its actuality."[13] These unequal relations are not well modeled by traditional contract theory because the trust is maximal, rather than minimal, and because the vulnerable party has very little punitive power.[14] We do, and should, trust precisely in those cases where we cannot control the other's response.

The centrality of trust to ethical thinking becomes quite apparent when we consider the social and personal costs of distrust. To the extent that we define ourselves through familial and friendly relations that presuppose trust, we risk losing our sense of ourselves when we fail to trust others. At the extreme, we can slip into a kind of paranoia. Sheer living becomes anxiety-ridden if and when distrust becomes a self-confirming attitude. Expecting others' ill will, we may construe every gesture of good will as an attempt to manipulate, to deceive or to harm us.[15] A fixed negative view of others may produce in us "a limited outlook insensitive to new information."[16] Constant surveillance and monitoring of others is extremely costly, as the Cold War showed only too well. Life within the private sphere proves difficult as parents are forced to stay at home or to miss work because they cannot trust a baby-sitter. Without trust, co-operative relations among professionals and clients, or businesspeople and their stakeholders, become difficult to establish or maintain. Society as a whole forgoes the goods the various professions promote (e.g. health, legal justice, and efficient use of capital). Distrust costs us our selves, our money, and our social goods. It even compromises our ability to know things. We routinely depend upon experts, reporters, teachers and others for knowledge.[17] Communicating our knowledge requires trust as well, because we look to presses, editors, and journals to review fairly our contributions and to disseminate them in an appropriate, timely fashion.

Still, granting the importance of trust to ethical theorizing, we may wonder whether we always should trust others. Human judgment is fallible. People report material selectively. Sometimes their memories are unreliable. They may have conflicts of interest or other commitments typically thought to make help, advice and/or knowledge suspect. Our trust may be unwanted by the trustee or may prove manipulative or excessively controlling. In such cases, trust may fail to respect the other person. These possibilities suggest there are some important distinctions to be drawn between a foolish faith and a reasoned trust or, more generally, between an ethical and unethical trust. While Baier and Govier do try to distinguish among forms of trust, they both tend to accept the trustor's expectations as legitimate instead of considering whether these expectations are well formed. This point brings me to the first problem with female ethics.

Problems with the ethic of trust

Problem 1: too much trust by trustors in their own judgment

For the moment, let us accept Baier's definition of trust as the trustor's expectation of benefiting from the trusted party's good will toward the trustor.[18] Implicit in this definition is a notion that the trustor sometimes will be justified in withholding trust. If and when the trustor thinks another is likely to harm or to try to harm her, she need not trust this party. Both Govier and Baier clearly recognize the possibility of harm and occasional desirability of mistrust. On this score, they differ markedly from some other theorists. Sissela Bok, for example, argues that the costs of deceit and mistrust are so high that we are *never* justified in deceiving another except in extreme cases—e.g. the murderer who is asking for directions for getting to his victim's house. On Bok's view, a society grounded in trust is the most desirable. The correlative is that mistrust is not justified insofar as such mistrust perpetuates a non-ideal, non-trusting society. As an ideal, Bok's vision may have merit. But, as Govier and Baier recognize, we are not living in an ideal society. Until we attain this nirvana, we are, they think, well advised to endorse measures and institutions that foster trust and to distrust those people who wish us evil or who may mean well yet still injure us. In fact, Baier and Govier themselves may be said to actively *mistrust* much of the theorizing of male ethicists, theorizing which they see as simplistic and sexist.[19]

Nevertheless, a profound difficulty arises at this juncture. While female ethicists oppose trust to distrust, the opposition is not so straightforward. *Every act of distrust is simultaneously an act of supreme trust by the trustor in his or her own judgment.* Mistrustors take their judgments to be incontrovertibly in their interest. The mistrustor's confidence in herself invites all kinds of abuses including, but not limited to, extreme self-righteousness, a propensity to make snap judgments and a loss of confidence in people who genuinely are worthy of her trust. Govier, for example, contends that distrust is "warranted when people lie or deliberately deceive, break promises, are hypocritical or insincere, seek to manipulate us, are corrupt and dishonest, cannot be counted on to follow moral norms, are incompetent, have no concern for us or deliberately seek to harm us."[20] On this view, we should always be on the lookout for persons who exhibit one or more of these behaviors. Yet this list is so sweeping that almost no one will be worthy of trust. Each of us is incompetent in some field. Are we to distrust a professor of history just because she is not a brain surgeon? Might it not be more reasonable to look to our own expectations and to modify them accordingly? Maybe we should trust people in some realms with some tasks and some information and not in other realms. Or maybe we need a more radical revaluation of our expectations. We all are sometimes incompetent even in our own fields of expertise. A doctor seeing a patient with a new disease will not know exactly what to do. The patient, scared and frustrated, may judge the doctor incompetent. But this judgment appears somewhat hasty and unjust given that no one can anticipate every new development or contingency in their area of competence. Female ethics' defense of trust is worrisome because nothing in the ethic of trust functions to turn the spotlight of moral scrutiny back upon the trustor's own expectations.

Note, too, how a rule-based or categorical mentality has slipped back in under the guise of trust. Matters such as incompetence, breaking promises, indifference or deceit are far from the categorical wrongs Govier takes them to be. There are plenty of people who have no concern for me because they do not know I exist. Those who do know me may sometimes lie to me, perhaps out of a good faith belief that they are helping me. They may go so far as to break promises. For example, you may have promised to help me jump-start my car. On the way over, you come across an accident. You break your promise to me in order to help the other person to the hospital. Do you thereby become untrustworthy? Not necessarily. I may see you as a conscientious, sensitive person of good judgment and repose even more trust in you in the future because you broke your promise to me in this case. In other cases, I may realize that the fault lies in my bad judgment as a trustor. My niece fails to bring back all of the groceries on the list. I trusted her to buy the groceries; she promised to do so. But I forgot that she did not know what kumquats were. Yes, the child broke her promise, but I erred in inappropriately reposing too much trust in her.

I accept that there may be times when we should not trust others. What I reject is a checklist approach to deciding when we are facing such a case. To mistrust others based upon some dubious list of allegedly categorical wrongs short-circuits the very process of communication and dialogue necessary for determining the conditions under which distrust might be warranted. We need arguments to establish whether mistrust is justified in some case; and we need to hear the perspective of those whom we are accusing of betrayal. To simply assume that distrust is justified under conditions X, Y and Z is itself unwarranted and hubristic on the part of the trustor.

The checklist approach will appeal only to those trustors who have absolutely no self-doubt about their own judgments. Yet if we are going to reserve the right to mistrust others because they have fallible judgment, surely we ought to apply this same standard to ourselves as trustors. Insofar as an ethic of trust sanctions distrust without ever casting a critical eye on the trustor's motivations and *modus operandi*, the ethic must be rejected as rather naive and inadequate. The standard for mistrust in persons requires mistrust in self. The ethic of trust fails to acknowledge, much less explore, such mistrust. Consequently, we are left wondering, as in the ethics of care and empathy, whether what we are enjoined to do is even possible. We are to trust, relying on others' good will, yet the ethic itself makes it likely that we will see ill will everywhere.

Problem 2: engendering resentment of others

As I noted in the previous section, the definition of trust offered by Baier and Govier tends to place us in the position of having to constantly scrutinize others for deviations from standards we impose, often without any discussion of these standards. We might agree that deceit, rationalization and such are generally bad. Yet surely we also must concede that what strikes us as deceit or rationalization might not appear as such to others. Govier would have us mistrust anyone who rationalizes, yet, as Mike Martin has observed, it is extremely difficult to specify precisely what constitutes rationalization.[21] The issue becomes: rationalization in whose eyes? A journalist might accuse an attorney of rationalizing his decision to keep his client's confidence. Yet the attorney may think he has a perfectly good reason for doing so and might offer a role-based analysis of the sort the journalist had never considered. One person's rationalization is another person's good reason.

In refusing to address the issue of perspective, ethics of trust tacitly import a spectator point of view they purport to reject. That is, they assume the existence of some objective, rational stance from which to judge the trustworthiness of others. While I shall argue later that there are certain processes and principles that can help us to make a reasoned judgment of people's trustworthiness, the possibility of such processes and principles must be established through argument. Simply assuming an objectivist stance is not acceptable. Nor is it desirable if it winds up suppressing the voices of those who are affected by our actions and who have an equal claim to living a thriving and good life within the community.

An ethic of trust, with its implicit objectivist stance, may actually provoke the very violence it is intended to overcome. Consider, for example, the case of manipulative trust. Assume the trustor, in effect, says to the trustee, "I trust you to do what I want and not to betray me." Such trust leaves the trustee with little freedom of action and may irritate him considerably. Or imagine the trustee's dismay when she finds that her trusting friend has decided to no longer trust her because she "rationalizes." Upon asking her friend what he means, he responds that there is no point in explaining his position because the friend will simply rationalize away this explanation as well. The once-trusted party is now stuck with the label of "betrayer" and has absolutely no recourse for appealing the possible injustice of the charge. Backed into the corner in this way, people may lash out in frustration. We must be careful, therefore, not to define trust in such a way that we paradoxically make a trusting society less of a possibility.

Problem 3: suppressing difference

We need to remember that, when we trust people, we do not, and cannot, fully specify with what exactly we have entrusted them. Those who accept our trust inevitably put themselves at some risk because they do not know exactly what behavior will conform to the trustor's expectations. A mother cannot tell a trusted baby-sitter everything this baby-sitter should do on behalf of her child or in the event of an emergency. According to Baier, the mother must rely upon the baby-sitter's discretion.[22] This reliance, though, is problematic because, even if the mother and baby-sitter have a verbal agreement as to what is to be done, the two still may disagree radically in practice. To the mother, "the children are to be put down to sleep at nine" may mean "they are to stay in bed from nine o'clock onwards." To the baby-sitter, these instructions may mean "at nine o'clock begin the arduous process of getting the children to go to sleep and then prepare for an hour's worth of drinks, story reading, bathroom trips, and so on." If the mother regards a firm bedtime as crucial for teaching children to conform their behavior to limits, the baby-sitter's more "laid-back" caring will not count as an appropriate use of discretion. But note that now we are saying that the trustee's discretion is appropriate if and only if *it exactly mirrors the use the trustor would make of his or her own discretion.* Since the trustee cannot read the trustor's mind; and since, even if the trustee could read the trustor's mind, the trustee might exercise discretion quite differently (assume, for example, that the trustor is vicious, the trustee virtuous), current versions of ethics of trust risk converting the trustee into a sacrificial lamb. The trustee is condemned to learn, *ex post facto*, that, in the eyes of the trustor, she has committed some horrible sin. She stands accused and convicted of being a betrayer of trust on account of some offense that other reasonable parties might not find all that blameworthy.

The trust ethic's definition of trust—as the trustor's expectation that the trustee will use his or her discretion in the manner which the trustor thinks good or appropriate—seems plausible only as long as the theorist concentrates on relations in which expectations are relatively clearly defined in advance of the interaction and where discretion is limited. I trust my mailman to deliver the mail daily because I know, and he has accepted, that he is bound by civil service regulations to do so.[23] The scenario becomes considerably more complicated when we ask what friends may justifiably do to or for each other. This case is more complex because some friendships evolve the terms on which they are conducted, with many misunderstandings along the way. Has my friend ceased to be my friend if she warns me that one of my cherished opinions borders on racism? She may intend to benefit me. Given her good will, she merits my trust under the Baierian definition. But her willingness to be confrontational may irritate me, lead me to impute ill will to her, and make me think I am perfectly justified in distrusting her (also on Baierian grounds).

To put the point slightly differently: the trust ethicists define trust in such a way that friendship and love mean seeking out someone whom we perceive as our equal and as having largely the same substantive commitments as we have. Stendhal may be closer to the truth when he writes that love does not seek equals but *creates* them.[24] Perhaps true friends make themselves equal by exposing themselves to one another's criticism and by consenting to mutual shaping. If so, the trustor's expectations in some cases will have to give way under the realization that these expectations are not well formed or appropriate.

Differences in class, culture, and race also complicate the picture. Once again female ethics of trust lose some of their plausibility when we widen our range of examples. Men and women who have lived abroad know full well how easy it is to violate another's expectations. The agent senses that he has committed a *faux pas*. He perceives that it would be a further gaffe to ask for an explanation as to which unwritten norms have been violated. On the Baierian and Govierian understanding of trust, the trusted party—the foreigner—is responsible for a breach of trust. The foreigner failed to use his discretion as the trustor would. Therefore, according to the ethics of trust, a betrayal has occurred. Since trust is a social good which we should maintain, the trustee ought, on this view, to seek the other's forgiveness.[25]

But is forgiveness really called for? Forgiveness presupposes that another is responsible for having given injury. Is the uncouth foreigner guilty of injury, given his total absence of malice and given the fact that what is perceived as injury may, in fact, not be such? His ignorance here seems inevitable, not blameworthy. After all, no human being has full knowledge of a relative stranger's expectations. At worst, the foreigner may be guilty of a kind of bad luck in happening to say something which diverged greatly from what the trustor found socially acceptable. How can he ask for forgiveness if he does not even know how he has offended? If an ethic of trust does indeed require that trustees always ask for the "betrayed's" forgiveness, then something is seriously wrong with the ethic's working definition of trust. As the above example shows, this demand frequently must appear absurd. Imposing such a requirement on the trustee is, I think, the result of ethicists insufficiently attending to the individuality and perspective of the trustee. As in the ethics of care and empathy, difference ends up being suppressed in this female ethic just as much as it is in traditional ethics.

Problem 4: the conflation of infant, adolescent and mature trust

Trust ethics mirror traditional ethics in a second way as well. The trust ethicists' perspective, like that of the care ethicists', unwittingly re-enacts the attempt by "male" ethics to make human interactions risk-free and completely within the control of the agent. Although Govier and Baier talk about the inevitable risk involved in trusting others, they continue to speak as though we can locate a god's eye perspective from which to assess others' trustworthiness. Hence, they contend that we are justified in mistrusting those who ignore or deceive us, who have conflicts of interest, etc. (see Problem 1). Trust becomes a rigid strategy for engaging with other people, not all that unlike traditional ethics' reliance upon inflexible contracts or maxims (e.g. the Kantian categorical imperative) to decide how to treat others. We run the risk of our relations turning into battlegrounds on which we fire charges of betrayal and think ourselves entitled to withhold trust as the ultimate weapon. Trusting becomes little more than a thinly disguised attempt to control the world and others' behavior in it.

At one point, Baier describes the contractual approach to human relations as that of an arrested adolescent.[26] This description is apropos; however, it equally applies to the account of trust she and Govier offer. To develop this claim, I must distinguish what I will call "infant," "adolescent," and "mature" trust. I use these terms to draw attention to key differences in various agents' self-perceptions and to important consequences of these differences for trust. I do not intend these stages as an exhaustive or natural schema of human development. Nor are they meant to track to chronological age. While all of us begin as infants with an infantile form of trust, it does not follow that all of us develop into adults exhibiting a mature form of trust. A 40-year-old could have an adolescent understanding of trust in the sense in which I am using the term "adolescent trust."

I begin with the trust of infants and young children. The child depends on its parents, but the child is not totally passive. Children are able to bond with their parents in part because the child is born already engaged with the world. The mouth seeks the warm breast; the eyes soon are able to look for and at objects; the ears distinguish the sounds of native speech from other noises in the first few weeks of life. Infant trust can be thought of as a primal belief that mother will return after she leaves the room, that nutritious food will be forthcoming when the infant cries, that the infant has a rightful place in the world. The world and parent are one for the child. Or, as the psychologist James Hillman puts it, the child is in Eden trusting God, the parent, "reliable, firm, stable, just, that Rock of Ages whose word is binding."[27]

The infant may experience doubt but there still is a trust where trust means something like "a fundamental belief that the world is a safe place, conducive to the trustor's thriving." If this belief is systematically denied; or if engagement with the parents does not get started for some other reason, then there may be a retreat into autism or a lack of development. If and when there is infant trust, however, it appears to be an engagement with the world in which the child has only to hope for something in order to have that hope confirmed. This infant trust is shared by animals who whimper when hungry and cry when their mother leaves the nest or burrow. In this sense, infant trust is what Santayana has characterized as a type of "animal faith."[28] The West's traditional mythical identification of childish trust with animal faith makes sense. In this world, the child can fly high like a bird. Icarus confidently soars with his father into the world beyond. Or, as in the John Updike story *Trust Me*, the child jumps from the bank or steps, flying through the air toward the father's arms.

Initially, then, trust is the agent's fundamental belief that the world is there to support the agent. While the child's belief is not reasoned, neither is it irrational. The belief exists and persists in the world of the hearth, the private realm of the family where members *do* look after each other simply because they are blood-related. The outside world, though, inevitably intrudes upon the child's world. The world does not always conform to the child's expectations. Parents die or abandon the child. (Interestingly, Updike designed the cover for the book in which his story *Trust Me* appears, a cover depicting a panicked Icarus falling from the sky.) Along with the child's developing sense of self comes an awareness of betrayal. (Or at least what the child sees as betrayal—therein lies the problem.) The parent knows that at some point he has to let go of the floating son, of the daughter on the bicycle. The child may panic as he begins to sink or as she wobbles on her bike. But the moment of separation is inevitable.

Adolescents may cope with the fear attendant upon this separation by trying to control the world. Stormy sessions with parents and other adults ensue as adolescents try to make the world accept them on their terms. These efforts typically merely reinforce the child's sense of distance between himself and the world. The world and the people in it remain stubbornly immune to his or her control. The adolescent may retreat into denial, refusing to accept this breach between the self and the world. Or paranoia may set in as others are characterized as demons out to oppose and frustrate the adolescent. Or he or she may begin to reflect on the nature and causes of betrayal.

This moment of reflection is vital. It is the hallmark of mature trust and is precisely what female ethics neglect. It is the mark of maturity to consider the possibility that betrayal is not the result of someone else's evil character but rather a consequence of the human condition of ignorance. I may betray your expectations because I did not know them. Or I may change my mind about some matter because I have had additional insight into it. If you are relying upon my maintaining the same position, you may be very upset. But such changes or "betrayals" are inevitable, given that people develop and alter their thinking as a result. The adolescent needs to learn to think about what constitutes good will on the part of friends and family members. If good will is that which promotes an agent's true self-interest, then the adolescent must learn to probe the difference between apparent and true self-interest. Others may act in our true self-interest, yet we initially may not comprehend their actions. If their actions have resulted in a genuine benefit to us, then it is hard to see how they have betrayed us. Thus, while Demeter is outraged by Pluto's betrayal in seizing her daughter, it is less clear that Persephone feels betrayed. Female ethicists interpreting this myth have forgotten that it is Persephone who chooses to eat the seeds that guarantee her return to the under-world and her separation from her mother. From Persephone's perspective, the betrayal may have been something of a blessing. Demeter's narcissism (see page 42) and her willingness to totally ignore what her daughter thinks suggest that Demeter herself has an adolescent understanding of trust to which Persephone no longer wants to be subject and from which she herself chooses to escape.

To generalize the point: mature trust grasps that trust is not violated simply because the entrusted party fails to fulfill the expectations of the trustor. *We cannot fairly answer the question of whether the trustor's trust has been betrayed without subjecting the trustor's expectations to critical scrutiny.* The trustor's expectations may be manipulative of others (e.g. limit others' development); they may be wildly inappropriate; or they may be fulfilled in some way not readily apparent to the trustor. It seems trust is truly violated only if the agent expects some good; if this expectation does not require the trusted party to act against his or her interests; and if, in fact, the trustee fails to provide the looked-for good. Mature trust differs from adolescent trust in admitting the possibility of error. It struggles to identify caveats of the sort just listed and to take them into account when forming expectations of other beings and of the self.

Female ethics of trust fail to address these problems. These ethics' view of trust leaves members of the community in a state of intense and constant irritation. This erethic outrage is reminiscent of adolescence. Our flying boy Icarus has yet to grow up. Nor does Baier's recommended strategy for coping with betrayal help us mature. As I noted earlier, she would have us forgive those who have betrayed us. Forgiveness seems at best an ineffective solution and, at worst, an immoral way of overcoming the trustor's anger at the perceived outrage. There may have been no injury (see Problem 3). Or perhaps the only party who can do the forgiving is dead. Many Holocaust survivors feel betrayed by the Germans who murdered their friends and family members. Yet, they contend that they cannot forgive the Nazis for these crimes because it is the victims alone who are entitled to do the forgiving. It is questionable as well whether the trustor can "will" forgiveness. The religious tradition has always emphasized that the trustor must pray for a kind of grace if forgiveness is to be possible. Furthermore, if the betrayed party is not to condone the betrayal, she must look for a change of heart in the other party.[29] This moral surveillance should arouse our suspicions. Is the trustor so wise that she knows all of the ways of the human heart, including the right ones for a person to adopt? Sometimes the trustor will demand an attitude that she herself is unwilling to adopt. Are we to erect moral relations of trust on such hypocrisy?

Furthermore, surely what we ultimately want is not the guilt of the betrayers, but their accountability. We want them to change their behavior to bring it more in line with what we think is acceptable. But, if a behavior change is what we want, what role is there for forgiveness? Surely it is more appropriate for the trustor not to seek the trusted's guilt but rather to explore the trusted party's motivations through dialogue. Then both parties may use standards to which they both agree to hold themselves jointly accountable.

Finally, there is something tyrannical about this demand that others change their hearts in order to be, as Kolnai puts it, re-accepted into the human community.[30] Such forgiveness looks like little more than an attempt by an adolescent trustor to return to the state of primal trust. Everyone is to be remade in the image of the betrayed. The offender is to change her mind or heart. Only when the offender exactly reflects the betrayed's own viewpoint is the offender to be forgiven. The world and the self thereby are again made one.

Of course, this identity is illusory. Having experienced betrayal, the self and its trust are changed forever. The self is in the world; it is not the world. Trust has transformed itself through its own trusting acts. We trust our parents to hold us in the pool; they let us go. We either accommodate ourselves to a world that demands that we arch our body in a certain way to float or we drown. The world requires that we come to grips with the fact that trust has as its correlative the possibility of perceived betrayal. We must analyze this betrayal to discover just how real it is. Forgiveness attempts to turn back time to Eden, the time when the child felt perfectly safe, by re-establishing a primal trust in which the self and world mirror one another perfectly.

This dynamic of forgiveness enacts the narcissism other studies of trust unwittingly have promoted. Supposed experts on trust tell us that we should try to gain another's trust by duplicating his or her gestures, facial movements, intonations, speech, etc.[31] In modern lingo, we should "validate" another party to gain his trust. Such an approach, though, risks locking trustor and trusted alike into a perpetual cycle of foisting inappropriate expectations onto the other, demanding validation, crying betrayal, and then seeking for a still safer person to trust. As they now stand, female ethics of trust promote an adolescent trust understood as the belief in the illusion that, if we just look hard enough for the right person or situation, we can find some place of total safety where we will never have to live with people who impede our will. They thereby contribute to the attempt to return to the sheltered home, to our blood relations, our gang, or our ethnic group. I worry that we will give up a contractual view of the community only to slide into a narrow-minded tribalism.

Problem 5: misplaced reliance on experience of institutions and strategies

Having focussed on some of the problems inherent in Baier's and Govier's treatment of interpersonal trust, I now want to shift gears and consider the strategies they propose for engendering trust. While both are weak on cross-cultural analysis, they do try to address the issue of how trust is best developed among persons within a given community. Baier questions whether there are or can be any rules (e.g. avoid these fifteen behaviors) or procedures either capable of or necessary for guaranteeing an agent's trustworthiness. Instead, Baier thinks we should look for institutions that have shown themselves reliable in the past. Then we should place our trust exclusively in these institutions or in others resembling them in structure. While there is no guarantee of absolute trustworthiness of any human institution, *our experience* has shown us, Baier contends, that the Supreme Court, elected for life, has proven more trustworthy than our allegedly more accountable elected Congressional offices.[32]

Once more we are up against the problem of perspective: who is making this assessment of "our" experience? Liberal academics may trust the Court; by and large, conservatives do not. Recent initiatives in Congress suggest that many ordinary citizens also do not trust court-mandated affirmative-action plans and would rather work for change through the House of Representatives. What is more, humans are fallible. It is doubtful whether any institution has been consistently free of conflicts of interest and prejudices. Baier's trustworthy Supreme Court has handed down plenty of decisions that appear to many to be racist or sexist. Appeals to "our" experience of institutions merely obscures the fact that some trustor (in this case, Baier herself) has applied some standard for trustworthy behavior. Before asking members of the community to place their trust in an experiential approach, the theorist needs to make this assumed standard explicit and to argue for it in the public domain. This defense will prove difficult because it is hard to see how experience could be a standard for judging others' trustworthiness given that the trustworthiness of our experience must itself be established by appealing to some other standard.

For her part, Govier acknowledges the dangers of relying uncritically on any institution. She, too, makes an appeal to experience. She favors (to a limited degree) engendering trust by employing certain strategies that have proven useful in the past—e.g. trying to reduce tensions in an arms race by taking care to

> announce a clear conciliatory initiative, carry it out completely reliably, on schedule, and make an explicit invitation to the other side to reciprocate—while not demanding a commitment to do so.... When reciprocation occurs, further acts should be taken, graded to the degree of reciprocation.[33]

This tactic, while moderately creative, does not solve the perceptual problem: who decides what is to count as reciprocation? As long as it is the trustor, the same old issue arises of hubristically misjudging other people. And it does so in spades. For we frequently view our own actions more favorably than others do. So if we are going to respond to the other in an in-kind fashion, we are putting ourselves on a downward spiral of increasingly hostile behavior. Instead of relying upon institutions or complicated strategies of graduated reciprocation to dissolve distrust, it may be better to simply choose to trust as a matter of policy.

Problem 6: the overlooked merits of trusting as a matter of policy

The ethics of trust proposed by Baier and Govier seek to identify some trait or some set of traits worthy of our trust. Sometimes they speak as if these traits can be identified analytically. For example, if a conflict of interest is a commitment compromising an agent's ability to fulfill her fiduciary responsibilities to trustees, then it seems to follow that we should not trust professionals or other parties who have a conflict of interest. Other times they talk as though there is no checklist for absolutely trustworthy behavior that can be compiled in a purely analytical fashion. Instead, we should look to what our experience tells us about the sort of people and institutions likely to prove trustworthy. However, in this case too, the presumption is that we can use our experience to identify some select, trustworthy features. So something akin to a checklist has slipped into the analysis in the form of an appeal to experience.

Thinkers like Mahatma Gandhi, H.J.N. Horsburgh (who developed many of Gandhi's ideas) and William James offer an alternative understanding of trust. In light of the many nuances of human behavior; and in light of our ignorance of others' motives and the possibility that we ourselves may know less about trustworthy behavior than we think we do, these thinkers argue that we should be less concerned to identify our would-be betrayers and more worried about whether our attitudes toward our fellow human beings interfere with our ability to learn from them. Thus Gandhi argues: "Nobody has ever lost anything by trusting people. Those who betray the trust put in them always lose something precious in spite of gaining millions. We lose something only if our soul is stained."[34]

Baier does not even consider Gandhian-style trust, while Govier treats Gandhi's stance dismissively. After all, people suffer losses through trust all of the time.[35] While it is true that neither Gandhi, James nor Horsburgh *demonstrate* that persons never lose anything through betrayal, I think their idea of trusting others as a matter of policy deserves a more sympathetic reading than Govier gives it. In fact, this strategy has, I shall argue, several advantages over female ethics' proposals for engendering trust.

What exactly is this strategy and what does it have to recommend it? In Gandhi's terms, we "stain" our souls when and if we adopt a strategy that keeps us from developing insights into ourselves and others. On Gandhi's view, we should evaluate our stances toward others in light of the effects these stances have on our ability to learn about ourselves and others. We should not allow our own mode of being to be dictated by other people's hatred of us or by their decisions to betray our trust. If we respond in a merely reactionary mode, we actually give our power and freedom over to our "betrayers." While we may not be able to *prove* that we are better off simply proceeding on the assumption that others mean well and will respond generously to our faith in them, we can adduce a number of arguments in favor of a policy of "willed trust."

First, trust seems to be unavoidable. We will frequently unwittingly rely on human beings or human processes to aid us, or at least not to harm us. A decision to self-consciously trust other human beings has the merit of making us more aware of the degree and extent to which we are always trusting. Furthermore, by choosing to trust, we accept our vulnerability to the actions of other human beings, a vulnerability that either is a part of trust (as Baier suggests)[36] or is entailed by it.

Second, some degree of self-suspicion is wise. As I have been at pains to point out, when we judge someone else untrustworthy, our judgment may be mistaken. If we are wise, we will treat our judgments of others' character as suspect. One way of doing so is to consciously choose to adopt a practical maxim to treat other parties as though they were capable of honorable actions. We may disagree with their opinions or actions. However, we will be more inclined to try to persuade them of their error if we see them as self-interested persons who, like us, are acting on their understanding of what is good, rather than as "bad people pursuing immoral ends through illegitimate means."[37] This cynical view easily turns into a self-fulfilling prophecy. I distrust you. You, in turn, feel justified in treating me dishonestly because doing so puts the two of us on the same moral footing. We are then caught in a mutually reinforcing cycle of cynicism and distrust.[38] By contrast, a policy of refraining from demonizing others has the advantage of keeping us in conversation with them and in keeping our own opinions in play. Who knows? We may discover that it is we, rather than our "betrayers," who have erred or acted less than honorably.

Third, adopting a reasoned policy of trust inclines us to listen to our peers and fellow citizens. If we are not afraid of them and try to avoid seeing them as bad people, we will make friends with them more readily. We will be more likely to preserve these friendships if we try to understand why our friends have acted as they have instead of immediately condemning them as evil. Friendship looks beyond justice. If we keep score of perceived hurts and joys, we will be inclined to do no more than the bare minimum for our friends and perhaps even begrudge them this. Attributing good will to them—or at least, seeing them as relevantly like ourselves[39] and giving them the opportunity to explain their actions to us— encourages our friends to remain our friends. These friends, in turn, can help us make better choices and perceive ourselves more accurately.

Fourth, if our "willed trust" enables us to establish and maintain friendships with persons who, like us, are willing to examine their behavior and assumptions in conversation with other people, then we jointly can evolve a process for keeping ourselves worthy of trust. Such "willed trust" is not merely the expectation of the trusted party's good will. It would be more accurate to say that trust is the expectation of the trusted party's *continuing* good will. No one trusts someone for the next nanosecond. The trustor looks to benefit from the trusted's good will for the foreseeable future. Trust, therefore, has the idea of longevity built into it. If so, it becomes important to ask: since future circumstances may arise which call into question your good will toward me, what justifies my trust in you now? A reasoned policy of willed trust goes some way toward answering that question. I trust you now for exactly the same reason I will trust you in the fore-seeable future: because you, like me, have shown yourself to be willing to subject your position to the test of critical argument.

The conversation in question will have to be of a certain sort. Parties will need an effective voice and the freedom to call into question any assertion or tenet they find unreasonable. In addition, the conversants will have to be willing to say what they really think. They will have to show some courage where courage is under-stood as the willingness to put themselves into play. Self-trust thus re-enters the picture less as a dogmatic commitment to one's own beliefs (see Problem 1) and more as an agent's reasoned confidence in her ability to follow a dialogue with others to a practical conclusion and then to adhere to mutually agreed upon propositions.

These features of conversation making for trustworthiness are themselves open to further exploration and refinement. I will say more about these features and their connection to mature trust in the next chapter. Here I simply would suggest that ongoing conversation with individuals seems the only viable way of gener-ating something like authentic trust (i.e. trust which, in principle, can extend into the foreseeable future). Relying on conversation to ground trust appears far preferable to the alternative strategies of relying upon social institutions or social solidarity. Social institutions may be corrupt, and, as we have seen, their trustwor-thiness often lies in the eye of the beholder (Problem 5). Nor will an agent's trust in solidarity with a group (e.g. with other trusting women or female ethicists) always conduce to a thriving life. Like institutions, groups that claim to speak for us may be deluded or may have their own interest in suppressing an individual's ideas. Richard Wright, a Marxist and supporter of group action, found that, in the final analysis, he had to rely upon his own voice to vent his concerns about the place of blacks in American society. He did not dismiss the concerns of other African-Americans about the possible negative effects of his portrayal of black rage in *Native Son*.[40] Nor did he kowtow to those who opposed his project. Rather he used the introduction of his book to *argue* that he could not be true to himself if he spoke only what other African-Americans, or whites, wanted him to say.[41] He trusted himself by putting himself into play. In terms of the above argu-ment, he showed himself trustworthy to the extent that he initiated and sustained a courageous conversation with others about his views and his methods.

Baier and Govier fail to consider the possibility of a "dialogical" trust in which interacting agents freely submit their beliefs about themselves and others to the test of conversation and do so in a spirit that does not demonize their partners in dialogue. These female ethicists instead opt for "evidentiary" trust—i.e. trust based upon trustees providing sufficient evidence of good will to merit the trustor's reliance upon and vulnerability to them. Since this "evidence" is always potentially up for examination, their approach leaves the trustor (and the trusted) bereft of any response other than irritation. The trustor imposes his or her expectations. If the trusted party gives "evidence" (in the trustor's eyes!) of betraying these expectations, then the trustor is warranted in stomping off in a huff. The evidentiary view seems rather childish: if you don't play the way I want and according to my rules, I'll take my marbles and go home. A quasi-contractual "male" view of the world has slipped in under the guise of trust.

Problem 7: confusing the public world with a macro-private world

I conclude with a final, related concern: the trust ethic, like other female ethics, has a strong existential bent. That is to say, the trust ethicist does not take the world as a given. The world can and does change in response to our thinking, actions and choices. Once we realize the importance of trust to human relations, we can choose to evaluate our actions and thoughts in light of their effect on trust. We can decide to set aside contractual models of human relations in favor of an ethic more sensitive to the needs of vulnerable persons and to the voices of the disenfranchised. Given this existential perspective, we would expect a trust ethic to be especially careful to emphasize the dynamic quality of the human condition and the importance of preserving a political realm in which many voices can get a hearing. Paradoxically, though, the ethic of trust's embrace of what I have been calling an "evidentiary" perspective is in some ways actively hostile to an existentialist understanding of human being and as politically naive as the ethic of care and empathy proved to be.

Existentialism distinguishes between a "who" and a "what." A tool (e.g. a hammer) or anything with a fixed and known nature serving a prespecified purpose is a "what." A human being, by contrast, is never a "what" but always a "who" because human beings are forever a question unto themselves. They do not have a fixed nature because who they are is disclosed through the debates in which they engage and the actions and choices they make in the public sphere. From the existential point of view, the political realm or the "public" is appropriately thought of as that space in which people appear to one another in their "who-ness."[42] If we follow female ethics' lead and construe the political sphere as one which caters to known human needs for shelter and food, we risk destroying the freedom that is the mark of the public sphere. We confuse the political world with the socio-economic world and effectively convert the public realm into one large tool-using household. This confusion by female ethicists destroys the political realm.

My point is not that citizens and their representatives cannot be legitimately concerned about their collective and individual economic well-being. A nation of starving people is not likely to be especially concerned about freedom or self-definition or other goods traditionally associated with public life. However, there are numerous reasons not to confuse the public realm and the private realm of intimates and of the household. In the first place, political problems transcend the household. The household is bound by bonds of blood. The political problem is how to forge community among potentially violent human beings who often do not know one another or who sometimes are extremely suspicious of people whom they do not perceive as kin. The by now familiar issue of the practicality of this ethic recurs. It is not particularly practicable to tell people to trust each other, and it is unclear how a Baierian or Govierian trust ethic would help us resolve a conflict in which two people are making vehement yet contradictory assertions about some event or policy or course of action. Are we simply to trust both parties even though they cannot both be speaking the truth?

Moreover, as I noted in Chapter 1, since a tyrannical state might meet citizens' physical needs better than a democratic one, the emphasis on a safe and nurturing environment imbued with good will deflects attention away from the possible merits of democracy. While democracy has its own problems, the relative merits of various regimes need to be evaluated, not prejudged. Ethics of trust prejudge the issue of the meaning and value of political life by commending safe, nurturing relations and by encouraging trustors in the dubious belief that they know what counts as evidence of another's good will. There is little sense in an ethic of trust of any value in a dialogue that has the capacity to bring us to radically redefine the self and its needs. This devaluation of dialogue is especially odd since it would seem to lie at the heart of the existential understanding of freedom and of human being.

In addition, to portray a concern with trusting relations as a women's issue turns women into a "what." Since who a "woman" is can be contested, there is all the more reason to fight for the idea of a distinctive public realm in which our "who-ness" as individuals, women, Americans, etc., is continually renegotiated. Converting the public realm into a macro-private sphere modeled on the household neglects the need for this struggle. Of course, my version of this public–private distinction could be contested as well. But that possibility only confirms my claim that female ethics err in treating "women" as an essence and in trying to inject "women's" issues from the "private" world into the "public" sphere. Such a strategy presumes we know exactly what we mean by "private" as opposed to "public." *That* distinction is precisely what is in doubt and should not be taken on adolescent trust.

Progress toward a more defensible ethic

Just as the ethic of empathy improves upon ethics of care, so the ethic of trust refines those of care and empathy in some important ways. Ethics of trust do not require us to appreciate every feature of every person. Our relations with people are given focus because the ethics of trust structure them around mutual expectations of good will. We are not simply listening *to* others. We are listening *for* signs of their good will toward us. In this sense, the ethic of trust goes further than ethics of care and empathy in motivating our interactions with others. Since we typically pursue relations we take to be in our interest; and since being the recipient of another's good will furthers our interest, the ethic of trust provides a reason why agents might actively seek to trust each other.

In addition to focussing and motivating interactions, this structuring has the merit of granting the self some independence from acquaintances, friends, family members, and fellow human beings. The self does not have to trust everyone. In principle, agents are entitled to set limits, refusing to extend trust to some persons or, at least, refusing to trust them on the terms these persons may be trying to impose. The ethic of trust is less likely to lock agents into abusive relations than is the ethic of care. There certainly is no requirement that people "move toward" others or empathize with them even when doing so will likely prove harmful or self-destructive.

Govier's and Baier's ethics of trust are more sensitive than ethics of care and empathy to the problem of risk posed by particularity. To say that persons possess an ineffable individuality means that we are not able to forecast their every act. The risks we run with one another are incalculable. To take one of Baier's real life examples: how could a woman know that her apparently nonviolent husband of many years would try to attack her as she lay in bed?[43] Although Baier and Govier both ultimately opt for an evidentiary view of trust, there are other moments when they seem inclined to argue for trust understood as a freely assumed stance of vulnerability to others that we adopt out of an awareness that we cannot avoid risk in our lives. We trust, and should do so, simply because living without trusting is impossible.

Perhaps the trust ethic's single greatest merit lies in the way in which it starkly poses the challenge of reconciling these two claims of justified distrust and of accepted vulnerability. For if we must accept our vulnerability, how can we set reasonable limits upon what we tolerate in others' behavior? It is tempting to respond that we can choose what risks we will run, refusing to be vulnerable to persons with conflicts of interest or persons who break promises, etc. But, as we have seen, these criteria are open to dispute and rule out as untrustworthy some of the very persons whom we perhaps should trust. Allowing the trustor to unilaterally impose her vision of appropriate behavior upon trustees is predicated upon an unrealistic, adolescent form of trust. Such trust threatens to subsume individuals into relations. The trustee is remade in the trustor's image, thus costing the self the very independence the ethic of trust has been at pains to grant the self. How, then, can an ethic both acknowledge and limit our vulnerability without requiring that infinite openness to other beings which Chapters 1 and 2 showed to be so problematic?

Finally, we still confront the political problem that has dogged all of the ethics examined thus far: how exactly does a theory of trust enable us to derive a politics capable of regulating relations among strangers? It is one thing to say that trust substitutes for punitive measures and that we should attempt to inculcate trust through our larger social structure of institutions and policies. It is a far different matter to grapple with the issue of what a community legitimately may do with people (e.g. convicted criminals) whom it has come to distrust, perhaps on dubious grounds.

While the trust ethic helps clarify some of the challenges any viable ethic must meet, we are still left with the question: can there be an ethic that: (1) requires each of us to properly appreciate other human beings' distinctive particularity; and (2) acknowledges the extent to which we are thoroughly interdependent beings; but that simultaneously (3) imposes limits on the extent to which we are obligated to be open to others; (4) engenders the self-suspicion necessary if our relations are to be free of manipulation, narcissism, self-righteousness and unjust resentment; and (5) provides for a rule of law and for political accountability? My answer is yes. The needed ethic is a dialogical one that shares features of both "male" and "female" ethics. To this ethic I now turn.

4

A DIALOGICAL ETHIC

For I am not only now but always the sort of person who trusts in nothing but the argument (*logos*) which seems to me, upon argued consideration, to be the best.

(Socrates)

We are left then with the question: if female ethics, as well as more traditional ones, are gravely flawed, by what ethic should we live? From the analysis of the preceding chapters, we can point to two features required for assessing our actions and choices. On the one hand, judgment must avoid invoking ethical principles that assume a god's eye point of view. As female ethicists have argued, human beings are not gods. No human being has an infallible view of all features of reality relevant to the question of whether some action is good. Each of us sees practical dilemmas and crises in a manner mediated by our concerns and experiences. An ethic that ignores this human reality of difference cannot be an ethic for humanity.

On the other hand, a practically useful ethic must supply some principles for judgment. By a "principle," I mean a concept capable of functioning as a non-arbitrary starting point for evaluating courses of action, choices, events and character and for arriving at a determination of who should do what. Without such principles, we will find ourselves committed either to accepting prevailing communal norms, which history shows can be corrupt, or to validating each and every individual's perspective simply because it represents somebody's experiential point of view. Since these perspectives may be ill-conceived, such validation will often prove harmful. And, if we are totally lacking any principles, we cannot mount an effective challenge to any position (or to any caring, empathizing, trusting) that strikes as unsound. Any challenge we might pose can be dismissed simply as a power ploy or unwarranted ideological attempt to impose our point of view (which is no better or worse than anyone else's) upon the questioned party.

Moreover, in the absence of any principles of judgment, the idea of persuasion and of a regulative ethic becomes incomprehensible. Every ethic tries to *persuade* listeners to adopt one way of thinking about actions in preference to some other way(s). The persuasive speech employed by an ethic always explicitly or tacitly

100

sanctions the determinations of reason over those of passion, feeling, imagination, or intuition. As Seyla Benhabib puts it, no ethical theory is or can be value-neutral on the role of reason.[1] We look to reason to make practical judgments because it alone considers various courses of action and alternative modes of deliberation and chooses among them in a non-arbitrary fashion. It prefers one course and form of deliberation to another for good reason. That is to say, thought finds itself compelled by thinking to take this or that stand because it grasps that it will not be satisfied by adopting an alternative position. All female ethics implicitly concede the privileged position of reason insofar as they *argue for* a certain mode of deliberation, citing reasons why agents must assess past, present, and future actions in terms of whether these actions accord with being a caring (trusting, empathic, etc.) person. Arguments like theirs, which aim at persuasion, are the stuff of ethical discourse. If speech were to cease persuading through reason, it would devolve into a form of thinly veiled violence, with conversants using words as weapons in a fight for victory for whatever point of view each party happens to hold. In other words, in the absence of reasoned judgment, the very violence abhorred by female ethicists would carry the day.

In this chapter, I shall argue that reasoned judgment requires principles. Insofar as female ethics inevitably accord reason a privileged position, the distinction between female ethics and a principle-based male ethics is misleading. Both require principles. The interesting question is: can there be an ethic of principles in which the principles acknowledge and genuinely respect various points of view while simultaneously providing for a reasoned and good resolution of practical crises confronted by particular agents? This chapter lays out my version of such an ethic. The ethic I defend is organized around those principles that thinking finds to be consistent with ongoing thinking.[2] I follow Hannah Arendt in taking thinking to be "the habit of examining whatever happens to come to pass or to attract attention, regardless of results and specific content."[3] Thinking so understood cannot take its bearings from an agent's experience of "the situation" because what the situation is must itself be evaluated by thought. In this sense, the practical thinking I want to defend is a mode of pure critical attention or care that proceeds without specific content or agenda. However, as I also show, this critical thoughtfulness fully respects particular points of view. To satisfy the demands it places upon itself, thinking compels the thinker to engage other human beings in dialogue. In other words, thinking determines itself to be essentially pluralistic. A defensible ethic thus turns out to be a dialogical ethic because thinking cannot ignore this pluralism and still be the thinking that it is.

Plato's Socrates, the man who knows that he does not know, exemplifies this thinking. Therefore, I want to develop the case for a principled, dialogical ethic by putting Socrates into a kind of dialogue with other ethicists, particularly female ethicists.[4] I will focus on Socrates' conversation with his friend Crito as portrayed in Plato's *Crito*. While there are a number of dialogues that could be used, I have chosen the *Crito* because it is relatively short and because it shows the two men arriving at a decision as to how best to act. It thus enables us to test the power of a principled, dialogical ethic to resolve a practical dilemma appropriately. In addition, since Socrates here explicitly treats the personal problem of whether he should escape from jail as a political one with implications for the rule of law and the good life in the city, the *Crito* encourages us to think about the truth of female ethics' oft-repeated claim that the personal is political.

My argument has two parts. Part 1 examines the beginning of the dialogue and points to some important similarities, as well as key differences, between the way in which a principled dialogical ethic and female ethics regard conversation. Part 2 formally sketches and defends four principles of a dialogical ethic and shows how they incorporate important insights of female ethics in a more defensible form.

Part 1: active listening, a precondition for ethical discourse and the good life

Crito comes to visit Socrates in prison shortly before Socrates is slated to die. He arrives before dawn, bribes the jailer for entrance, and then waits for the sleeping Socrates to awaken.[5] When Socrates awakens, Crito urges Socrates to take his advice to escape prison in order to be saved.[6] Socrates allows Crito to make his case without interruption. In the language of female ethics, Socrates is "open" to Crito's argument. Unlike some traditional ethicists, Socrates does not censor his friend's speech by imposing any advance restrictions on the type of questions either he or Crito may ask or on the considerations either may advance.[7] Instead, he treats Crito as a fellow conversationalist who may have some important insight into how Socrates should best act and as someone who, therefore, should be allowed a full hearing. In the ensuing conversation, Socrates accords to Crito all of the privileges he claims for himself (e.g. the privilege of raising objections: seeking clarifications, etc.). He repeatedly grants Crito ample opportunity to counter any and all of Socrates' responses with objections or further questions. In fact, Socrates goes out of his way to raise the sort of objections he thinks Crito would find compelling.[8] In short, this conversation between friends exhibits the formal traits of open access and mutual reciprocity argued for (or assumed)[9] by female ethics.

It resembles female ethics in substance as well as in form. The discussion touches on matters belonging to the personal realm (e.g. family matters). Crito and Socrates consider whether Socrates is being a good father if he dies and "abandons" his children.[10] The question of responsibilities to friends—another major topic in female ethics—comes up as well: should not friends be willing to sacrifice for each other? Are not friends obliged to help one another, even if this obligation conflicts with a given regime's laws?[11] Finally, the discussion honors the contribution of the imagination to our ethical thinking by respecting the highly idiosyncratic, imaginative visions of the conversants. For example, Socrates appeals to a dream he has just had as evidence for his position that he will not die on the morrow, as Crito claims, but rather two days' hence. While Crito is not persuaded by this dream, he allows Socrates to introduce it into their discussion.

Despite these major similarities between a dialogical ethic and female ethic, some telling differences between the two emerge early on in this conversation. There are five key differences.

Difference 1: focus not on consequences

From the beginning, Socrates displays an acute, general attentiveness to dimensions of his interaction with Crito. He wants to know not merely why Crito has come to visit him around dawn but also how Crito managed to get into the prison before visiting hours[12] and why Crito did not wake him upon arriving.[13] Socrates does not judge Crito's responses immediately. However, the subsequent argument certainly suggests that Crito, in contrast to Socrates, has not been particularly attentive to what he is doing. Crito claims he gained access to the jail by doing a good thing for the jailer.[14] But if bribery is against the law, and if we should avoid breaking the law, then perhaps bribing the jailer is not such a good action after all. Similarly, if the best way to spend our life is in conversation, then Crito's choice to sit around and indulge in self-pity while Socrates sleeps may be a poor choice.

The open-ended quality of Socrates' thoughtfulness is striking. His thinking proceeds without reference to results or consequences. On this score, it diverges markedly from the needs-oriented thought central to female ethics of care.[15] While Crito prides himself on caring for his friend Socrates and puts all of his energies into what he is sure is a caring action—helping Socrates escape—Socrates remains aloof from such concerns. It is not that Socrates has no interest whatsoever in consequences. On the contrary, by the end of the dialogue, it is apparent that Socrates' thoughtfulness enables him to identify possibly evil consequences (e.g. harm to the jailer) that Crito does not even see. Socrates is able to see the broader picture concerning consequences, though, precisely because he is not committed to any substantive end apart from being as thoughtful as possible. This suggests that any caring or trusting totally focussed on the needs of others paradoxically may turn out to be uncaring and untrustworthy because this focus substitutes for a more general attentiveness capable of disclosing considerations relevant to assessing the agent's action or choice.

Difference 2: stress on active listening

This attentiveness goes hand in hand with an active listening different in quality from the more passive, open receptivity stressed by female ethicists. Socratic listening is *discriminating* as well as open. Socrates listens for the *reasons* Crito has for urging escape. And Crito, aware of Socrates' focus, struggles to provide them.[16] By a "reason for action," I mean, first, a motive that an agent finds compelling enough to act upon. We think it odd if an agent claims to have a reason for doing X (e.g. buying a lottery ticket), determines that X is possible, and then fails to do X. Second, a reason for action is a publicly expressible motive: (1)

that, in principle, can be challenged by other speakers who doubt whether the motive in question is one that the agent should act upon; and (2) that the agent in question is prepared to defend and to act upon if this defense proves satisfactory to him as a thinking being. Thus, a mere liking for doing X is not a reason for action insofar as this liking is nothing more than a preference. This preference is contestable by others who may claim that the agent ought not to have had this preference. To address the question of why the agent has this preference rather than some other preference or none at all, the agent must invoke some consideration other than the liking or preference. For it is precisely the wisdom of having this preference that is being contested. To put the point slightly differently: citing a reason for an action stops the probing regarding why an action was or is to be done. (It must do so or otherwise we would need another reason to determine why some reason was decisive and would find ourselves in an endless regress.) Invoking a preference does not stop this probing because this liking remains contestable. Therefore, invoking a preference is not equivalent to citing a reason.

It should also be noted that, strictly speaking, a reason for action coincides with *a good reason* because a good reason is one capable of satisfying thinking (i.e. the agent's and other objectors' thinking) by meeting objections posed by this same thinking. "Reasons" that fail this test of thinking show themselves ultimately not to have been reasonable, even though they may have appeared as potential reasons before they were examined. As a result of this failure, thinking rejects them as motives, not finding anything in them capable of compelling the thoughtful agent to act in accordance with them.

Insofar as Socratic discourse is a practice of giving and listening for reasons for actions and choices, Socratic discourse contrasts sharply with conversation on the female ethics' model. Although it is not yet clear what sort of consideration qualifies as a good reason, we can say that Socratic discourse is practically good insofar as it aims at arriving at a judgment as to whether the agent(s) has a good reason to adopt some course of action. It is dubious whether the same can be said about conversation on the female ethics' model. These models take conversation to be practically good whenever conversants are in an equal, voluntary and open relation with one another.[17] If I say I want to do X because I like X, and you retort that you prefer I not do X because you do not like my doing X, this non-coerced conversation qualifies as good on the female ethics' model. But it is hard to see how it can be good, given that nothing in this mode of conversation orients conversants toward the truth regarding the best course of action. Instead, we have two agents engaged in what will likely be an ever-escalating battle of wills.

Difference 3: search for truth

In addition to reflecting a general attentiveness and to seeking reasons, Socratic discourse exhibits a third distinctive feature. On this view, people listen to each other not because they owe each other respect but because, as thinking agents, they want to determine how best to act and speak. In other words, they want to find a good reason for their action. If a good reason is one that is capable of meeting objections satisfactorily, then it follows that thinking agents in search of a good reason will want to hear possible objections to proposed courses of action. Since different objections will occur to different people because they see the world differently depending upon their age, gender, social status, history, etc., the search for a good reason necessarily takes the thinker into the realm of appearances. As agents, we cannot act for a good reason unless we can discover such a reason, and we cannot make such a discovery without both: (1) considering objections coming from particular people (e.g. Crito) who see the world in their own idiosyncratic way; and (2) attempting to discover what might be right in their position.

Female ethics equally insist upon the need to hear and to make a good faith effort to genuinely grasp the particular perspectives of other individuals. These ethics favor dialogue because it gives people the opportunity to share their individual perspectives and lets individuals be the distinctive and unique persons they are. But it is important to see that female ethics do not value dialogue because it has the potential to yield truth but rather because it respects individuality. The dialogical ethic, by contrast, places an interpersonal truth at the center of what makes dialogue valuable and respectful. If it is indeed true that what each person accepts as true reflects his or her individual experiences, it must be equally true that not all truth is contingent upon individual perspectives. For what is the status of this *truth* regarding the relation between truth and individual history? This *truth* about an unavoidably personal dimension to truth is not to be understood as merely *my* or *your* truth. Here we are maintaining not only that all truth reflects individual experiences insofar as the truth reveals itself to particular people, but also that this claim about an intrinsically personal dimension can withstand objections we or others might raise. Therefore, from the dialogical ethic's perspective, when we talk with each other with a view to discovering a good reason for acting, we are not simply being open to the other party's perspective. We are actively listening to the idiosyncratically expressed proposals, justifications and objections offered by our interlocutors with a view to uncovering a non-idiosyncratic truth capable of withstanding the test of critical dialogue.

This dual mode of listening and probing is a practically good and reasonable way to engage in conversation with other people because it is this mode which makes conversation worthwhile. If conversants were not listening for an impersonal truth, the most they could hope for would be an exchange of one set of prejudices for another.[18] In that case, there would be no reason to bother to talk with others as opposed to remaining silent because nothing of value could be gained. What is more, if we did not think it was possible to learn any truths from them, it is doubtful whether we have truly respected our interlocutors. Listening would be little more than a rather patronizing exercise in condescending to hear the other party out because he or she is different from us. So, once again, somewhat paradoxically, it turns out that a more critical form of dialogue provides a better (i.e. more compelling) reason to talk with and listen to each other than do the female ethics that settle for being open and sensitive to people's individuality.

Difference 4: quest for consistency

There is a fourth dimension to the active listening characteristic of Socratic discourse—a search for consistency. Although female ethics are right that there is no particular virtue in being consistently pig-headed and that, therefore, consistency is not everything, it does not follow that consistency is of no value in ethics. A desire for consistency is extremely important if we accept that a conversation's worth lies (at least in part) in helping conversants to discover a good reason for acting, speaking or judging one way rather than another. Recall that a reason to act is a non-arbitrary, thought-satisfying determination supporting one course of action over others. The thinking person finds the reason satisfying and is compelled to act upon it precisely because the determination it makes is non-arbitrary. We initially are engaged in thinking about our actions by a belief that one course may be better than another. If we knew, or believed that we knew, that there was absolutely no basis for preferring one course to another, we would have no reason to think about our options. A coin toss would suffice to guide us. So, to the extent we are thinking about our actions, we are *already* committed to the possibility that one course of action can be shown to be better (i.e. more satisfying to reason) than another. And, if we are so committed, then we cannot be indifferent to contradictions we encounter in our practical reasoning. For, if we find ourselves claiming that some course of action A both is and is not to be preferred to course not-A, then we either must seek to resolve the contradiction or resign ourselves to acting upon an arbitrary preference. However, such resignation is not practically viable because we already implicitly rejected it when we initially engaged in conversation and in reasoning.

The opening encounter between Socrates and Crito illustrates the problem quite nicely. As I noted above, Socrates hears Crito out. But what Socrates and the active reader hear is speech filled with contradictions. Crito says a person should not care about money when the life of a friend is at stake,[19] but shortly thereafter he reveals himself as a wealthy man quite attached to his funds. He appears to have calculated rather carefully the personal cost of helping Socrates to escape[20] and hints that Socrates should spend someone else's money.[21] Furthermore, although he claims to be Socrates' best friend, Crito contends that Socrates' children will grow up as orphans[22] if he rejects Crito's advice, remains in prison and dies. Why, though, won't Crito, this supposedly great friend, take care of Socrates' children, given that he clearly has the funds to do so? Moreover, if Socrates takes Crito's advice and flees to Thessaly,[23] Socrates' children will be orphaned by this course of action as well. So how can Crito consistently advocate Socrates' escape? Note, too, that Crito insists that a person should not beget children if he is going to abandon them.[24] This claim is extremely peculiar given that Crito has children and has just proclaimed himself willing to die in order to save Socrates.[25] Crito's closing plea is equally bizarre. Having advanced all of these reasons in an effort to persuade Socrates, Crito ends his speech by urging Socrates not to think anymore about his plight. Socrates should stop considering and instead immediately act to save himself.[26] But what, then, was the purpose of advancing *reasons* if not to persuade Socrates to do the right thing? Insofar as being persuaded to do the right thing presupposes that the agent trusts in the correctness of a projected course, surely Crito's reasons need to be considered to see whether they withstand objections. To tell Socrates not to consider the reasons undercuts Crito's own practice of having offered them.

Considering the reasons further is especially important because Crito makes a number of important assumptions in advancing his case. He assumes that people have the power to harm one another;[27] that the people in Thessaly will treat the fugitive Socrates better than the Athenians have;[28] that we should regulate our lives by public opinion;[29] that living, rather than living well, is the end of life.[30] If these assumptions are false, the two men may find themselves involved in a contradiction if they act upon them. For example, Crito wants Socrates to be better off than he now is. He, therefore, advises flight to Thessaly. But given that the Thessalians, too, may decide to kill Socrates, Crito's option can hardly be said to be preferable.

Contradictions and problematic assumptions like these are potentially present in any person's position. As reasonable people, we will want to concern ourselves with the consistency of our positions if we are to have any hope of leading satisfying lives. Good conversation is not merely a matter of an open and trusting exchange. Good dialogue aims at establishing a reason for conversants to trust each other. Crito asks Socrates to trust him to act in Socrates' best interest. But why should one friend trust a colleague who shows contempt for deliberation[31] and who has failed to think through the implications of his own recommendations? Unreasonable trust is as suspect as the lack of trust criticized by Govier and Baier. While female ethicists have argued that the process of becoming personally engrossed with people is necessary in order to acquire the "specialized knowledge of their context, history and needs that permits us to fully care for them on *their* terms [author's emphasis], rather than ours,"[32] there is no particular virtue in such engrossment if these others' terms are pathological, evil or destructive of human thriving. We should not free ourselves from the too restrictive formalism of traditional male ethics only to enslave ourselves to the ethically inappropriate responsiveness and unreasonable trust of female ethics.

Difference 5: desire for closure

Finally, Socratic discourse aims at achieving some closure, some judgment concerning how best to act. This desire for closure is implicit in the act of listening for a good reason to act one way rather than another. From the Socratic perspective, having a good reason is equivalent to having arrived at some closure because a reason just is a non-arbitrary determination sufficiently persuasive to satisfy thought and to move it to act upon this determination. By contrast, some female ethics try to make a virtue of indeterminacy. Conversations are said to be good primarily because they give us a chance to connect with other people and to express our point of view. This view treats practical options as if they were infinitely negotiable. Such clearly is not the case. Socrates must decide now whether to escape from prison. If he does not leave, he will die shortly. Obviously, after he is dead, he cannot revisit his decision. The fact that he has reached the decision by means of an open and trusting conversation with equal access and mutual reciprocity does nothing to assure us or him that his decision to stay in prison is a good one. Nor is it of much consolation to Socrates once he is dead and buried that others can re-examine the decision *ad infinitum*.

In summary, a defensible ethic is, as female ethics claim, dialogical. However, *it is dialogical in a certain way*. On the one hand, a good conversation does not place advance restrictions on what parties can discuss. On the other hand, it is not infinitely open. Good conversation requires participants to both give and listen for reasons supporting a judgment as to how they should act, including how they should engage one another in conversation. Good actions, in turn, are those which are supported by good conversation. It may be objected that this under-standing of conversation and action is too narrow, too solipsistic, and too impractical. Does not this view of discourse ignore those cooings and smiles and all of the other important exchanges between parents and their young child, exchanges that are not reason-giving but which are nevertheless crucial to a child's wellbeing? And is there not a danger that an agent will equate the demands of reason with the demands of *his* reason, proceed upon what satisfies his thinking, and dismiss other people's concerns and objections? How exactly does good conversation make for closure? Seeking a reason for action is a far different thing from finding such a reason. At best, an analysis of Socratic discourse would seem to yield a theory of discourse, not an ethic capable of resolving practical crises.

These are serious objections. However, I want to defer addressing them until after I have said more about what a critical dialogue looks like. There are four important principles the dialogue must observe if it and the choices it yields are to be good. Although these principles are formal, they possess a suppleness lacking in deontological and utilitarian ethics. They thus are able to preserve the open responsiveness to people's individuality and to allow for the imaginative playful-ness so valued by female ethicists while enabling conversants to arrive at a reasoned judgment as to how best to act. At the same time, because the principles embody a demand for thoughtful consistency, they are able to check the preju-dices and avoid many of the problems arising in ethics of care, trust and empathy. Each of these four principles of a critical dialogical ethic is articulated in and well exemplified by the dialogue between Crito and Socrates. Therefore, I will continue to treat this dialogue as exemplary. Each of the four sections below states a principle, shows how this principle improves upon female ethics, and explores some possible problems with this principle.

Part 2: principles of a dialogical ethic

Section 1

Principle 1: recognize that all opinions of all people may not be equally practically good

After hearing Crito's plea to escape from prison, Socrates asks whether people ought to esteem the good opinions of the wise and ignore the bad ones of the foolish.[33] After all, does not the athlete heed the praise, blame and opinion of the one who is a physician or trainer, instead of the opinions of the many?[34] Crito agrees that the athlete does so and concedes that "in questions of right and wrong and disgraceful and noble and good and bad . . . we [ought] to follow and fear the opinion" of the one who knows about such things.[35] Who exactly is wise about such matters, Socrates does not say. He rightly treats the existence of such experts in the human good as hypothetical, claiming only that, *if* there were such an expert,[36] then it would be important to listen to him or her.[37] Whether such an expert exists with whom we could consult would have to be established by argument.

Indeed, Socrates' own analogical argument plants some seeds of doubt. In a sense, an athlete already must be an expert herself in order for another expert to be useful. Whether the *doctor* or the *trainer*[38] is the right person to consult depends upon whether this particular athlete's problem is one of restoring health or maintaining it through exercise. If the athlete errs in the assessment of her problem, she is less likely to be helped by the expert she has sought out. And, even if there are experts for particular technical problems (e.g. setting a broken arm), the athlete still faces the problem of ordering a variety of particular goods into a good life. Whether the handball player with the broken arm should have her arm put into a cast if doing so keeps her from an important civil rights event is a question of competing goods a doctor would not be qualified to answer.[39] Reliance on experts alone appears unlikely to resolve all of our practical quandaries. For these reasons, Socrates is right to leave open the door for "any number of interpretations of the nature of moral knowledge. It may be productive or theoretical. It may also be 'non-technical' or dialectical."[40]

However, the analogy, although problematic, is practically significant in two ways. First, Socrates suggests that *as a matter of fact* we routinely discriminate among opinions, seeking the advice of the doctor and not the quack, presumably because we think some opinions are better than others and that it is in our self-interest to know to whom we should listen. The claim that "not all opinions of all people are equally good" is thus an expression of a belief that is regulating our actions, whether most of us know it or not. Second, the mere possibility that there are relevant and important objective differences in the goodness of persons' opinions is ethically significant. It means that thinking necessarily has a role to play in the living of the good life, because the only way we can determine whether this possibility is an actuality is through a further act of thought. In other words, thinking raises possibilities that necessitate further thought on the part of the thinker who initially has entertained these possibilities. By calling attention to the possibility that not all human opinions are equally good, Socrates establishes thinking's need for further thinking. Raising the possibility provides thought with a reason to continue thinking about this possibility and about other possible needs of thought itself.

I term the recognition of this possibility "Principle 1" (P1) of a principled ethic of dialogue. P1's value does not lie in its ability to substantively specify all of the components of a good life. We can agree with Socrates and Crito that a knowledgeable doctor's opinion concerning treatment is "good" but this agreement does not tell us much about the character of the good life. We do desire health, so we might infer that the good must be something we desire. But we still do not know what health is nor what exactly we are desiring when we seek to be healthy. So this claim sheds little light on the nature of good living. Furthermore, since some desires may not be good, we cannot simply equate "the good" with "whatever we desire." What the precise relation is between the goodness of something and its desirability is precisely one of the questions we would need to explore.

P1's significance and value lies rather in its ability to aid and motivate such an exploration. Its worth resides in what I will call its *critical dialogical value*. In contending that P1 has critical dialogical value, I mean that it expresses a condition for ongoing, thoughtful discussion of whatever particular crisis or issue the conversants are confronting. P1 expresses such a condition because it constitutes thinking's discovery within itself (e.g. in the athlete's reasoned choice to seek out a doctor in preference to a quack) of a reason to continue thinking. Without such a motivating reason, thinking would not occur. And if thinking were to cease (or never to begin), then the conversants might very well fail to seek out good advice. They would settle for listening to bad advice and might come to grief as a result. Socrates' own situation is a case in point. Although Crito advises Socrates to stop thinking and to flee immediately, such advice now looks unsound in light of P1, a principle Crito accepts. For P1 means that thinking agents have a good reason to keep on thinking. If doing so is in their interest as thinking beings, then Crito's advice to Socrates goes against both men's interests.

Thinking's discovery within itself of a reason to continue thinking has practical consequences for how discussants should conduct their conversations. P1 entails that discussants distinguish between conversations in which they simply mirror each other's positions or use the conversation as a way to validate their initial stances and conversations devoted to trying to discover which opinions are truly worth heeding. The distinction is necessary, because, while there may not be any wise opinions, the only mechanism we have for deciding the issue is a conversation of the second sort. So the very attempt to think through the possible existence of better and worse opinions involves the discussants in the very sort of dialogue that this attempt makes necessary! Or, to put the point more paradoxically, the distinction between the two types of dialogue is necessitated by the mere possibility that there are better and worse opinions.

Furthermore, the belief that there is an important distinction between the two types of dialogues itself qualifies as a *better* belief than the opinion that all beliefs are equal. It is better in the sense that it is more satisfying to the thinker: (1) who, as thinking has just shown, is already committed to making choices that discriminate between those who possess relevant practical knowledge and those who do not; and (2) who understands that, while this commitment might be ill-founded, the only way to examine the commitment is by engaging in further thought with a view to determining whether in fact some beliefs are better than others. The thinking person will be inclined by thought (i.e. have a reason), therefore, to govern his or her life in light of this belief rather than in light of what the many happen to say is good.

Of course, we do not always think. At least part of the time, we act like Crito, regulating our actions by the inherited beliefs we share with other members of our culture, subgroup, and family. Such reliance on inherited beliefs is perfectly understandable given that we have all grown up under the tutelage of laws and parents. The laws reflect the values of the many persons who have legislated (or at least accepted) these laws. Our parents, in turn, reflect the values instilled in them by these laws. P1 is practically significant because it has the effect of distancing us from our habitual beliefs and conventional power structures. If and when we and our conversational partners think P1 and assent to it, we implicitly commit ourselves to a life of examining our inherited beliefs with a view to judging which beliefs are better than others. The principle works to move us from the unthinking place where we habitually exist to a different plane of thoughtful living.

P1 has critical dialogical value in one other sense. Introducing and thinking of P1 within a discussion provides the discussants with a reason to converse with each other. Our discussion partner may be wiser than we and able to offer the intelligent advice that our own actions show that we value.[41] This incentive to engage in dialogue extends to conversing with ourselves. Other people may not be any wiser than we are or than we could become through our own efforts. In fact, if we are to accurately assess the worth of other people's advice, we must be reasonably confident that we know how to do this assessment. So the same reason for talking to others necessitates that we converse with ourselves, examining our beliefs with a view to determining which are the best ones. It is no accident that Socrates' attempt to persuade Crito to accept P1 diverts Crito from his plan to get Socrates to flee immediately and re-channels Crito's energy inward. The introduction of P1 is an invitation to Crito to begin to consider whether his own beliefs regarding the best way to live are well founded.

P1's critical dialogical value would seem to constitute a good reason to accept P1. Acceptance of P1 is, in turn, of practical import. If we understand thinking as the human capacity to entertain an idea as a possibility and to then recoil upon itself in order to examine the implications of this idea,[42] then P1 appears to be a necessary condition for thoughtful discussion. And, while it may be true that thinking so understood produces no creed,[43] it does not follow that thought does not play a central role in the conduct of a good life. Insofar as thinking discloses the conditions needed for thoughtful and satisfying discussion about practical matters, it both makes such discussion possible and motivates us to engage in it. This outcome is itself a practical consequence.

It is important to stress that P1 is not a transcendental condition for dialogue that every rational person allegedly must accept in order to be part of a conversation. P1, as well as the other three principles I discuss later, come up as part of conversation between Socrates and Crito, a conversation in which we as readers participate when we ask ourselves whether we have reason to accept the claims these men are making. Socrates asks Crito whether he agrees that not all opinions of all people are equally good (P1). Crito does not have to consent. The rest of us who are participating in this discussion are similarly free to challenge at any time any assertion that is made, including claims as to the existence of necessary conditions for an ethically good dialogue to occur. That is *not* to say that there are no such conditions. I have been developing a case for the existence of them. It *is* to say that these conditions, if they exist, are not somehow "beyond" questioning. In fact, as I shall argue shortly, the best reason we have for accepting the four principles of dialogue Socrates offers is that these principles do not close off objections. Instead, they make for a conversation that is capable of continually circling back on itself and revising prior principles in light of possible objections. If P1 and other principles come to appear to us to be necessary conditions for dialogue, it is only because and to the extent that the principles themselves clear the way for their own possible subsequent revision. So to say that a principle is necessary for discussion cannot mean that everyone would find it logically impossible under any circumstances to deny the truth of the principle. Rather it is to say that those people who are part of the conversation about principles making for good dialogue and good choice have discovered through the conversation itself what they consider a good reason (i.e. a compelling or necessitating consideration) to accept these conditions.

Revisions to female ethics suggested by the acceptance of principle 1

While a dialogical or conversational ethic preserves and agrees with many of the important insights of female ethics, it also improves upon them in many key ways.

IMPROVEMENT 1: REFINING THE TELEOLOGICAL ORIENTATION
OF CARING, TRUSTING, AND EMPATHIZING

A dialogical ethic rooted in P1 is, in one sense, perfectly open-ended. By itself, P1 does not provide all the insights we need to make good choices. Nor does it impose advance restrictions upon what issues can be discussed or what concerns advanced by discussants. These matters must be decided through discussion with others. In this respect, this open-ended dialogical approach resembles discursive female ethics. In another sense, though, the dialogical ethic I am defending is strongly teleological. That is, the dialogue favors and furthers actions directed toward a specific end (in Greek, *telos*). What is this end? A dialogical ethic requires that our thinking honor the demands thinking imposes upon itself when giving itself reasons for action. First and foremost among these demands is the need for thoughtful discussion with other people directed toward ascertaining which opinions about the good, right and noble are worth esteeming. This thoughtful discussion of opinions and positions culminates in a judgment that some are better than others—namely, those consistent with P1 are better than those that are not. More generally, the examined life is better than the unexamined one, although additional thought and judgments are needed to determine what exactly is entailed by living the examined life, at this time, at this place, and with respect to this practical problem. While P1 leaves the substance of the examined life relatively undetermined, it is teleological both in requiring that we live the examined life and in specifying how we should approach our choices.

Female ethics generally are teleological as well. Their teleologies are of two types: *substantive* (i.e. positing highly specific, concrete goals) and *process-based* (i.e. the end is nothing but involvement in a process). The dialogical ethic's form of teleology is superior to both. To see why, consider Ruddick's substantive ethic of care. Ruddick takes mothering as the paradigmatic form of caring and argues that mothering has three specific goals.[44] The true mother struggles to meet her child's material needs for clothing, food, shelter, and security. She also fosters her children's emotional and intellectual growth by encouraging their awareness of personal strengths and weaknesses. Finally, she tries to socialize her children by training them in values most likely to make them genuinely productive members of a good society.

In what does such training consist? This question is obviously tricky because these "social" values are contestable. Ruddick herself worries that a mother unwarrantedly may impose her vision of a good life on her child.[45] To correct for this possibility, she suggests that mother and child jointly work out a mutually acceptable position. With this move, Ruddick substitutes talk of process for any judgment concerning what it means to be a productive member of society. This move toward process is not necessarily bad. Ethical judgment of the sort I have been arguing for involves a process of dialogue. However, we need to be clear as to the form and limits of this ethical judgment. Ruddick is not clear. She imposes few checks on this process of parent–child mutual accommodation apart from a requirement that the mother accept her children for who they naturally are.[46] This injunction to accept the child's "true being" is not very helpful, given that our identities are constantly subject to re-evaluation, especially the more thoughtful we are. To the extent Ruddick's talk presupposes a static identity, it needs to be further scrutinized. And therein lies the problem. Ruddick's maternal ethic of caring has no equivalent of P1 to encourage examination of this and other assumptions. This lack is worrisome because we know of all too many cases of

113

people (e.g. murderers) who have worked out a mutually acceptable arrangement with their mothers to support and even lie for them. Behind many warlike men and women stand mothers who are all too willing to defend their sons' and daughters' aggression.[47] What is needed is not an ethic of acceptance but an ethic that encourages both adults and children to be critical and gives them a reason to be so. P1 does both; the maternal care ethic does neither.

A similar problem plagues the more feminist ethics that identify care with liberation. These ethics promote one end or goal—freeing women from exploitation and domination. What qualifies as liberation is unclear: is it withdrawal from intercourse with men or does it require engagement? What exactly is exploitation? Do feminist ethics entirely escape the charge of being exploitive? In light of such difficulties, Jaggar reasonably insists that the feminist proceed critically, but she does not show how a commitment to liberation encourages, much less requires, a critical perspective.[48] A dialogical ethic rooted in P1, by contrast, is critically teleological and therefore provides a way of exploring these all important questions regarding the nature of liberation and exploitation. Feminist ethics may be wrong, for example, in their assumption that the worst of all possible fates is being oppressed by someone else. Perhaps, as Socrates consistently maintains, the worst life is the unexamined life. Indeed, perhaps it is thoughtlessness that leads to oppression. Until this latter possibility is ruled out, no one is entitled to confidently proceed as though being treated unjustly by other people is the life most to be feared.

At the other extreme are those female ethics that refuse to specify any end to human existence and instead make participation in some process into the end itself. Meyers, for example, favors human thriving and thinks that such thriving is guaranteed if agents try on a succession of other perspectives. Friedman argues for understanding friends as partners who challenge one another's perspectives and offer advice. Friends share a process of learning from one another but ultimately each friend still chooses as she sees fit. Neither thinker believes that there is, or even could be, an end to human life that an agent could discover through conversation with other people. Each party must create her own value in her life. What matters most is that the agent participate in processes that in some way foster this self-creation while preserving other people's ability to freely create themselves.

These process-based accounts are problematic because they presuppose a value-neutral autonomy. These ethics respect various agents' autonomy but only in a very "thin" sense of the term. Individuals honor each other's and their own autonomy by struggling to truly hear the positions of others and by receiving an equally attentive, non-prejudiced hearing of their own opinions. The process of exchanging information and points of view is everything. It is hard to see, however, how the result can be termed "good." An agent may proceed to try on a series of pathological perspectives; or the two parties (e.g. Crito and his friends who have agreed to liberate Socrates) may agree, without much thought, that some course will be mutually beneficial. Unless these parties' conversation thoughtfully examines the issue of what makes for a good life, the question will remain: what reason does the agent have to place any confidence in the resulting position and/or course of action? In the absence of such a reason, we cannot even be sure that this supposedly respectful exchange has not actually harmed one or both discussants. As others have noted, when we consult friends or peers, we usually desire more than their opinions. For this reason, "autonomy is not best realized by non-directiveness and value neutrality."[49] We want an argument that some course of action will, in fact, lead to satisfying living.[50] Whether our "non-directive" colleagues and friends know it or not, the "facts" they choose to share with us reflect a number of judgments and assumptions concerning relevance of information, the meaning of advice, the nature of friendship, etc. The facts always presuppose some vision of the good life. The truth of the vision animating both the facts and beliefs of our counselors (i.e. our friends, family members, doctors, lawyers, etc.) is precisely what is at stake, especially when people are in crisis or in conflict with others. It is intellectually unsatisfying to talk about arriving at some "richer" position through hearing others not because such talk is unscientific but because it begs the hard, yet practically central, question of how we are to adjudicate among often competing beliefs and assumptions concerning how we should best live. As I argued in the first half of this book, after we analyze a problem from different perspectives, the difficult task of synthesizing a judgment remains. Process-based female ethics concentrate on analysis and largely ignore this problem of synthesis.

While much more needs to be said regarding how exactly a dialogical ethic performs this adjudication, P1 is an important step in the right direction. In Socrates' example, the athlete seeks out the advice of the doctor or trainer not to hear some opinion he may or may not heed but to obtain thoughtful advice he willingly chooses to follow. Nor does he adopt this advice simply because it offers a different perspective. He seeks out and submits to the trainer's or physician's directive because it is the product of relevant intelligence being brought to bear on the athlete's problem. By "relevant intelligence," I mean that the advice speaks to the problem at hand and does so with the recognition that the problem is, in part, how to lead a satisfying human life. Doctor and trainer do not advise how to preserve mere biological existence. The healthy or thriving, satisfying life, not biological persistence *per se*, is the end that motivates the athlete's search for advice and the doctor's or trainer's offer of that advice.[51]

People can and do disagree over what should count as a thriving life. Nevertheless, the fact that we seek the advice of other human beings with a view to altering the quality of our life tells us something important about our choices. It suggests that the end of our choices is not to stay alive but to live a life of one sort (call it the "good" life). If so, we already must be committed to making choices in furtherance of the good life. And what sort of choices are these? They must be choices that reflect an agent's awareness that some opinions may be better than others (e.g. the opinion that the end of living is the good life, not life *per se*). The better opinions are those that are formed and tested through principled discourse committed to discovering the meaning and nature of good living, acting and discussing. Less good opinions are those which are not so formed and evaluated. Almost all beliefs of female ethics must be deemed less good because these ethics offer no mechanism for encouraging sustained teleological thoughtfulness. They settle for talk of being critical or "open" but do not examine in detail what exactly it means to be thoughtful. A dialogical ethic, by contrast, provides for a critical teleological focus. This ethic evaluates practical options and choices in light of whether they are consistent with the self-imposed demands thinking must meet in order to be satisfied. Since the evaluation is done with an eye toward determining which choices most conduce to a satisfying life, a dialogical ethic has a synthetic power absent in female ethics.

Problems with principle 1

P1, while suggesting this important modification to female ethics, is not without its own difficulties. Three are particularly troublesome. By itself, P1 is still far too formal to be of much concrete practical help. If, as I argued above, any ethic worthy of its name must provide insight deemed relevant by those facing a practical difficulty calling for judgment, then this principle does not constitute an ethic. Do thoughtful persons committed to P1 escape from prison in order to avoid what may be an unjust death sentence or do they remain in jail? Do they oppose a just war or not? Do they file a sexual harassment complaint against a co-worker or simply change jobs? The connection between thoughtful, principled dialogue and good judgment of a particular situation or dilemma is underspecified.

A related concern runs along the following lines: might not an agent simply declare himself to be thoughtful and exempt himself from conversation with others, especially if he believes, perhaps wrongly, that other people are not especially thoughtful? Even if, as I shall argue shortly, an ethic of dialogue presupposes a form of thinking that is essentially pluralistic, what holds agents to such pluralism? After all, female ethics have arisen in part out of a perception that the reasoning extolled in traditional ethics has tended to be monological in character and has not shown itself to be especially sensitive to difference among particular persons. The ethic of dialogue as described thus far seems as though it, too, could easily fall prey to a frighteningly rigid logic of principles.

Finally, the reader legitimately may wonder whether this ethic of principled dialogue constitutes very much of an advance over female ethics. The ethically good agent sounds remarkably narrow in her outlook. She self-consciously makes choices in furtherance of the good life for herself. But what about the good life for other members of the larger community? Are these two one and the same? If so, in what sense? I criticized some female ethics for reducing the political realm to a series of two-party encounters. Could not the same charge be leveled at the dialogical ethic I am here defending? To address these concerns, we must consider a second important principle.

Section 2

Principle 2: never act unjustly

Having obtained Crito's consent to P1, Socrates makes a new beginning by advancing a second regulative principle: agents should never act unjustly.[52] He concedes that "there are few who believe or ever will believe this."[53] However, he argues, "those who believe this, and those who do not, have no common ground for discussion (*koinē boulē*—literally, common deliberation), but they must necessarily, in view of their opinions, despise one another."[54] On the face of it, this assertion is rather dubious: why should this principle, rather than some other, be the necessary ground of common deliberation? Why does this principle moderate hate? How do we know what is unjust? Might there not be cases where injustice should be met with injustice? How can Socrates establish this principle as a practical precept without considering a variety of cases? Although questions like these are legitimate, we should consider in what sense the commitment to never doing wrong (P2) might indeed be a necessary condition for common deliberation before dismissing it out of hand. The principle underpins common deliberation in at least five ways: (1) in its imposition of an absolute demand upon all agents; (2) in its negative formulation; (3) in its focus on injustice; (4) in its demand that agents live responsibly by acting consistently with this principle throughout their lives; and (5) in its practicality. I will take up these points in the order listed.

The demand is obviously absolute. P2 states that persons are *never* entitled to act unjustly or, equivalently, to do evil.[55] Acting unjustly is prohibited even in the case where the agent is returning evil for evil.[56] This prohibition makes sense when we remember that what qualifies as an injustice is disputable. If we acknowledge that some opinions concerning how best to live are better than others (P1), then we implicitly admit that our own beliefs regarding justice and injustice may fall into this class of less good opinions. We may have erred in determining either when an act is unjust or when an unjust act is justified; the distance between "us" (i.e. the good and the just) and "them" (the bad and the unjust) may not be as great as we thought.[57] To admit this possibility of error is to concede that we need to converse with fellow human beings who are equally committed to arriving at a sound opinion about the matter at hand and who may have discerned a problem or factor we have overlooked. Adopting the principle to "never do wrong" thus provides individuals with a reason to engage in these crucially important conversations. Moreover, it obligates them to engage in these conversations in a certain way. In assenting to P2, agents hold themselves accountable for responding to each and every objection that some action of theirs is unjust, irrespective of the objection's source.

So P2, like P1, turns out to have critical dialogical value. When agents subscribe to P2, they bind themselves to submit their actions and their thoughts about these actions to public scrutiny. In effect, they agree to live their lives in the public sphere. The thoughtfulness required by the dialogical ethic thus differs from moral thinking in Kantian or utilitarian systems. These latter two systems permit and encourage individuals to make *private* determinations of the good. By contrast, P2, taken in conjunction with P1, imposes a requirement upon agents to live their lives in sustained dialogue with fellow human beings who similarly strive to avoid injustice.

Like P1, P2 is best understood as a demand thinking imposes upon itself. P2 is a reason thinking gives to itself for thinking, and thinking specifically about justice. The opinions directing our lives may be flawed, including any belief that it is sometimes morally permissible to commit injustice. If so, then the only belief that we can safely hold is one that calls these other opinions into play and whose goodness lies in its ability to do so.[58] P2 is exactly such a belief. It forbids us to rest easy with our opinions. Agents who subscribe to it stand in sharp contrast to those who feel themselves entitled to commit justified injustices and who thereby absolve themselves of responsibility for injustice. The person who does not accept P2 may say at any time, "Sometimes it is right for me to commit an injustice. The case at hand is a case in point." If anyone objects, she can override their objections. For, while doing so may be evil, she believes it is sometimes permissible to do evil. In other words, this person can also rationalize a practice of dismissing objections as a permissible act. The objector can gain no purchase for his position because P2 grants this purchase, yet it is precisely P2 that his conversational partner refuses to accept. Her principle—"It is sometimes permissible to perform unjust actions"—insulates her from the need for further thought. Her principle might be analogized to the principle that "The agent should accept the current state of affairs because whatever will be, will be." Arendt condemns this latter principle as fraudulent on the ground that it relieves the agent of any need to judge and to act.[59] I am suggesting that the rejection of P2 is similarly unethical because, in spurning P2, we absolve ourselves of the need for the thinking that enables us to draw and defend distinctions crucial to living a good life.

We can now grasp the sense in which P2 provides the basis for common deliberation. Those who reject P2 may opt out of common deliberation at any point, citing their belief that they are entitled to sometimes act unjustly. Only those agents who commit to P2 have a reason to engage in sustained deliberation. P2's negative formulation is significant in this regard. If we were to reformulate P2 as "Always act justly," we might be inclined to think we already know what justice is and that therefore we could stop thinking, cease conversing with our fellow human beings, and proceed to institutionalizing mechanisms for securing justice. The focus on avoiding injustice in every circumstance promotes ongoing common deliberation in a way the positive formulation does not.

This last observation brings me to the third and fourth important features of P2; its focus on injustice and its demand on agents to live responsibly. Recall that P1 appeared problematic because it appeared to allow individuals to make private determinations as to the character of the good life and right actions without being in any way accountable to other people affected by these determinations. P2 speaks to this problem by putting each of us into relation with every person who wishes to object to our actions, be that a neighbor or someone in China who thinks she is being wronged by us. On this score, the ethic is thoroughly relational and public. However, this relational quality does not come at the expense of a teleological orientation. P2 preserves the teleological orientation of P1. It commits us to a *lifetime* of holding ourselves responsible for *never* doing wrong. It also binds us to trying to persuade others to adopt P2 because we need other people's insights if we are to avoid wronging them and ourselves; and P2 makes joint, responsible deliberation possible.

Like Socrates, I am aware that many persons may never assent to this second principle. In fact, unless they think about what is entailed by the possibility of being wrong in their beliefs about the best way to live, they almost certainly will *not* accept the principle. For, as we have seen, P2's goodness lies in its critical dialogical value, and this value reveals itself only to persons who engage in critical dialogue. This point brings me to the fifth feature of P2—its practicality. While some people will never adopt P2, it does not follow that the principle has no practical force. On the contrary, it is practical in at least four ways. First, P2 is a standard for thoughtfully judging the goodness of all stances and actions (past, present, or future). Those consistent with P2 satisfy a thinking human being and are thus better than those which are inconsistent with the principle. Second, the standard helps us to identify just actions. Actions consistent with P2 are equally consistent with the possibility of common deliberation devoted to identifying and avoiding possible injustices to members of the community. The two must be consistent because it is the discussants' commitment to P2 that makes common deliberation possible; such deliberation, in turn, must aim at avoiding wrong-doing or the discussants will be in violation of P2 to which they are committed. Third, while some people may not explicitly agree to P2, they are in fact committed to P2 insofar as they desire a satisfying life. In other words, P2 applies to their actions whether they recognize it or not. Fourth, P2 enables human beings to arrive at a *shared* judgment regarding what is right and wrong. It thus has the practical effect of fostering community of the best sort—an ethically reflective community. It is no accident that the *Crito* shows Crito and Socrates using P2 to arrive at a shared judgment: Crito concurs with Socrates' assertion that Crito must be judged to have acted "wrongly" in urging Socrates to forego thoughtful consideration and to act instead out of fear of death.[60] Such a course might involve both men in wrongdoing and thus put them in violation of P2 (which both have endorsed).

Revisions to female ethics necessitated by the adoption of principle 2

As with P1, P2's further specification of the principled dialogical ethic suggests a number of additional ways to improve female ethics.

IMPROVEMENT 1: OFFERS A MUCH NEEDED FOCUS TO HUMAN INTERACTIONS

We have seen that female ethics emphasize being open to other people in their full individuality. Surely, though, we ought not to be infinitely open. Raising a child well means foreclosing some options (e.g. beating on a brother; stealing the family's grocery money). It also means directing the development of the character of our children and friends toward some end, instead of celebrating choice *per se*.[61] I am not claiming that we are entitled to impose our vision of the good life on others. But I am saying that our interaction with our friends and family should be centered upon the question of how all of our actions and deliberations promote or thwart good living. At this point, I want to speak to one of the objections I deferred for later consideration. The question was whether a dialogical ethic could yield any important insight into child nurturance, given that children are not as sophisticated reasoners or speakers as adults. While there are unquestionably differences in sophistication between parents and children, Socrates' conversations with the young Theatetus and Lysis[62] demonstrate that even children can be taught to be skeptical about their initial positions and can be trained in the discipline of joining others in the effort to find and defend still better positions. In other words, they can be initiated into a life lived in accordance with P2. If we fail to engage ourselves and our children in such a search, then neither of us will develop the thoughtfulness necessary to achieve insights into the character and merits of the good life.

I would add as well that it is hard to see how any person can achieve any real autonomy if he or she fails to learn disciplined thinking. Autonomy always presupposes some control by agents over their own actions. Without the focus and direction bestowed by P2, our character is nothing more than the product of a series of "open" encounters with intimates and strangers. Any sense in which our character and those actions we are led by our character to perform are under our control tends to evaporate. They cease to be our "own" as well. As Midgley points out, making moral choices and judgments are a matter of "committing ourselves to a decision which issues from and expresses our wider attitudes, and which has to be more or less consistent with the rest of our lives." Although this consistency is never complete because we ourselves have not fully articulated these beliefs, "we still need to make [this consistency] as complete as possible, because the state of chaotic looseness between our various thoughts and actions is not just painful—it is destructive to our individuality, our personal identity."[63] In the absence of disciplined judgments, we lose our identity and thus any claim to authoring our "own" autonomous actions.

The dialogical ethic rooted in P1 and P2 provides for this needed discipline, but not at the expense of closing down or shutting off conversation with others. Both principles function to preserve the thoughtful give-and-take of assertions and objections necessary for leading the good life. Furthermore, the ethic avoids the charge of relativism. As we have seen, P2 is absolute.[64] One of this dialogical ethic's most important insights is that openness is best preserved not by a rela-tivistic acceptance of others' individuality but by the unyielding commitment to never do wrong. A female ethicist might object at this point: is not this focus perhaps too restricted? For example, Socrates would have Crito concentrate only upon the question of whether an escape from prison would wrong the Athenians.[65] According to Socrates, other questions, such as the costs to those who fund his escape or the effect of execution upon Socrates' civic reputation and upon his children, should not figure in their common deliberation.[66] But, our female ethicist may object, why are these factors irrelevant, especially if the main-tenance of our connections with others is, as Socrates himself concedes, important to living well? With whom do we converse if not our friends, family, and fellow citizens? Why then should we not care for them?

My response has two parts. First, addressing these questions requires conversing with others and with oneself. The dialogical ethic does not preclude raising the above objection; however, P1 and P2 still must regulate such a conver-sation because they make this discussion possible. Therefore, establishing these principles and exploring their meaning and implications qualifies as the first order of business. Second, it may very well be that, upon thoughtful examination, not all issues will prove equally important. The objector unwarrantedly presumes we know the value of civic reputation or what it means to act in the interest of our children when she sets up these issues as competitors to the focus on never doing wrong. As I have insisted throughout this book, ideas like "caring for one's chil-dren" do not carry their meaning written on their face. What such a phrase means is contestable and must be considered and judged through an ongoing dialogue made possible by P1 and P2. The point, then, is not that these alternative concerns are totally irrelevant. In fact, Socrates himself returns to all of them at the end of his talk with Crito.[67] The point is rather that their relevance should be judged only after the interlocutors have become clearer on the meaning of the just and good life. Such clarity can be achieved only if we accept P1 and P2.

To reiterate: the dialogical ethic makes continual thoughtfulness our central priority. In doing so, it focusses practical deliberation more than female ethics do. Female ethics, especially those of care and empathy, require agents to be open to any and all possibly good courses of action or ways of being in the world. As a result, these ethics leave our choices infinitely calculable. What I decide to do after today's encounter with you may look evil by the standard of tomorrow's encounter with someone else. On this score, female ethics are akin to utilitarianism. Utilitarianism enjoins agents to do that which results in the greatest possible happiness of the largest number of people. Since the agent may have overlooked some possible course of action capable of yielding even more happiness, utilitarian ethics produce decisions that are subject to being overturned the next moment.

The dialogical ethic, by contrast, judges our past or proposed actions good as long as they are consistent with ongoing thoughtfulness. Agents do not have to evaluate any and all possible courses of action in order to act well. For example, Socrates and Crito consider whether it is better for Socrates to stay in prison or to bribe the jailer and to flee to Thessaly. However, they do not entertain the possibility that the two should murder the guard in order to escape or that Crito should administer poison to Socrates so that he could die at the hands of a friend. The dialogical ethic asks only that agents critically evaluate the courses of action that occur to them at the point of time of the discussion. Note, though, that this narrowing of focus does not make the conclusions they draw arbitrary nor does it render their choice infinitely calculable. By acting in a way consistent with ongoing thoughtfulness, the agents have acted well. Nothing they do has foreclosed the possibility that someone else will suggest yet another course of action they have overlooked. If and when this other suggestion surfaces in a conversation, the agents will be well positioned to consider it because nothing they have done will have precluded future deliberation. By acting in accordance with the principles of the dialogical ethic, they insure that this additional deliberation can occur. The narrowed focus of the dialogical ethic yields non-arbitrary choices without requiring the agents to consider all possible courses of action, a task that is humanly impossible in any case.

IMPROVEMENT 2: PROVIDES FOR A MORE APPROPRIATE OBJECT
OF TRUST AND CARE

Baier, Noddings, Gilligan, and Govier all would have us trust and care for other persons. While there are many difficulties with this position, two are especially salient for assessing the relative merits of a dialogical and female ethics. First, as we have seen, interpersonal trust and care are not intrinsically ethically good. While trust may foster associations capable of teaching us skills of sensitivity and co-operation, these same associations may equally train us in evil. The militia movement preaches its own view of caring, as does the Mafia. Within each of these groups, members may display attitudes quite similar to those between a loving parent and child or between friends. Sometimes interpersonal care and trust may not extend to people outside of the group. They seem to co-exist comfortably with the promotion of a culture of hate. Second, as long as trust and care are understood only as (or, at least, largely as) interpersonal virtues, they contain a built-in tendency toward self-righteousness.[68] As the prior chapters demonstrated, female ethics allow the trustor or caregiver to define what counts as the good will of the trustee or as active responsiveness on the part of the caregiver. Thus, an American businessman might go to Japan and try to make a sale. The Japanese, who seek to build extensive rapport before they form a business relation, may counter with an offer to go out for dinner and drinks. After three days of wining and dining, the American businessman may conclude that the Japanese are not showing him good will but merely leading him on. Under a Baierian or Govierian ethic of trust, the businessman is perfectly justified in concluding that he has been betrayed and storming off in a huff. Clearly there is a crucial issue of who gets to decide what constitutes good will or a loving act of open attentiveness.

A principled ethic of dialogue, modeled on Socratic discourse, avoids both the problem of self-righteousness and of the possible immorality of care and trust. The ethic accepts that human beings trust themselves and each other and that they routinely give and receive care, but it calls these modes of care and trust into question. Conversants who are committed to never doing wrong (P2) must consider the possibility they have erred in their trusting and caring. Perhaps what they had previously accepted as moral trust and care are not such. This doubt leads to further questions: When is trust truly moral? Who can provide insight into this issue? Arriving at sound answers to such questions requires that we converse with others with a view to finding answers capable of meeting our and their objections. Both we and our conversational partners must commit to P1 and P2, principles making this conversation possible. *But committing to these two principles is equivalent to binding ourselves to care for and to trust in the argument.* The dialogical ethic thus might be said to treat principled conversation, rather than the other person, as the true object of trust and care. Trust can still be thought of as the expectation by the trustor that he or she will be the recipient of the good will of that which has been trusted. But now good will (i.e. beneficial will) is seen to inhere in and be expressed through critical conversation instead of residing in the unexamined beliefs or intentions of some other person.

In a similar vein, we may continue to think of interpersonal care as appropriately attending to and as being responsive to the insights of other individuals. However, insofar as it is the commitment to P1 and P2 that gives conversants a good reason to listen to each other, the parties' primary focus needs to be on whether their discourse accords with these principles. The focus belongs on the quality of the discourse because the interlocutors' receipt of each other's insights is both made possible and mediated by this discourse. It should be noted as well that the interlocutors place their trust in principled argument *as a matter of reasoned policy*. This shift from interpersonal trust and care to trust in and care for the argument is thus simultaneously a shift away from evidentiary forms of trust to policy-based trust of the sort argued for in the prior chapter.

IMPROVEMENT 3: CHECKS THE TENDENCY TO MIRROR OTHERS' POINTS OF VIEW

From a dialogical ethic's point of view, opinions are not good because we want them to be true, because some group of people happens to subscribe to them, or because we find them empowering. Rather they are good insofar as they reflect wisdom. Of course, we may err as to who is wise. It is exactly this possibility of error that should incline us to suspect our point of view and our own "wisdom." However, the dialogical ethic I am defending does not require skepticism. That is, we need not view all opinions as equally dubious until some subset of true opinions can be established. On the contrary, the dialogical ethic begins with the possibility that some opinions are in fact better than others (P1). Recognition of this possibility serves as a prod to further thought and as an incentive for agents to call their own opinions into question. A dialogical ethic does not demand that we be skeptical about the possibility of knowledge; it does admonish us to be careful not to take ill-judged positions on matters and to be cautious in our choice of interlocutors.

In particular, the dialogical ethic warns against any tendency to interact only with those others who strike us as kindred spirits or as people we can care or trust. (Recall Chapters 2 and 3's analysis of the tendency of interpersonal trust and care to become self-righteously selective.) From this ethic's perspective, the problem with a breakaway movement that refuses to speak with others is not, as some have argued,[69] that this spurning encourages an irresponsible withdrawal from more general public discourse and a disengagement from political issues of general concern. The stance of a separatist group might well prove, upon discursive reflection, to be more responsibly political than some other courses—e.g. participating in the political processes of an exploitive regime. But the key words here are "upon discursive reflection." By refusing to talk with persons outside their group, the separatists shut themselves off from potentially edifying discussions. Whether this separation is just or unjust cannot be decided *prior* to principled conversation with these other people. In refusing to even try to have a principled conversation with their fellow citizens, the separatists risk living a life committed (perhaps unconsciously) to opinions destructive of the good life for all concerned parties. By trusting in their group's outlook, such agents also risk getting caught up in a mob psychology. Adopting a dialogical ethic gives people an important psychological distance from whatever ideology happens to be popular among the groups in which they travel.

IMPROVEMENT 4: IMPOSES SOME LIMITS ON INTERPERSONAL CONNECTIONS

We need, then, to take care not to lightly sever relations with people whom we judge, perhaps mistakenly, to be untrustworthy, careless or politically misguided. On the other hand, being connected to others is not desirable in and of itself. We need to be connected in the right way. In particular, our conversation with each other should be oriented toward jointly finding a reason why we should act one way rather than another. Committing to P2 is especially important in this regard. For, as we have seen, it is discussants' concern "never to do wrong" that provides them with a reason to talk with one another and to continue to do so in the future. In the absence of such a commitment on both sides, conversation is likely to break down and end with parties despising each other.[70] For this reason, Socrates is right to seek Crito's assent to P2. P2 represents a lower limit, a minimal condition for conversation to occur.

Or perhaps it is even more accurate and illuminating to think of P2 as a specification of what it means to hold a conversation. If and when one party has no qualms about acting unjustly, then it becomes questionable whether he or she truly participates in a conversation at all. A person may talk at the other person, but a conversation is more than a mere exchange of sounds. We can imagine two tape recordings played one after another. These successive speeches do not constitute a conversation. Even if the first recorder records the sounds emitted from the second recording, we still have not heard a *conversation* because there is no possibility that the first "speaker" will persuade the second to adopt the first's point of view. Conversation is meaningful verbal exchange that provides reasons for why conversants should think one way rather than another. If one of the parties refuses to consider reasons and shows himself *in conversation* to be unpersuadable, then it is pointless to require as Noddings does[71] that both parties continue to stay in dialogue. No dialogue or conversation is occurring in such a case.

P2's relevance to the possibility of genuine conversation should now be obvious. As long as parties reject P2 and are willing to do wrong, they may not be persuadable. Their misdeeds may take the form of attempting to silence or to in some way abuse the would-be persuader. In such cases, no real conversation can occur. The would-be persuader is under no obligation to continue to interact with this party because she is not ethically bound to submit to abuse or to waste time better spent talking with someone else. Thus a dialogical ethic would side with those Holocaust historians who refuse to appear on talk shows to "converse" with neo-Nazis who deny that the Holocaust ever occurred. It is largely irrelevant whether the exchange would be free and voluntary or even whether the historians and neo-Nazis extend to each other reciprocal privileges (e.g. opportunities to rebut, etc.). Contrary to what some female ethicists have claimed, these features do not suffice to guarantee that the exchange will be ethical or respectful of difference. What is relevant is whether a real conversation with the neo-Nazis can occur. That is dubious, given that members of this group have shown in past public "discussions" that their "opinion"[72] that the Holocaust never occurred is not amenable to being changed by historical evidence to the contrary. Their steadfast denial of the Holocaust begins to look like an attempt to silence Jewish victims a second time—first, there was the murder of millions of Jews; now there is the denial that the murder ever occurred. Surely the Holocaust historians—many of whom are Jewish—are justified in being suspicious of any "conversation" that has the effect of making them collaborators in their own silencing. Furthermore, by appearing to debate the neo-Nazis, the historians may inadvertently legitimate their opponents' propaganda. To debate with such persons makes it seem as though there really is some question as to whether millions of Jews were murdered in World War Two. Since the historians do not doubt the facticity of the Holocaust, they can hardly be obliged to participate in a "conversation" that implicitly commits them to a position the exact opposite of the one they actually hold.

It might be objected that this line of reasoning contradicts my earlier argument against separatists who desire to speak only with people resembling themselves. However, the two cases are different. The separatists withdraw on principle and not as a result of actually talking with those whose company they shun. The historians in my example have arrived at their conclusion regarding the neo-Nazis through past attempts at discussion with members of this group. If a neo-Nazi showed himself through discussion to be amenable to persuasion, then the dialogical ethic would no longer support the historians' refusal to speak with this person. But, as long as participation results in the interlocutor harming herself, refusal to participate is warranted by P2's injunction against harming anyone, including oneself. The dialogical ethic does not accept that the historians who refuse to talk with the neo-Nazis are somehow less "caring" or "empathic" than their neo-Nazi opponents who are "open" and are willing to "discuss" their position on talk shows. Indeed, to the extent that the caring and empathy defended by female ethics are predicated upon the possibility of a *genuine* exchange between parties, these female ethics presuppose a dialogical ethic of the sort I am defending. For the dialogical ethic looks to whether a real discussion is possible. In the case of the neo-Nazis, a dialogical ethic would judge the historians to be the more truly caring of the two parties in their concern for conversation, for the truth and for helping mankind to avoid future wrongdoing. The historians, not the "open" neo-Nazis, display the commitment to P2 that makes for thoughtful conversation, not just sound bytes.[73]

Clearly we need to go beyond talk of inclusion and focus on what constraints on interactions are required in order to make them genuinely respectful and meaningful. A dialogical ethic, therefore, is the most sympathetic to those female ethics that impose some substantive limits on caring and trusting. To see why, let us return to Govier's ethic of trust.[74] Govier cautions against trusting those who have conflicts of interest. I previously criticized her for failing to realize that when and whether an immoral conflict exists is disputable. Conflicts of interest should be a topic for discussion, not simply something that a trustor imputes to others. This criticism still holds. However, the dialogical ethic treats Govier's concern about such conflicts as warranted. *Always* trusting others cannot be an unqualified virtue or obligation since persons are not bound to place their welfare in the hands of parties who would harm them. (To do so would be to violate P2, which prohibits any wrongdoing, including harming oneself.) If we take a conflict of interest to exist whenever the agent has an incentive to act against the welfare of a client or trustor whose welfare he is pledged to promote,[75] then the trustor justifiably is concerned about apparent conflicts of interest. If and when an agent takes no steps to minimize or eliminate this conflict and fails to address the concerns of a trustor who accepts P1 and P2 and who thus is herself willing and able to have such a conversation about the perceived conflict, then we may infer that this agent is not committed to never doing wrong. The trustor would thus be justified, under the dialogical ethic, in being cautious about trusting or caring for such persons.

IMPROVEMENT 5: RESPECTS TRANSCENDENT CHARACTER OF
HUMAN INDIVIDUALITY

P2 improves upon female ethics in a fifth way. As the prior chapters demonstrated, some versions of female ethics tend to reduce the human being to a social

126

relation. Meyers' analysis of empathy is an important advance over these other ethics because her account, though riddled with difficulties of its own, rightly stresses the power of human individuals to grow beyond existing social relations and mores. With such growth comes the potential to change these relations and mores to make them more compatible with the vision the individual is evolving. P2 both acknowledges this transcendent power of the human being and serves to goad individuals to examine the values inscribed in their communal laws, relations, and mores. If these values appear pathological or harmful, the individual who is committed to never doing wrong will find herself compelled to seek new values by which to live and, to the extent possible, change the laws and social relations to make them more just.

To be fair, some female ethicists have been concerned to empower women to make these changes. These thinkers have rejected various versions of care ethics on the ground that the care being promoted may not be all that healthy and that women can (and should) find a better ethic by which to live. For example, Card, Hoagland and Friedman have criticized Noddings' and Ruddick's celebration of maternal care. They fear the maternal role will constrain women and limit their freedom[76] because this role has evolved within a patriarchal culture that is insensitive to women's interests. Friedman praises friendships because they have the capacity to move us beyond societal prejudices. Our friends challenge us to find our own defensible values, even if this search means scuttling widely accepted norms and practices. They also support us in the adoption of these alternative values.[77] To the extent female ethicists like Friedman and Card want to preserve a dialogical space in which individuals can challenge prevailing cultural norms, a dialogical ethic supports their efforts. Indeed, the conversation between the two friends—Socrates and Crito—is a fine example of the power of friendship.

But the dialogical ethic goes a step further. It not only preserves such a space honoring the *right* of an individual to criticize these norms.[78] It requires individuals to speak up, to argue for their positions. A person must acquire a voice of her own and be responsive to others. While people are not required to object to everything said by someone else, acquiescing out of laziness or fear violates P2. By remaining silent, the person shows that he is not concerned to avoid wrongdoing. Since the only way we have to identify and to avoid wrongdoing is to have conversations with other people who share our belief that we never should do wrong (P2), refusing to speak out of laziness or fear is itself a wrong. It destroys the only mechanism we have for identifying and rejecting bad and foolish opinions that are inconsistent with living well. Striking as it does at the heart (or soul)[79] of the good life, non-participation should be avoided. It is a threat to our self-interest, as well as to other people's wellbeing, because the self discovers its interests through principled dialogue. Since P2 prohibits doing any wrong, including injuring oneself, P2 entails that non-participation is to be avoided (unless silence itself is functioning as a form of principled dialogue[80] or unless it becomes apparent through dialogue itself that non-participation is necessary to avoid harming oneself or others).[81]

Problems with principle 2

The addition of P2 addresses some of the problems with P1. P2 explicitly links the good of the individual with the good of others, thereby rebutting the assertion that the dialogical ethic is too self-centered. In addition, it clarifies the relation between ongoing thoughtfulness and judgment. P2 functions as a standard by which agents may judge their own judgments, as well as those of others. Judgments not consistent with P2 fail the test of thoughtfulness thinking imposes on itself. Moreover, by requiring agents to remain responsive to other people's objections, P2 speaks to the concern that someone will simply declare himself thoughtful and opt out of the conversation.

Still, it remains to be seen whether the standard can be applied to a particular situation and yield concrete direction. For example, it is not yet clear whether Socrates should leave prison or whether Crito should aid and abet this escape. An ethic of dialogue somehow must flesh out what is involved in the envisioned escape if we are to evaluate this particular act by this particular man. Can this ethic do so, and if so, how? And how exactly can this dialogical ethic be politicized? If all of us are to try to spend our lives in principled conversation, some provision must be made for talking with each other about larger public policy issues. That, in turn, would seem to require some way of rendering the conversation national or public in its scope. I previously criticized some female ethics for their failure to look beyond relations with intimates to the larger political scene. Is not a dialogical ethic vulnerable to the same charge?

A related issue turns on the relation between P2 and the laws. In Chapter 2, I noted that human societies look to the rule of law to establish and enforce appropriate relations among strangers who are not bound by blood and kinship and who cannot reach out in a personal way to care for, trust in or empathize with each other. Some such rule seems necessary. But what then, under the dialogical ethic, is an agent to do if the laws appear to mandate performing a wrong action? If we should never do wrong, then presumably we should not do so even when it is legally required. Yet shouldn't we also consider whether it is right to violate the dictates of the laws, especially since the laws provide the social framework in which principled dialogues occur? The agent seems caught in an insoluble dilemma. What would the dialogical ethic direct the agent to do in this type of case (actually faced, e.g. by many citizens in the former East Germany)?

Finally, we might question whether the dialogical ethic I have been defending truly respects the individuality of other people. The ethic does not draw its standards/principles from the experience of agents but insists instead upon judging an agent's experience through principled dialogue. A particular agent's description of her experience is not necessarily infallible. To the extent that principled dialogue provides the only way to appropriately assess the weight to be given to this first-person testimony, the dialogical ethic insists upon filtering agents' experience through the lens of principled dialogue. So, given that these principles arise in the demands that thought imposes upon itself; and given that this thinking must be generically human in order to ground shared judgments of the right and the wrong, how can an individual or her experiences retain any particularity within this ethic?

I do not think these difficulties are insurmountable; but additional elaboration of the dialogical ethic clearly is needed. This elaboration takes the form of yet another principle.

Section 3

Principle 3: abide by the laws one has agreed to obey

After Crito assents to the proposition that human beings should never do wrong, Socrates asks whether persons should do what they have agreed to do, provided it is right.[82] When Crito concurs, Socrates presses him then to "consider: whether, if we go away from here without [persuading the political community (*polis*)], we are doing some harm and doing it where it is least justified and whether we are or are not adhering to what we agreed was just."[83] Crito does not understand the question, so Socrates responds by asking Crito to imagine that the laws and constitution of Athens have come to Socrates and asked him what he is proposing to do: are you, Socrates, proposing to destroy the city? Do you imagine that any city can exist if legal judgments are to be nullified by individual citizens? Have you forgotten that the laws are responsible for your birth and nurture? We, laws, are your parents, and you and your ancestors are our slaves and offspring. Therefore, what makes you think you are entitled to oppose us and retaliate against us, given that you had no such just claim against your father or your master?[84]

In simplified form, the argument is as follows: agents should abide by their agreements when these are just. As citizens, we have entered into a tacit agreement with the regime and its laws. We entered into this agreement simply by virtue of being the product of the regime's laws regulating citizens' birth and education. In addition, we have benefited by their nurturance and, therefore, it is just that we should abide by the pronouncements of the legal system under which we live. A number of objections might be advanced against this line of reasoning: in what sense can the relation between citizen and regime be termed an agreement? Agreements generally imply voluntary consent. Yet children have no consent in the matter of their birth and education. Furthermore, laws understood as conventional statutes often conflict. Which law should we obey in such a case? And in what sense could the laws be the parents of a philosopher like Socrates? As a thinker, Socrates gave birth to himself. Elsewhere he portrays himself as raising the objections leading to his distinctive mode of reasoning.[85] The laws did not provide this philosophic nurture; he nurtured himself. So how can thinkers be bound to abide by this alleged agreement? Also, what are we to say about those cases in which persons (e.g. slaves, abused children and wives) do not receive the wonderful education in music and gymnastics valued by Socrates?[86] It is hard to see why such persons would be obligated to abide by any alleged agreement with the regime responsible for their rearing, particularly once they have reached the age of reason. True, children are not the equals of their parents.[87] Children grow up, though, and may come to judge parental pronouncements unjust. If we think grown children are entitled in some cases to oppose their parents, why should these parental laws be exempt from such opposition? Indeed, why should the relation between a citizen and a regime be modeled on the parent–child relation at all? This view seems quite paternalistic and leads to yet another problem: how can Principle 3 (P3)—obey the laws to which one has consented—possibly be reconciled with the adult thinker's independence of judgment provided for and cultivated by P1 and P2?

While P3 is not unproblematic, it is consistent with the rest of the argument. Like the other two principles, P3 has critical dialogical value. This value is both *specific* and *general*. P3 shifts the conversation about the right way to act from a conversation between two private persons (i.e. Socrates and Crito) to one between the laws and all citizens. Every member of a community grows up under some laws (written or unwritten) regulating matters such as maternity/paternity and the education of the child. P3 can be read as asserting that relations between parent and child, which often are portrayed as a natural, private family matter, have a political dimension. For example, if biological parents rear the children they have, it is only because the laws have not removed these same children from parental custody. We know of systems in which childcare personnel rear children (e.g. Israeli kibbutzim) or which do not permit parents to have more than a certain number of children (e.g. China). P3 reveals a political dimension to relations (e.g. familial) we like to treat as private.

This revelation renders Crito's plan to help Socrates escape highly problematic, and therein lies its *specific* critical dialogical value. For it is *Crito* who first invokes the idea of familial duties. He insists Socrates must escape if Socrates is to fulfill his duty to raise his children.[88] If there are universally binding familial duties as Crito has claimed, and if the laws are our parents, then Crito, as well as Socrates, owes the laws obedience. On the one hand, if Crito is to be consistent in his denial that any duty of obedience is owed to the parental laws, he must revisit his prior position on familial duties. On the other hand, if Crito grants the force of this claim by the law, he must re-examine his present assertion that people are not obligated to obey legal pronouncements whenever they think them unjust. Children do not have a right to second-guess every decision of their parents. In other words, even if Socrates' analogy between the laws and parents is weak on some scores, the stance he takes on the law still qualifies as ethically good when assessed in terms of what it does (i.e. when it is evaluated dramatically). Regardless of whether Crito accepts or rejects P3, P3 places him in a position where he must treat his belief *as the belief that it is*. He is not logically warranted in continuing to treat his set of contradictory beliefs as knowledge. Granted, this judgment is made from the perspective of the reader who already distinguishes beliefs from knowledge. Still, persons arrive at such a distinction only if they come to suspect that their beliefs may be inadequate. Socrates' argument is designed to foster exactly such a suspicion in Crito by leaving him with no place where he can rest easy.

P3 possesses a more *general* dialogical value for the rest of us as well. If the laws are responsible for what we like to think of as *our own private being*, then *all* of "our" opinions are thoroughly conventional, a product of the laws (the Greek word for laws—*νομοι*—refers to conventions and mores as well as formal regulations). This conventionality does not mean our entire belief system is wrong or of no value. But it does mean that, when we search for knowledge in accordance with P1 and P2, we must in principle be willing to examine the whole of our beliefs. Examining only a few opinions—e.g. those concerning care or empathy—will do little to help us avoid wrongdoing if all of our beliefs are marked by a conventionality we have failed to recognize precisely because our personalities are so thoroughly a product of these same conventions. In order to live well, we need a self-understanding capable of leading us to engage with the whole of our belief system. P3 makes for such a self-understanding. It places our entire belief structure in relation to the whole system of conventions (NB: the laws appear in the plural throughout this dialogue) regulating our entire life.

This principle, like the other two, arises from thinking's recoiling upon itself. When we reflect, we discover that our thoughts originate as after-thoughts. Thinking about wrongdoing (P2) leads to thinking about whether it is wrong to do what the law prohibits (P3). This line of reasoning, in turn, lets us see how our thinking builds upon that of our ancestors. Our forerunners embodied their thinking about the humanly good life in the laws. These laws subsequently have become the basis for our own life and our thinking about our existence. Through thinking, we can partially escape from our conventional, inherited opinions. In fact, to identify our thoughts as conventional is already to begin to effect an escape. For, if the laws are the product of human thought, then presumably our thinking can lead to changes in these same laws if and when we find them unjust, contradictory, etc. The very argument that makes us beholden to the laws simultaneously makes the laws our offspring. Our escape, though, is never complete. Even though P3 enables us to recognize the conventionality of all of our opinions, it does not change the fact that we refine our thoughts by examining whether they are consistent with other beliefs we hold. Since we cannot examine all beliefs at the same time, we inevitably rely upon inherited, conventional opinions at various points in the thinking process.

P3 makes this mutual dependence of thought and the laws/conventions explicit. Thought's dependence on the laws is captured in the claim that we are bound to obey the laws insofar as they are our parents. This principle assumes an absolute form because the relation between thought and the laws is not always a chosen one. The effects of the legal system are so pervasive that they become virtually invisible to us. We end up obeying the laws regardless of whether we intend to do so. One might say, therefore, that P3 is less a normative claim than a statement of fact—we are bound to obey the law simply because it does not occur to us to do otherwise. Even when we think we are choosing to disregard the law, we may still be adhering to it. Again, the example of Crito is illuminating.

Crito bases his claim to be acting well upon his belief that biological persistence *per se* is the best of all existences. He will "save" Socrates from the laws' unjust verdict by keeping him alive;[89] Socrates' children, too, will benefit because they will have a father to provide food and shelter for them.[90] Crito's reasoning ignores the extent to which caring, parental, "biological" activities depend upon the existing law. Socrates and Crito each are responsible for the rearing of their children because the Athenians' law and tradition has allowed them to be. But it could be otherwise. We can imagine alternative systems of childrearing—e.g. the communal childrearing practiced in Sweden and Israel. So, although Crito does not realize it, his vision of his and Socrates' future lives as fathers assumes the continued existence of the Athenian legal system responsible for legislating who shall rear and educate children. Crito's vision of continued persistence presupposes a specific legal system that his own actions undermine. He is oblivious to this problem precisely because he has not considered what he owes to the laws—i.e. he has failed to consider P3.

The point could be rephrased as follows: most people hold the conventional position that biological persistence constitutes the good life. The laws, which the majority support (explicitly or tacitly), reflect this love of *bios*. Since the laws habituate citizens to think like them, it is not in the least surprising that Crito overlooks the role the law has played in his own world view, possibly to his own detriment. With P3, Socrates has forced the laws' role as controlling convention into the open by pitting Crito's (and our) conventionality against itself. To paraphrase Pogo: in this dialogue, we have met the enemy, and he is us.

In exposing the laws' hold over thought, Socrates simultaneously discloses the converse sense in which the laws are dependent on thought. As I noted earlier, if we become aware of the conditioning role the law plays, we can begin to liberate ourselves from an unthinking, childlike obedience to it. We become the creators of our own destiny. At this point, the caveat of P3 becomes relevant: we are bound to obey the laws *insofar as they are our parents*. If and when we cease to be in an unthinking, childlike relation to the laws, the laws cease to be our parents and our obligation to them correspondingly changes. P3 thus anticipates its own subsequent revision. I will say more about this changed relation and the revision of P3 in a moment, but first it is important to see that there are two important problems with P3.

Problems with P3

P3 binds the agent to obey the laws, yet the laws may be unjust. After all, they are the product of human speech and action. Those legislating may have failed to distinguish between belief and knowledge (P1). They may not have been concerned about never doing wrong (P2). Consequently, P3 would seem to involve agents in a contradiction. P3 appears compelling to agents who are thoughtful by virtue of their commitment to P1 and P2. Yet P3 involves these same agents in a potential contradiction with P1 and P2. How is the thoughtful agent to resolve this contradiction?

Furthermore, adherence to these principles is supposed to lead to the good life. Yet—to return to the objection posed earlier—why should slaves who are beaten by their masters,[91] women who are abused by their husbands, or children who are exploited by their parents be obligated to obey laws sanctioning their oppression? By observing P3, the oppressed arguably wrong themselves, thereby violating the second principle of never doing wrong. By requiring absolute and unqualified obedience, P3 appears to weaken the link between these principles and a thoughtful, satisfying life, the very link that makes these principles ethically good. A revision in P3 is needed in order to avoid these inconsistencies. Not surprisingly, Socrates quickly alters P3 to yield:

Principle 3a: obey the law, persuade it to change, or take advantage of a legal right of exit

The problem then with P3 is that it leaves no space for the thinking from which it arises and draws its critical dialogical value. The reasons that P3 would have us consider in order to obtain our obedience cannot command the obedience of those who consider these reasons! In entering into a dialogue modeled on Socratic questioning and answering, the laws have embarked upon an attempt to persuade. They aim at convincing thinking beings that, after thinking, they will find the laws' reasoning more compelling than other possible lines of reasoning. Implicit in this invitation to consider and assent is the possibility of dissent. Consequently, the laws cannot reasonably require obedience on the ground that they are our parents and are entitled to treat us as children who have no right or privilege of dissent. Indeed, the need to permit dissent has been implicit from the beginning of this discussion with its introduction of P1. P1 effectively drives a wedge between belief and knowledge (P1), making the difference apparent to us as thinking beings. Beliefs, like parents, control us because they have not been questioned. The moment they are questioned, they lose some of their persuasive hold over a thinking being. What matters is what thinking finds itself compelled to assert, not what others claim to be true.

P3, therefore, must be revised to allow thinking to reconsider and dissent from its prior thoughts. Thought needs the opportunity to regulate behavior through further thought. Therefore, thought appropriately makes the implicit right of dissent in P3 explicit in P3a: We must obey the laws' commands *or use our legal option of trying to show the political community* (πολις) *and fatherland* (πατρις) *by persuasion what is really right.*[92] In obeying P3a, we follow the example of the gods and men of understanding (νους), who revere the laws and their country (which is a product of these laws) more than their parents.[93] Socrates' reference to the gods at this point highlights a major shift in how we should think about the laws. Since some of the gods have no parents, the gods can hardly revere the law on the ground that the law is like their parents. Rather, the gods, as well as the men of understanding with whom they now are linked, must honor the law because of what their intellect has disclosed to itself.

Our society's conventional laws merit our allegiance only if they clear a space for the thinking capable of discovering what sort of life is worth living. When the laws fail to do so, they are not legitimate. Thus, under the terms of P3a, groups such as the Jews, gypsies, and homosexuals under the Nazi regime were not morally obligated to abide by the Nazi regulations because the Nazis did not give them an opportunity to register dissent but instead killed them. The Native Americans in the United States similarly were not under any ethical obligation to abide by the laws forbidding certain native religious practices because they were not allowed to present arguments against these laws. This line of reasoning would apply to slaves or oppressed women and children who have no political power or right to dissent from the laws that are exploiting them and would free them from any obligation to obey these laws.

This shift in ground between P3 and P3a signals thinking at work. Thinking about the laws and the basis for our obedience has circled back on itself and queried the truth of the principle it had accepted previously (i.e. P3). P3a, the afterthought of P3, is explicitly reflexive. Thinking dissents from itself in requiring for itself the privilege of dissenting. P3a clears the way for future revisions in the law akin to P3a's revision of P3. For, of course, P3a brings new thoughts in its wake just as P3 did: why should the mere fact of having been persuaded to a course of action guarantee its goodness? Consent is worth little if it is compelled, obtained through deceit or given when there has been no time for forethought. And persuasion may be impossible if prevailing attitudes result in the speaker not being taken seriously[94] or if listeners' bigotry means speakers have no real chance of altering the commitments of the powers that be. In cases of systemic oppression or under-representation, persuasion may not be a viable option. What does a person do then?

Simply complying with the law appears unreasonable. The law might be wrong. Compliance might lead us to harm ourselves and diminish our ability to lead the good life. Consequently, we must now add a caveat to P3a: we are bound to obey the law only if we have had an opportunity to argue for change in the laws and if we have a legal right of exit from the regime[95] in the event we judge persuasion to be impossible. This legal right of exit is crucial if the laws are to retain their status as a standard for good behavior. If the standard of right is nothing but what someone or some group says it is, there is no standard: "For if law is anything which Power elaborates, how can [law] ever be to it a hindrance, guide or a judge?"[96] By providing a legal right or privilege of exit, in addition to guaranteeing an opportunity to persuade the laws of their wrongdoing, the laws acknowledge the ever present possibility of error on their part and concede to the individual the right and power to follow his or her own judgment.

The revised P3a acknowledges the breach in which the thinking individual dwells. Neither fully a part of community nor fully apart from it, thinking individuals freely obey the laws because, and to the extent that, the laws allow them to leave *and to live elsewhere*. This right of exit must be viable. As Socrates notes, individuals must be mobile[97] and must be allowed to leave the community with enough possessions to make a life elsewhere.[98] Under this revised P3a, individuals would not be obligated to obey the laws if the laws permit authorities to confiscate their property upon departure. A viable right of exit would probably entail that workers' pensions be portable. If they were not, then older workers' ability to leave the community and start a new life elsewhere would be compromised. P3a might necessitate easing currency restrictions in the United States and elsewhere in order to permit citizens to take their wealth with them. The principle might even obligate a regime to provide for a viable right of exit by paying departing citizens the funds necessary to travel, feed, and clothe themselves abroad (e.g. by prepaying exiting citizens the net present value of social security benefits/pension benefits).[99]

We certainly could debate what constitutes a truly viable right of exit. Unlike Athens, the United States and most other countries do not have extensive colonies they can force to accept self-exiled citizens. Moreover, if we were to follow Athens' example and grant convicted criminals the option of exile in lieu of imprisonment, might we not be accused of wronging other regimes by dumping our problem citizens upon them? It is not obvious that there can be a viable right of exit in the modern world. We might wonder as well whether P3a is truly fair to dissenters. Might it not be better to give the dissenters a right of revolution instead of a right of exit? At least that way dissenters would have a chance to establish and live in a government more to their liking.

I do not raise these objections because I think they are decisive. Countries already admit "criminals" from abroad (e.g. the United States received Solzhenitsyn; Canada took in American draft dodgers during the Vietnam War). They could negotiate more treaties allowing exiting citizens to settle in one another's lands. No doubt it would take time to arrange for such treaties, but they surely are not impossible. The modern world did not have extradition treaties a hundred years ago but now it does. Laws can and do change in response to individuals' thinking about these laws. The refinement of P3 into P3a is exactly such a change. If people come to think that the legitimacy of their laws hinges upon the existence of a legal right of exit, appropriate changes in the laws could be initiated.

The second objection regarding the dumping of problem citizens on other countries presupposes knowledge we do not have. Whether an outgoing "criminal" committed a wrong act would have to be carefully considered. Persons condemned by one community might be welcomed by others who have evaluated the "crime" more thoughtfully. One person's murder is another's just killing. Or, to take an example from Noddings, one man's just adherence to the law is another woman's uncaring act.[100] What we are to call a given act is precisely what must be determined through critical speech. Socrates rightly hedges when he describes the escape proposed by Crito as "running away or *whatever it should be called*."[101] Furthermore, even if the self-exiling person has done evil acts, these actions occurred in a particular context. If the person's history in a particular context is partially responsible for the person performing the condemned deed, this same person may cease to be a threat if treated differently by another community.

The third objection regarding a right of revolution hardly qualifies as decisive either. It is true that the dialogical ethic I have been defending does not grant agents a legal right to attempt the violent overthrow of the laws of the community in which they are currently residing. However, nothing in the dialogical ethic precludes people from voluntarily going into exile and then trying to persuade others to join them in founding a new community or from organizing an assault on the regime of their former homeland. Revolution fomented from without may be legitimate, although agents would be bound by the dialogical ethic to consider the possible effect of such plotting on the laws and welfare of their new homeland. I would add that the dialogical ethic permits civil disobedience (at least, some forms of it). The laws generally do not say that a person cannot perform a certain act. Rather they say that, if an individual chooses to do this act, he or she must suffer certain consequences. Therefore, persons may refuse to obey a certain law as long as they willingly submit to the lawful consequences of their disobedience.

In any case, my aim is not to raise and dispose of all possible objections to P3a. I mention these issues in order to show how crucial P1 through P3a are for critical discourse. All are grounded in the need thought discovers in itself for further thinking. Discovering and considering objections (as we have been doing throughout this chapter and will go on doing) confirms this need for an ethic with principles articulating the thinking person's interest in acting in a manner consistent with ongoing thoughtfulness. P1 through P3a do exactly this. Unlike the Kantian categorical imperative or the utilitarian's principle of utility, their value does not lie in their ability to decide some issue and close down all further discussion of it. Instead, their worth resides in their power to lead agents to engage in critical conversation and to *judge* their position in as thoughtful a manner as possible. This last point brings me to the first of five ways in which P3 and P3a modify and enhance female ethics.

Revisions to female ethics necessitated by principles 3 and 3a

IMPROVEMENT 1: CHECKS TENDENCY TOWARD VIOLENCE AND MANIPULATION

The dialogical ethic acknowledges that individuals inevitably bring their own experience to bear when assessing how they or others should act in some particular situation. Differences in experience partially explain why an action or event is frequently described and responded to so variously by different people. Women who have endured rapes usually feel more passionate about prosecuting rapists than do those who have not been violated. They will emphasize the rights of victims, while a person falsely accused of rape likely will stress the rights of the accused. However, this difference in experience is not the only factor affecting how particulars are described. More thoughtful persons also understand particulars differently. For the more thoughtful agent, the only ethically good description and judgment of an act or character is one that demonstrates an awareness of the contestability of the description. This person accepts an ethic only to the extent that it allows agents full scope for arguing over how the act or character in question should be described and requires them to think about the meaning and conditions of such an argument. Thoughtful conversants consent to P3a (i.e. to obey the law if and as long as the laws provide for dissent and a legal right of exit) because they understand P3a's specific virtue. P3a provides for maximal contestability by admitting the possibility that our experiences can lead us astray and that we humans sometimes draft irresponsible laws, fall prey to dangerous passions, and pass ill-formed judgments on our fellow citizens. Recognizing our inclination toward violence, thoughtful citizens embrace P3a and push for laws imposing restraint upon both legislators and citizens by denying any legal right to kill people who are perceived to be lawbreakers unless the accused have been guaranteed a viable option of leaving the community and have refused it. Those who abide by P3a are able to attain some distance from their own point of view. The dialogical ethic provides for a measure of intellectual doubt that caregivers, trustors, and empathizers frequently lack and that can lead them to harm those who are at the receiving end of their attention and concern.

The dialogical ethic does not require agents to pretend they have no special interests connected with their gender, class, race, or religion. Like female ethics, it accepts the idea of specific, motivating interests. It is questionable whether it makes any sense to speak of non-specific interests divorced from the particular commitments responsible for our individuality.[102] Furthermore, the dialogical ethic itself arises out of a particular and individuating commitment to consistent thoughtfulness. It is precisely this commitment that distinguishes Socrates from his friend Crito. Where the dialogical ethic parts company with female ethics is over the issue of how we are to understand good conversation. Female ethics accord parties an equal and reciprocal right to air their views and to vent frustrations. In effect, female ethics grant all affected parties "standing" in the dialogue. But being permitted to expound a point of view does not necessarily move the venting parties any closer to shared judgments. As some corporate diversity training sessions have demonstrated only too well, employees who try to get others to share their feelings of humiliation and anger may be led to commit possibly unjust actions (e.g. when a woman allegedly grabbed a male co-worker's crotch so that he would know what it felt like to be sexually harassed). Expressing grievances may lead to a kind of escalating competition among conversants as they compete to see who has been more victimized by their respective experiences. One need only view the "conversations" on afternoon talk shows to get a sense of how common and real this danger is.

A principled dialogical ethic requires more than the expression of various points of view. Yes, conversants are entitled to state their concerns but the dialogical ethic requires them to admit as well that their concerns may be misconceived and that they may not understand their situation as completely as they believe they do. They may have something to learn from their fellow citizens. By giving people a good reason to talk with each other and to continue doing so for the foreseeable future, P3a substitutes the possibility of persuasion for violence. P3a thereby interrupts the cycle of escalating violence so common in our exchanges in a way female ethics as conceived to date do not.

IMPROVEMENT 2: PROVIDES FOR ESCAPE FROM UNJUST RELATIONS WITH OTHERS

A recurring theme of the previous chapters has been the need to avoid morally obligating people to remain in abusive relations. In defining the self as a set of interpersonal relations and binding the self to continuously work at these allegedly defining relations, many versions of female ethics risk sentencing people to life imprisonment in hellish marriages or friendships.[103] P3a guarantees a right of exit from these relations as well as out of the country. P3a arises out of the understanding that the thinking person is not obligated to do anything inconsistent with continuing thoughtfulness. If a woman is being terrorized by her spouse or lover, she is not going to be able to spend much time in quiet thought. In such a case, she is entitled under the dialogical ethic to leave the relation. At a minimum, the laws would have to allow for divorce in order to qualify as legitimate. Moreover, if this right of exit is to be viable, the laws must provide for adequate child support should the exiting spouse need financial assistance in rearing the couple's children. If one spouse is stalking the other, a viable right of exit might require governmental provision of an alternative identity through a program such as the US government's witness protection program.

The dialogical ethic has the merit of getting us to think about the meaning and importance of a right of exit. Moreover, it strikes a fine balance between the opposing dangers identified by female ethicist Gilligan and the more traditional Hirschman. Both of these theorists connect a right of exit with a right of autonomy. They think individuals have a right of exit because ultimately people are entitled to have their own point of view. Gilligan worries, though, that this right may encourage individuals simply to opt out of relations. People may feel entitled to assert the autonomy so prized by traditional male ethics and sever connections with other people whenever affairs do not go their way.[104] For his part, Hirschman favors a right of exit because it lessens people's fear of speaking their minds. People know they can leave if their co-workers or fellow citizens turn hostile and reject them. Without such a right, persons easily could be exploited by those with more power.

The right of exit I am defending is able to speak to both of these concerns precisely because it is not based on a right of autonomy. People are entitled to a legal right of exit because thinking reveals that each of us may err as to where the good lies and may harm others who do not deserve our ill will. On the one hand, the right of exit in a dialogical ethic does not imply that it is just or right for persons to sulk whenever things do not turn out as they wish. It simply allows them to leave the community and to live elsewhere if persuasion fails. On the other hand, under this ethic, people owe each other the attempt at persuasion. Perhaps the dissenter is the one in the wrong. P3a wisely avoids giving the dissenter a *liberum veto*—i.e. a veto permitting one member of a community to stymie a project to which all others agree.[105] This project may be just; in which case, interfering with it on the strength of what may be little more than whim would be unjust. By shifting the ground of the right of exit, the dialogical ethic speaks to both Hirschman's "male" and Gilligan's "female" concern: individual voice is respected but not at the expense of halting or sabotaging all measures undertaken for the common good. It is honored as the human voice it is— sometimes thoughtful, sometimes erring.

IMPROVEMENT 3: RECONCILES CARING WITH POLITICAL
RESPONSIBILITY

Previously Socrates had asserted that a child had no more right to disagree with or escape from its parents than a slave from its master. Now we see that the only requirements that human beings are obliged to honor are those arrived at through a conversation with built-in viable rights of dissent and exit. If laws are to be legitimate, all persons subject to the laws must be treated as equal peers of those who speak for and enforce the laws. This reasoning, in turn, suggests that parental rule is legitimate only to the extent that parents keep in mind that they are rearing children to be their peers before the law. If so, ethically good parenting requires considerably more than that the parents be "caring" in the female ethicist's sense of this term. For female ethicists like Noddings, Gilligan and Ruddick, caring means giving the child scope to express personal values or preferences while teaching the child to honor other people's right to be similarly expressive and to nurture all living things with which the child is in relation. The ethic I am defending requires something different. The just and caring parent is one who teaches the child not merely to be expressive but to think, test, and honor the truths that dialogical reasoning reveals. The caring parent holds the child responsible for thinking. In the dialogical ethicist's eyes, not to do so borders on child abuse. The child has a practical need to be able to judge the particular actions, events and character, all of which must be characterized through shared discourse that keeps circling back on itself. Children need practice in thinking; and they can acquire it only if those close to them insist upon it in their interactions with the child.[106]

What holds the adults who rear the child responsible for thinking? The idea of a tacit or implied contract between the political regime and those subject to its laws does so. The existence of such a contract does not preclude debating the various conditions under which such a contract would be valid. We have just seen that there are several possible grounds within the dialogical ethic itself for invalidating the contract. The point is rather that the only people who can and will have such a debate are those who are willing to entertain the possibility that they do have choice (and have made choices in the past) with respect to their relation with the political regime. If we think of ourselves as simply victims of politics or of law, we will fail to consider both whether we have been complicitous in an unjust system and how we could alter the system to make ourselves less responsible for any injustices. As Robin Dillon has observed, the status of victim is not particularly empowering.[107] However, if, like Socrates, we think of ourselves as having entered into a binding agreement with the laws to either abide by them or persuade them that they are wrong, then we are driven to contemplate whether we are acting unjustly in violating the laws and to develop an argument one way or the other. We are not warranted in simply asserting, as Crito does, that we have been wronged by the state (by the "system," etc.) and consequently are entitled to respond however we desire without any responsibility to the regime whose laws we may be breaking.[108]

P3a preserves our responsibility to think by insisting that we have had an agreement with the state for our whole lives and, by implication, have been making choices throughout our lives in accordance with, or in violation of, this agreement. In effect, Socrates is claiming that the personal is thoroughly political. Each of our acts upholds or weakens the regulations and mores under which we live. Some laws may deserve to be overthrown. But the only way we can make that determination well is by thinking. In the terms developed above, the argument for a tacit agreement has "critical dialogical value" because it holds us responsible for thought without ruling out in advance arguments we might want to cite as evidence that any such agreement is not valid in our particular case. It honors human thoughtfulness by making it incumbent upon us to think and by holding us responsible for the results of our thinking.

IMPROVEMENT 4: LAW IS A PARTNER FOR LIFE

As I noted earlier, many female ethics locate the value of our life in tending to other persons' needs. Other people are the primary object of our trust, care, and empathy. Earlier I criticized female ethics for requiring an individual to be over-involved in other people's lives and for failing to provide the party who is at the receiving end of all this care or empathy with any power to challenge the caregiver's position. Now I would add a concern about the caregiver herself. If she spends her life being responsive to others, what then happens to the value of her life when friends and family members die? If she lives to care for and to empathize with them, then when they are dead, why should she care to keep on living?[109] P3a, by contrast, gives individuals a reason to remain engaged with the world. If we are to live well, we need to be in conversation with the laws throughout our life, questioning their meaning and the justification of their dictates and trying to persuade legislators to revise the laws when they appear to be unjust. Socrates is right, therefore, to portray himself conversing with the laws. Both the dialogue with the laws and the laws themselves will last, as long as we take care not to destroy them through a thoughtless belief in a right to violate the law whenever we make a private determination that the law has wronged us. The laws can be our partner for life, enduring long after friends and family have passed on. By binding us to enter into persuasive conversation with the laws, P3a gives us the means to lead the good life of dialogical responsiveness to which we committed ourselves when we accepted P2. Whether we lead a satisfying life depends on our thoughtfulness, not upon whether our friends and family chance to die before or after us.

IMPROVEMENT 5: CARE AND TRUST ARE INTEGRATED INTO A LARGER POLITICAL AND DEMOCRATIC STRUCTURE

In addition, P3a integrates care and trust into the political structure of a community. Earlier we saw how care and trust were dependent upon other activities and institutional arrangements. Clients, for example, are willing to trust professionals because of a whole web of beliefs regarding the responsibilities of professionals. Patients trust doctors to be on call and to provide coverage when the physician is away. These professional ethics, rooted in a professed willingness to serve a particular good, make patients' trust reasonable. These ethics are supported in turn by a common law tradition concerning the nature of the professional–client relation, confidentiality, etc. Activities of caring, trusting, and empathizing are never freestanding. If these valued human activities are contingent upon particular political structures and laws, then we need to care for these underlying factors as well.

Ironically, although female ethics criticize traditional ethics' emphasis on autonomy, they themselves treat the self as remarkably free of any political or institutional influence. By equating private and intimate human relations with the political realm, these ethics overlook the role of institutions in these relations. P3a corrects this oversight. It binds agents to think continually about the law and the many ways in which it controls and supports both the institutions and structures in which agents operate and their self-understanding. P3a does not (and cannot) list every societal institution, arrangement, or structure in need of examination. What P3a *does* do is make it incumbent upon agents to regularly consider the possible relations between their various practices and roles and those structures and institutions guaranteed by the law.

This responsibility devolves equally upon everyone subject to the regime's laws. Furthermore, all share an equal privilege of either attempting to influence the laws by dissent or exercising their legally guaranteed and viable right of exit. In this sense, the dialogical ethic is essentially democratic in spirit in a way that many female ethics are not. As I argued in the first half of the book, there could be trusting or caring relations within a totalitarian regime. Indeed, a totalitarian regime might be more effective in meeting people's perceived needs than a democracy. A dialogical ethic differs from female ethics insofar as it integrates care and trust into a democratic regime and refuses to say these practices are good unless they are consistent with P3a.

141

Problems with P3a

Despite these numerous strengths, several outstanding objections to P3a remain. How can the ethic actually enable a particular agent to decide upon a course of action? An obligation to remain consistently thoughtful sounds like an invitation to postpone a decision forever. For example, can P3a determine whether Socrates should remain in prison? If anything, P3a might be said to complicate his options. For now it looks as though the laws themselves, to demand his allegiance, must guarantee him a legal right of exit. The escape Crito advocates apparently is Socrates' by right. In a case like this where both options appear to be morally permissible, is the agent's choice simply arbitrary?

How, too, are we to reconcile adherence to P1 through P3a with respect for human individuality? These principles express the demands human thinking imposes upon itself. If human thinking as such were not characterized by a reflexive circling that discovers conditions for its own operation within and through this self re-tracing, then I could not have traced the logic of Socrates' argument and the reader could not have followed in the footsteps of my argument. By employing such generic principles, do we not risk eviscerating the particular of all of its particularity? Another worry: if these principles are grounded *in our own thinking*, is it accurate to say we are following the *law*? It seems more as though we are adhering to the dictates of our own thinking. If that is the case, hasn't this dialogical ethic voided the political of all meaning, the very charge I earlier leveled against female ethics? These concerns can be countered, but to do so, we must appeal to a fourth principle thinking uncovers within itself as a condition for ongoing thinking.

Section 4

Principle 4: consider whether principles 1 through 3a apply in one's own case

Having just argued that individuals either should obey the law or try to persuade the laws to change and leave if and when persuasion fails, Socrates poses a rather startling question. He asks whether perhaps he of all men has not made this agreement (ὁμολογίαν) more emphatically (ὁμολογηκώς) than all other Athenians.[110] The question is surprising because it calls the truth of P3a into question. If Socrates has agreed to P3a *more* than others, then perhaps others have not agreed *at all* to this principle. Maybe they have discerned some falsity in it and do not find it as necessitating as I (and Socrates) have been portraying it. If that is the case, it hardly seems right to require them to obey a principle that might be harmful in their eyes. And how can one person agree *more* than another? Agreement would seem to be an all or nothing sort of affair. One either agrees or one does not. Now it looks as though, even if persons have agreed to P3a, they may not be all that bound to adhere to it. Are we left, then, with no practical principles, no ethic, no basis for shared judgment regarding the goodness of actions?

142

Although these questions initially appear to weaken the case for the dialogical ethic, reflection reveals the exact opposite. Another circling back should come as no surprise. Thought breeds after-thoughts. This insight was what led to the positing of P3a. If P3a somehow shut down all further questions, then we would have cause to worry. It would thereby destroy its own *raison d'être*. Moreover, Socrates' query as to whether *he* actually has agreed to abide by P3a does not deny the legitimacy of P3a. The query instead distinguishes two questions: (1) the question of the circumstances and conditions under which a legal system's claim to be obeyed is legitimate; and (2) the question of whether these conditions obtain in a particular individual's case. People are obligated to obey the laws if and when these same laws provide them with an opportunity to dissent and with a legal right of exit. However, this abstract claim does not decide the question of whether, *as a matter of fact*, some particular person has been extended this opportunity and this right.

Slaves (whom Socrates mentions three times in passing)[111] are a case in point. If the laws do not consider slaves to be persons, or if slaves are not given an opportunity to oppose the laws' enslavement of them, then P3a could be invoked as a good reason why slaves would not be bound to obey the law. However, although P3a functions as a principle—a reasonable starting point—to use in assessing the slave's situation, it does not address the issue of who is ethically entitled to do this assessing. P4—"Consider whether P1–P3a apply in one's own case"—is crucial because it speaks to precisely this issue. P4 claims that we always need to hear from the particular person (e.g. the slave) whether he or she agrees to being bound by the principles of this dialogical ethic.

P4 makes explicit the need for the individual's assent, a need that has been implicit all along in the dialogical form. The laws seek Socrates' consent to their claims; Socrates seeks Crito's agreement regarding the rightness of the agreement between Socrates and the law. These two discussions are isomorphic. This identity is not accidental. The laws converse with Socrates because they must. The rule of law is necessarily dialogical because the laws must command the assent of those who think about the rule of law and, as we have seen, *this thinking is itself dialogical*. Just as the laws must return to Socrates after making the case for obedience and ask whether Socrates in particular agrees to abide by P3a, so must Socrates turn one last time to Crito and probe as to whether Crito has any further objections to Socrates remaining in prison.[112] Crito's experiences may lead him to have objections or questions Socrates has not considered. The only way to know that Crito is satisfied is *to ask Crito*.

From the dialogical ethic's perspective, it is invalid to argue that Crito, Socrates, or anyone else must have consented to some set of practical precepts because any reasonable person would do so. This sort of move, common in traditional social contract theory, is unacceptable because it treats thought as though it were a closed system, a monologue capable of establishing certain conclusions beyond anyone's doubt. But whether some conclusion is certain cannot be decided by proclamation. The only way to put a conclusion beyond others' doubts is to let the doubts of others into the ethic. The dialogical ethic does this in the form of P4; traditional ethics do not.

So, this final principle of asking individuals to consider whether the previous principles apply in their own case turns out (like the other principles) to be grounded in thinking itself. The ethic begins with the insight that there is a difference between good and bad opinions and that others may have better opinions than we do (including opinions about what makes for a good opinion!). To consult with these other people, therefore, is the thoughtful thing to do. Questioning and answering—the living, spoken dialogue—is the medium for this exchange of opinions and explorations of doubts and objections. Nothing else can substitute for this exchange, not even an artificial written imitation of a dialogue (more about this point below).

P4 makes space for the living dialogue with individuals in all of their particularity. What is more, it does so without making the dialogical ethic relativistic. To see how it accomplishes this, it is necessary to consider Socrates' closing argument in some detail. Socrates concludes he has agreed to obey the laws because he never tried to leave Athens. Apart from a stint of military duty, he has spent his life in Athens. He has traveled less than the lame and blind,[113] not even going to festivals outside the city.[114] He was pleased with the city's education and nurturance of children and chose to rear his own children in Athens.[115] He never journeyed in order to know other cities or their laws.[116] Although Thebes and Megara and other cities are well regulated (εὐνομοῦνται),[117] Socrates was perfectly content to remain in Athens. Clearly he was not at odds with the laws, bucking them or trying to escape from their jurisdiction. On the contrary, when explicitly presented with the legal right of exit, he voluntarily declined it.[118] Having accepted the laws' pronouncements on other matters in his life, and having rejected the right to exit the city, he contends that he is now bound to obey these laws under the terms of P3a.

Notice that Socrates does not claim that everyone would be so bound. In fact, the argument Socrates makes for why he is bound seems almost designed to force the issue of whether other people would arrive at the same conclusion in their case. Socrates did not leave the city,[119] but Plato did on numerous occasions. Socrates did not visit other regimes as part of political theorizing. Plato, however, went to Syracuse, investigated the rule of Dionysus, and tried to establish a regime modeled on the good regime explored in the *Republic*. Socrates had children in the city; it is unclear whether Plato did. Athens allowed Socrates to go about having principled dialogues for seventy years. The city has even allowed him to have conversations with his friends within prison. The very fact that Socrates has had this long, satisfying life in Athens binds him to it. From the perspective of a man at the end of his life, it makes little sense to leave the city that has provided him with the freedom to discover what constitutes the good life— the best freedom possible—in search of a better city. To be free of the city would be to leave the city of his freedom. But, from Plato's perspective, life in the city could be said to look quite different. Plato is relatively young at the time of

Socrates' death. It is fine for Socrates to say that he can take satisfaction in knowing that it is the men of Athens, not the laws, which wronged him. However, if Plato stays in Athens, he must look forward to many years of living among these very same men, men with the power to alter the laws. If they have been so thoughtless as to wrong his friend, might they not be so thoughtless as to abolish the legal right of exit and the other features of the laws that command the assent of thinking men and women? I do not claim that these considerations would justify a decision by Plato to leave the city. I am arguing rather that these and other possibilities may occur to Plato and other similarly situated persons and lead them to conclude that they are not bound to obey the laws. It is, therefore, critical to ask the particular people confronted with a practical difficulty how they view this difficulty—i.e. to accept P4.

If someone were to reach an alternative conclusion, it would not mean P3a is not an ethically good principle. Nor would it follow that we should give up on ethical principles entirely and simply go around polling people and assenting to whatever judgments they make. P3a is important because it is only by accepting P3a's legitimacy that a person is driven to try to apply the principle in his or her own case. If Plato or someone else were to conclude that he personally had not consented to obey the laws, it would be because he had accepted P3a as an ethically good precept potentially relevant to his circumstances. Therefore, a different conclusion does not establish the relativity of all ethical principles. What it reveals instead is the need to distinguish between the question of the conditions for abiding by our agreements (P3a) and the question of whether these conditions have, in fact, been met in a particular person's case (P4).

The need for this distinction arises because an individual's thought is both generic and highly particular, bearing the mark of individual character, spirit, and experience. As I noted above, any argument will inevitably embody generically human thought. Anyone (including female ethicists) who advances and publishes an argument hopes to persuade by means of a logic that others find compelling. What other thinking beings will find compelling is what they can reproduce in their own thinking. The principles of a dialogical ethic are reproducible because they are grounded in the generic human capacity for thought. This reproducibility in turn becomes the basis for possible agreement to these principles. It also enables Plato and his readers to think their way into Socrates' and Crito's reasoned decision not to escape to Thessaly and, in Plato's case, to imaginatively reproduce the conversations between these two old friends. However, this same grounding in thinking introduces a rift, a breach between Socrates and other thinking beings. In thinking about life and action, the individual inevitably considers *her* life and *her* experiences. These are the ones most available to her. Doubts and objections drawn from her life will differ from those raised by someone else. In fact, it is this difference that justifies referring to persons in the plural. If we were all living a generically identical human life, there would logically be one living being, not the many beings presupposed in the plural "persons" (or "individuals"). In thinking about its own thinking, thought finds itself compelled to accommodate this difference. It accommodates it in the form of P4. Thus far from being a concession to relativism (understood as the claim that there are no necessary ethical principles to which all human beings are subject), P4 is a necessary accommodation imposed upon all of us by our generic thinking.

This dual generic-particular quality of thinking accounts as well for why agents must be said to obey the laws and not merely the dictates of their own thinking. In one sense, this disjunction is false. The talking laws' argument for obedience; the argument Socrates has within himself and reproduces in order to engage Crito in this dialogue; the argument Plato has within himself and reproduces as the *Crito*; the internal conversation I have been having and am reproducing here as an argument with the text—all of these arguments are necessarily isomorphic. Each is able to trace or reproduce the other by virtue of thinking's generic quality. On the other hand, they are all different because of the individuality of the concerns and objections a particular person feels compelled to address. My concerns have been informed by a long-term, ongoing dialogue I have had with myself and others regarding the merits and dangers of female ethics. Others will raise their own objections based upon their concerns. Laws are legitimate to the extent that they make room for this inevitable variety of objections and responses. From a dialogical ethical perspective, the laws are owed obedience not because they always accord with our own individual way of thinking but because they acknowledge and protect the diversity immanent in human thought. This protection both constitutes the rule of law and gives this rule of law its political character. The law belongs to this diverse community of human beings. If we equate the law with the dictates of our own individual thought (i.e. with our autonomy), we destroy the political. What is more, we unwarrantedly grant ourselves the functional equivalent of a *liberum veto* because we think we are entitled to legitimately disobey any law that does not conform to our way of thinking.

Revisions to female ethics necessitated by principle 4

IMPROVEMENT 1: AGENTS CAN CHOOSE WITH INTEGRITY WITHOUT REQUIRING THAT EVERYONE ELSE MAKE THE SAME CHOICE

The dialogical ethic enables us to make sense of the traditional virtue of integrity. I suggested earlier that a concern for integrity was an essential part of making moral judgments because when we judge how best to act, we are defining our sense of our self and our identity as well as selecting a particular course of action. It matters, therefore, that our present choice be consistent with our other beliefs and attitudes.[120] The dialogical ethic enables us to achieve such consistency. Agents who abide by its principles gain an integral wholeness to their lives because every act is subjected to dialogical examination. Since this dialogical examination takes its bearing from the single aim of disclosing which opinions are the best ones by which to live, these examined acts become melded into one life with the single end of sustained thoughtfulness.

We may rarely, if ever, achieve this ideal of continual examination. The Socrates of Platonic dialogues always may be, as he claims, the same.[121] But perhaps such consistency is reserved to an artificial character. Most of us slip into dogmatic assertion from time to time. Nevertheless, it remains true that we do value this trait of integrity. The dialogical ethic has the merit of preserving a place for the virtue of integrity. It is thus an improvement upon female ethics that embrace a vision of a fragmented self.[122] By depriving the self of any core being directed toward a single *telos*, female ethics make it difficult to understand why an agent would even have a stake in life, much less moral judgment. Who is this self who is supposedly thriving as a consequence of opening herself to a succession of encounters with others? Moreover, even supposing such a self to be a coherent idea, why should this self bother to think or deliberate? No conclusion she reaches has any stability. It is likely to be completely overturned by the next perspective she encounters and empathically assumes. Besides, is not this view of an entirely open self a bit disingenuous? While I have no doubt of female ethicists' sincerity in valuing openness, many hold strong feminist positions as well. Their feminist commitments include, but are not limited to, an insistence upon hearing from women of their own experience, upon seeing the political dimension of what has been dismissed as personal or private, and upon listening to those who have been marginalized. There certainly seems to be a core self who holds to these commitments!

The dialogical ethic accounts for why we value integrity without forcing us to assert that all agents are bound to choose the identical course of action or be judged to be lacking in integrity. P1 through P4 enable Socrates and Crito to come to a shared and reasoned decision regarding the best course of action: it is best for Socrates to stay in prison and to die at the hands of the Athenians. The principles make it possible for other thinking beings to understand and to accept that Socrates' decision to stay in prison is necessary if he is to continue to lead a thoughtful good life. Yet P4 simultaneously grants that equally thoughtful human beings might find themselves compelled to escape were they the ones in prison. The possibility of this disagreement does not mean one party has integrity while the others do not. Or that one party is rational, while others are not. Under the dialogical ethic, disagreeing parties may each possess a rational integrity insofar as integrity consists in making the self's actions and speech as harmonious with principles of consistent thoughtfulness as possible.

IMPROVEMENT 2: DIALOGICAL ETHICS MAY BE MORE
CONSISTENT WITH EMPATHY, TRUST AND CARE THAN FEMALE
ETHICS

The dialogical ethic seems to be more consistent with true empathy than female ethics that pride themselves on promoting openness and engagement with others.

147

In Chapter 2, I pointed to the danger and naiveté in conceiving of empathy as a pure openness to others, as a receptivity unaffected by the agent's own concerns and outlooks. We never attain a perfect mind-meld with others. Even if we could, it would not be desirable to lose ourselves and our independent discretion in a unity with others who may not know as much as we do about living well. What *is* desirable is a shared, consistent thoughtfulness about the good life and the role thoughtfulness plays in such a life. By deriving its principles of action from the nature of human thinking as such, a dialogical ethic enables us to act, think, and speak with others and to do so in a way productive of good, critical judgment. Furthermore, since human thinking has an individual element as well as a generic quality, this focus on thoughtfulness carves out a space for individual contributions. Unity is not achieved at the expense of either individuality or good judgment. Indeed, it is precisely the Socratic focus on human thought as such that both discloses the individual element in all thought and permits a Plato (and his readers) to enter into and evaluate the life and world view of a particular man like Socrates. What is most generic about human beings—their thinking—turns out to be what is the most individuating.[123]

In addition to preserving empathy as a value, a dialogical ethic recoups female ethics' emphasis on the importance of trust and compassion in a more defensible form. As long as the primary object of trust and care is another person, these activities will prove as destructive as they are constructive. Unless we care for and trust in critical dialogue, we will accord a privileged status to our point of view as to how others should behave. The god's eye point-of-view condemned by female ethicists will return surreptitiously in the form of the trustor or caregiver (or trustee/cared-for) who unilaterally declares what qualifies as care or good will. We are already seeing this return as female ethicists spin out quasi-rule-based ethics of care, trust, and empathy (see Chapters 1–3). The surreptitious introduction of these rules means that female ethics fail to honor what I take to be one of their own key insights—namely, that living requires trusting and trusting, in turn, involves an incalculable risk that cannot be anticipated in advance by some set of supposedly comprehensive rules.[124]

The dialogical ethic concurs that there is such risk in trusting and gives two reasons for it. First, from infancy on, we are already always trusting each other in ways we do not suspect. Consequently, we are vulnerable to being betrayed. We cannot anticipate and counter every threat. Second, as I have repeatedly stressed, we tend to trust our own perspective in an uncritical and potentially very dangerous way. For both of these reasons, we cannot avoid the risk that accompanies trusting. What we *can* do is alter the form of the risk we run. Instead of placing our trust in persons, we can shift our trust to critical dialogue. Making such a shift is reasonable. Although thinking inevitably brings unanticipated afterthoughts in its wake; and although listening to other people can yield unexpected and perhaps upsetting insights, the dialogical ethic has the advantage of confronting the incalculability of risk head on and providing us with a way of coping with it. This ethic provides principles for disciplined thoughtfulness instead of mandating rigid rules for how to behave in various situations. The ethic thus enables agents to respond flexibly as they make new discoveries about the situation in which they are operating.

In addition, the dialogical ethic wisely does not pretend to calculate the incalculable. It accepts that we will sometimes trust and then later feel ourselves betrayed. It differs from female ethics, however, in obligating us to consider whether betrayals by others are truly such or whether we have misjudged their actions. The dialogical ethic does not guarantee happiness. What it does do is deflect the rage that leads us to feel entitled to unilaterally declare that others are traitors and the enemies of our happiness. Whether they are truly enemies depends upon whether we have analyzed their behavior correctly. P1–P4 makes good judgment possible in part by obligating us to step back, to think about these alleged wrongs, and to discuss them with the "offender" instead of indulging our anger.

Finally, the dialogical ethic may even prove truer to the idea of interpersonal care than care ethics. If true interpersonal caring is a practice of both seeing and affirming the essential relatedness of all human beings, then the dialogical ethic must be judged caring. This ethic reflects and encourages a sense similar to the Buddhist's and Confucianist's deep feeling that all beings are akin to one another. From the dialogical ethic's point of view, all persons share the fundamental human condition of being both able to think and to err. In this sense, we all belong to the same family. We are, as the female ethicists claim, essentially related. Confucius called this sense of belonging to the same family *jen* and said that *jen* is always nearer than it appears. The dialogical ethic offers its own twist on *jen*, rooting the experience of it in thinking itself. Through thinking we are led to affirm P4, a principle honoring the generic and particularistic dimensions of the thought we share with others. Since being in the same family means being both generically akin and individually distinct from the other family members, we can say that *jen* is fully present at the moment of thought. At other times, it is indeed "near," just waiting for us to think and to realize it. Far from being hostile to care, the principles of the dialogical ethic may be the glue that binds us to each other most securely.

Conclusion

A dialogical ethic is a viable alternative to both traditional and female ethics. It incorporates key insights from each, while avoiding many of the difficulties inherent in their approaches. One of the recurring themes in this book has been the contestability of positions asserted as certain. The history of ethics largely has been one of disputes. I see no reason to think that these disputes will ever cease. In fact, if thinking always has an intrinsically individual element, these disputes necessarily will continue as new generations of thinkers are born. The best we can hope for is an ethic that builds this contestability into its principles. The dialogical ethic does so, and, for that reason, it seems to be the most viable of ethics.

CONCLUSION

It is within the nature of philosophy that the truer it becomes the less it is able to round out or complete itself.

(Karl Jaspars)

You may not be able to complete the work but that does not mean that you are not required to start it.

(Emil Fackenheim)

In a famous Zen parable, the master and his disciple are strolling through a forest. They hear a woodcutter cutting down trees. The disciple rejoices in the beautiful sounds of the clean chopping strokes resounding in the forest. The master immediately chides him for missing the truth: the sounds only make obvious the deep and lovely silence of the forest. No doubt the master is, in one sense, quite right. The analytic incursions we humans make too often result in a fragmentary understanding of our world. We confuse our perceptions or insights with the whole of reality. The last two decades of women's critiques of traditional ethics have shown how often thinkers have employed highly selective methods and abstract frameworks that not merely gloss over but even suppress important insights of people, especially those who historically have had little political power. Insofar as our perceptions compose our social reality, it is fair to say part of reality itself has been suppressed. As one Zen commentator puts it, the "hewing sounds of the woodcutter's axe are clearly audible and delightful to the ears, but they are so at the expense of the basic silence of the forest."[1]

Of course, this interpretation of the master's wisdom is itself a "chop" at the meaning of the parable. There are other, complementary interpretations worthy of consideration. We might ponder, for example, the importance of the axe's chopping and of the disciple's attention to it. After all, the master is prompted to offer his interpretation only because the disciple has dared to share an observation. It is the disciple's remark—the stroke, as it were, of his axe—that prompts the master's counter. Failure to make any observations or assertions concerning experience would equally lead us to miss the forest's silence. Sound is relative to silence, but the converse is true as well. Perhaps it is only when the strokes of thought are the cleanest and most incisive that we have a chance to grasp the unspoken assumptions, features and preconditions of our thought.

We should be leery, therefore, of rushing to condemn reason and analysis. Since all speech is an incursion into the whole of which we are speaking, female ethicists err when they attack traditional ethics for being selectively abstract. Female ethics are abstract as well and take their own analytic stands on such matters as the definition of care, trust, empathy, etc. Instead of attacking all abstraction, we should focus our attention on the character of the principles to which we appeal. As the prior chapter showed, there are different types of principles, some of which make conversations more inclusive, others less so. We need to ask: do our principles help to cultivate an attentiveness to the whole when we employ them? Or do they function to exclude other people's insights or to mislead and harm in other ways? This question needs to be asked of female ethics as well. For all of their talk of holism and inclusion, female ethics reproduce much of the rigidity and repression they ascribe to traditional analyses because they ignore individuals' erotic longings, lock people into potentially manipulative and violently abusive relations, and provide little or no basis for challenging other people's perspectives and prejudices. As we have seen, female ethics are not always all that responsive to individuals' concerns and insights.

As should be clear by now, I accept many of female ethics' criticisms of Kantian and utilitarian ethics. My aim has been to incorporate their insights into an ethic—a dialogical ethic—with all of the strengths of female ethics but fewer of the difficulties. Rather than rehearsing all of the advantages of this dialogical ethic, I want to close by identifying a few key differences between the way in which a female ethic and this dialogical ethic would handle some concrete practical difficulties. I will consider four cases—two which are personal, one professional, and one explicitly political.

Case 1: Heinz and the druggist

In her book *In a Different Voice*, Gilligan compares how boys and girls respond to the following scenario: Heinz, a man with a very sick wife, needs a certain drug to save her life. Heinz cannot afford this drug and his local druggist refuses to sell it to him at a lower price. Jake, a youthful participant in Gilligan's study, sees the ethical dilemma as one of logically working out which right should trump when they come into conflict. Jake argues for Heinz's right to steal the drug. The right of Heinz's wife to live trumps the druggist's right to make $1000 from the sale of this drug. Amy, by contrast, argues that Heinz should not steal the drug. She locates the ethical issue in the quality of Heinz's relation with his wife. If he steals the drug and has to go to jail, his wife might be abandoned and be worse off than before he stole to help her. Furthermore, Amy wants Heinz and the druggist to converse with one another. She assumes that every person has a voice that deserves to be heard and that through conversation the two parties can arrive at some other mutually acceptable arrangement.[2] Claire, an older participant,

151

reasons like Amy. She equates "responsibility with the need for response that arises from the recognition that others are counting on you and that you are in a position to help."[3]

Gilligan applauds the young women's recognition that they are connected with others and need to care for that connection in their actions.[4] According to Gilligan, their reasoning qualifies as ethically good—as a genuine ethic—because it respects individuals in all their particularity. Heinz does not need to apologize for trying to meet his wife's needs. It is only right that he do so because it is in our relations with intimates that we have the most opportunity to exhibit caring.

From the perspective of the dialogical ethic, this judgment is suspect on at least four grounds. First, notice how the female ethic of care takes the description of the action in question as unproblematic—Heinz is acting to benefit his wife. But is this the correct description of the act? Although female ethics emphasize the need to hear from people in their own voices, we never hear Heinz's wife's opinions about her husband's quest for this life-saving drug. The wife's voice is silenced because the care ethic tacitly privileges the perspective of the caregiver. Heinz may think of himself as caring. However, if Heinz's wife is reconciled to her death, or if she is actively opposed to him even thinking about stealing the drug, then Heinz's zeal looks rather different. A dialogical ethic would require that we talk with all parties whose interests are at stake in the case because their contributions may affect how we describe the act we are being asked to judge.

Second, whether any of the participants' responses qualifies as good is difficult to judge because the interviews with them are so short and do not probe very deeply into what exactly is being claimed. It looks as though Jake treats the ethical dilemma as a quasi-mathematical problem to be resolved simply by identifying and appealing to a hierarchy of rights. But if the interviewer had varied the scenario slightly; or if Jake had been permitted and encouraged to ask his own set of questions, Jake's response might have been very different. For example, are we really to believe that Jake is so enamored with the language of rights that he would argue that *every case* is analyzable in terms of competing rights? Suppose the druggist had asked Heinz to work in the pharmacy for forty hours in return for a month's supply of the drug but Heinz had refused because he thought the job of a clerk was beneath his dignity. Or suppose the druggist has explained to Heinz that he is already supplying free drugs to neighborhood children with leukemia and cannot afford to give Heinz drugs as well. Would Heinz then have had the "right" to steal the drug? When confronted with such a line of questioning, Jake might change his position, reconceiving of rights in light of the character and past history of Heinz, the druggist and any other involved agents. A single question does not establish that Jake is committed to a quasi-mathematical treatment of all ethical problems.

The care ethic's treatment of Amy's and Claire's responses is equally problematic. They are portrayed as exhibiting an ethic of care because they would have Heinz acting in such a fashion as to preserve his connection to his wife. The care ethicist would have us believe that, as long as Heinz acts in a caring fashion, Amy would judge his behavior morally correct. This inference is unwarranted. Suppose that, on his way to asking the druggist for help, Heinz punches a homeless man in the face when the man asks Heinz for a quarter. Heinz's concern for his wife might strike Amy or Claire rather differently now. Heinz seems less interested in preserving connections with others simply because they are needy human beings and more intent upon saving his wife irrespective of the costs to others. Or what if Heinz tortures the druggist in order to learn where the life-saving drug is kept? Do we want to claim, as the "caring" Claire does, that Heinz "should have done *anything* to save [his wife's] life"?[5] Would Claire herself stick with this claim?

My point is that female ethics assume a description both of Heinz's dilemma and of the participants' response to it. Heinz's contemplated act of saving his wife is characterized in complete isolation from the rest of the actions comprising his life. The participants' responses, too, are represented as final positions instead of initial thoughts that might be substantially altered under further questioning. Almost everyone would praise "an act saving a life," but these same people would almost certainly condemn "the torture of an innocent party to obtain a life-saving drug for an elderly wife."

The female ethic rushes to judge an act or response "caring," failing to ask further questions that might significantly affect the assessment of the act, of the response and of what it means to live a good life. A dialogical ethic, by contrast, begins with the principle that a good practical judgment cannot be reached unless: (1) parties affected by the action (e.g. Heinz's wife; the druggist) in question have a chance to voice their concerns; and (2) all parties to the dialogue (e.g. Amy, Jake, the interviewer) are committed to never doing wrong. This commitment motivates the interlocutors to vary the description of the action being judged in order to insure that they understand fully what the action is. Since female ethics in their present form lack any principle capable of introducing a critical perspective, they settle for an unexamined characterization of actions or policies and risk endorsing courses of action that would not withstand additional scrutiny.

Third, female ethics provide no mechanism for actually resolving a practical problem. In this case, we are told that the ethically good, caring solution is to talk with parties to the problem and, through conversation, to find a solution acceptable to all persons. How exactly, though, is a resolution to be reached? Heinz or the druggist may adopt a position and refuse to budge from it. For example, we can imagine Heinz claiming that the wife he loves is entitled to the drug as a matter of right. Heinz may self-righteously refuse to even entertain the pharmacist's suggestion that Heinz work for him in exchange for the drug or that the two join forces and lobby the legislature to subsidize drugs because many elderly people are unable to afford life-saving drugs. Unlike female ethics, the dialogical ethic recognizes that parties may be unable to arrive at a mutually acceptable solution unless they commit to certain principles that make for ongoing, thoughtful conversation. It realizes that such commitments constitute an important check on caring, which can easily become an excuse for treating others badly. Heinz may appeal to his care for his wife in order to justify terminating the conversation with the druggist. The dialogical ethic requires us to focus upon what commitments, attitudes or habits are required in order for responsible conversation to occur.

This last comment points to a fourth, related difference between the way in which female ethics and a dialogical ethic approach practical problems. Although female ethics ask us to acknowledge the fundamental human condition of interdependency, these ethics do not provide any strategies for building and reinforcing community. Granted, it is important to hear various points of view and to take care to heed the concerns of those whose voices have so often been ignored. But it is equally important to figure out some ways to achieve the consensus necessary for accomplishing projects requiring co-operation. The dialogical ethic introduces a disciplined way of dealing with objections that simultaneously makes it possible to resolve differences of opinion.

Recall that the ethic begins by asking conversants to admit that there are better and worse opinions and that discriminating between the two is necessary in order to live a good life (P1). To the extent we as conversants believe in such a difference, we are committed to considering a variety of opinions about the matter at hand with a view to determining which opinion is better. We are not entitled to simply arbitrarily reject a position contrary to our own. That position might prove, upon examination, to be better than our own. If the thinking person who has accepted P1 is to be satisfied with her stance, she must either modify her original position to incorporate whatever seems true in the other person's position, show that this alternative position has consequences or implications neither party wants to endorse, or demonstrate that her original position has already anticipated and adequately addressed the other person's concern. If conversants proceed in this fashion, obtaining each other's consent at each step of the way, then their thinking will evolve together. At each point in the conversation, they have a joint stake in their conversation and are able to arrive at a mutually acceptable description of their problem and resolution of it.

I am not claiming that all conversants will be able to have this sort of conversation. On the contrary, as we saw in Chapter 4, such a conversation is not possible unless people are willing to accept certain principles. My point is rather that the dialogical ethic provides for principles, which, if they are accepted, foster consensus and community. Verbal exchanges *per se* will not lead to Heinz and the druggist reaching an accord. In fact, "conversation" may drive them further apart if each adopts a rigid position or self-righteously concludes that the other party is untrustworthy. It matters *how* they talk with each other. The dialogical ethic recognizes this dimension, while female ethics do not sufficiently do so.

Case 2: the graduate student and her grandmother

For my second example, I want to examine care ethicist Rita Manning's autobiographical case of the graduate student who is torn between, on the one hand, doing graduate work in philosophy on the West Coast and, on the other hand, staying on the East Coast to care for an aging grandmother who has no other living relatives to look after her.[6] I have already remarked on how odd it is that a female ethic devoted to hearing other people's perspectives expressed in their own voices completely ignores these voices when it tackles a practical dilemma. While we learn that the graduate student is conflicted, we do not hear much about what the grandmother thinks about the impending move. If the grandmother thinks she can manage on her own and is horrified at the prospect of her granddaughter forfeiting life-enriching education, then it seems a little perverse to think of the move as an uncaring abandonment or desertion of the grandmother.[7] The dialogical ethic would explore whether the granddaughter is according herself a status (i.e. crutch to an elderly relative) that the cared-for party may find offensive. Unless and until the grandmother is given a chance to speak for herself, the suspicion remains that the well-meaning granddaughter is wronging her grandmother in her description of her problem.

The dialogical ethic cannot specify the best solution to this problem. The grandmother and granddaughter must reach their own solution because only they can determine what problem, if any, they are facing. From the grandmother's perspective, there may not even be a practical problem. She may be perfectly happy to see her granddaughter enter graduate school. Although the dialogical ethic cannot solve their problem (if indeed it is such), the ethic would emphasize the importance of the two women committing to the principle—never do wrong (P2). It is this unconditional commitment that leads each of us to listen to what others have to say. We must listen because these others may argue that an act of ours wrongs them in ways we never suspected. If we are to avoid wrongdoing, we must be responsive to their concerns. Without this commitment to P2, the granddaughter and grandmother may simply impute positions to each other and end up harming one another.

Moreover, from the dialogical ethic's perspective, the very fact that there are so many questions concerning the right description of this case supports a decision by the granddaughter to pursue her interest in philosophy. Surely additional thinking and philosophizing hold out the promise for gaining clarity about exactly these sorts of issues. If so, then getting a graduate degree in ethics is not best described as an act of self-caring at the expense of others but rather as an act of caring for the argument, an argument benefiting grandmother and granddaughter alike by helping to disclose what actions are right and which ones wrong. Seen in relation to the possibility of an ongoing thoughtfulness, the choice to get a graduate degree and to spend time with fellow students who want to think through practical dilemmas may very well be the right choice, even if it means leaving behind a loved one (who, incidentally, possibly could be moved closer to the granddaughter in the event her condition worsens).

Like female ethics, the dialogical ethic does not think of "morality as a compact, impersonal action-guiding code within an individual"[8] bur rather as a shared process of discovery and interpretation in which individuals continually adjust their positions in light of what others have said and done.[9] What the dialogical ethic adds to female ethics is the insight that, *if* the woman's choice to pursue graduate studies is right, what makes it right is the conversants' understanding that this choice accords with the principle of continuing thoughtfulness. It is not right simply because the woman took her grandmother's supposed needs into consideration. People can be overly responsive to each other. Nor is it right because the woman felt *angst* at making the choice but then finally asserted her right to care for herself. Merely feeling *angst* is no guarantee of right action either. A vicious person may feel internally tormented over a missed opportunity to rob or maim. Nor is the choice morally right because the woman acts upon some alleged right to care for herself. Even assuming that it makes sense to speak of a "right to care for one's self," this right would still have to be exercised at the right time, in the right place, and with respect to the right person to qualify as praiseworthy. Identifying the right time, place, etc., will require continuing thoughtfulness, and it is this thoughtfulness, therefore, that would seem to be the source of any rightness the act may possess.

Case 3: the needy student and the professor

Female ethics frequently discuss the student–professor relation. For example, we are told that the right-acting professor is the caring person who tailors her teaching to the needs to her students.[10] Thus, if a student wants more time to write a paper, the professor should extend the deadline or provide additional help to the student. The dialogical ethic certainly does not argue for denying such help. However, unlike the female ethic, it would not accept the student's description of his problem at face value. Once again the ethical problem is one of arriving at a sound description of the problem. And, once again, the unconditional commitment to avoid wrongdoing comes into play, pushing the two parties to thoroughly analyze exactly what the practical problem is. If the student admits to bad work habits, extending the deadline may not help the student. If he wants to succeed in the workaday world, he will have to learn to work to deadlines. By insisting on a firm deadline, the professor may provide the training the student needs in order to become more responsible. Or, if further conversation reveals that the student's problem is less one of time management and more one of language difficulties, then the best way to assist him may be to refer him to a language tutor.

In addition, the professor will want to explore how committed the student is to avoiding injustice. If this is the third or fourth time in the quarter the student has asked for some special dispensation, the professor may well wonder whether the student is not trying to use her in some way. The professor is not bound to be the student's doormat or to harm herself by taking time away from her projects to provide ineffective help to this student. Nor is she bound to accommodate this one student if doing so will be unjust to the rest of the class.[11] If her expectations were clear; and if the student did not challenge these expectations, then the professor legitimately may ask the student if he thinks it is fair that he gets an addi tional week to do work everyone else had to perform in less time. This question gives the student a chance to challenge the professor's expectations while at the same time holding the student accountable for not placing the professor in an untenable position.

The student may retort that these course requirements are reasonable for the majority of students but not for those who, like him, do not have English as a first language. The professor who is seriously committed to avoiding wrongdoing must then weigh this response. The dialogical ethic would require as well that she consider whether the student had a viable right of exit (P3a) from her class. Could the student leave the course without penalty once he realized that he could not successfully meet the professor's expectations? If not, then the legitimacy of the expectations is questionable for reasons elaborated in the previous chapter.

As in the other cases, it devolves upon the participants to address their own problem in their own voices. I am not proposing a single key to all problems. To borrow a phrase from St Augustine: I want to stir our souls, not test our ingenuity as lockpicks.[12] My aim, therefore, is to identify what I take to be important and suggestive differences between the way in which female ethics and the dialogical ethic approach practical issues. This example highlights one crucial difference. By introducing the principle of avoiding wrongdoing into our conversations, the dialogical ethic identifies a number of issues connected with power dynamics (e.g. the question of whether the student needs help because the professor's expecta- tions were unreasonable or maybe even coercive; the question of whether the student's demands are resulting in harm to the professor), issues which are completely ignored by female ethics because the latter assume some description of a situation and then demand that agents put all of their energy into caring for, or empathically receiving, persons whom they characterize as needy.

Case 4: the accused son and his mother

Still other differences between female ethics and the dialogical ethic emerge when we think about a case involving criminal charges. Let us suppose that a neighbor approaches a mother on the block and accuses this mother's eighteen-year-old son of raping her fifteen-year-old daughter. A female ethic of care would have the mother empathically listen to her son's account. If he denies the charge; and if the two have a history of mutual trust, then presumably the mother should continue to trust him in order to preserve the mother–son connection.[13] Although the law may require she report a possible crime, female ethics permit agents to violate the law in the name of preserving connections.[14] So, as far as some female ethics are concerned, the matter can come to an end with the mother's act of caring and trust. (It might be objected that the care ethic would require the mother to take positive steps to care for the possible victim as well—I will return to this objection shortly.)

The dialogical ethic requires more of all agents than that they act to preserve their connections with other people. The dialogical ethic obligates agents to act in a manner consistent with ongoing thoughtfulness. Therefore, the mother ought not merely to accept her neighbor's charge against her son. What happened between the two teenagers may not be clear. Did her son assault the girl? Did the girl seduce him? Did the two even have intercourse? On the other hand, the mother ought not rush to her son's defense in an effort to preserve the mother–son connection. If her son did assault this young woman, then it may be best for all parties that he live with the consequences of the deed, including some form of detention or imprisonment. This possibility, too, will have to be considered if wrongdoing is to be avoided.

So, at the very least, we can say that adopting a "caring" approach of empathically receiving whatever the son or daughter says, irrespective of the thoughtfulness of their claims, would not be a good approach. Merely accepting the son's or daughter's possibly misleading descriptions of the contested event could harm the teenagers by encouraging them in injustice. Moreover, such "caring" does nothing to address the girl's and her mother's sense that the girl has been violated and that some response commensurate with this violation is needed. In fact, insofar as a female ethic lets the mother rest easy with her empathically caring response, the ethic undermines the criminal legal system designed to protect people from being victimized.[15]

If the mother should neither uncritically accept nor rush to rebut the rape charge against her son, what would the dialogical ethic have her do? As in the other cases, the general strategy is one of trying to hit upon some line of questioning capable of orienting all involved persons' lives toward greater thoughtfulness about their commitments, values, accusations, and responses. For example, the mother might ask her son whether *he* thinks he harmed the neighbor's girl. By asking such a question, the mother shows herself to be committed to never doing wrong. If she simply had assumed her son was in the right (or wrong), she might have erred. Choosing to ask this question creates an opportunity for her son to challenge her own thinking regarding both what is right and what occurred between him and the young woman. He may say "no" and proceed to explain that she invited him to have sex with her. Or he may say that she threatened to accuse him of rape if he did not disclose the secrets of some mutual friend and then made good her threat when he refused to betray this trust. Or he may admit to having forced himself upon the girl and then proceed to try to defend such force. We simply do not know in advance of some discussion what the event under discussion is. The event always is interpreted by involved parties. Until we hear their interpretations from their own mouths we cannot be said to have thought about the event in which these parties are participants.

By asking to hear the son's story in his voice, the mother does not forget the girl's charge of rape. On the contrary, by asking whether the son thinks he has acted wrongly, the mother insists upon public accountability. She acknowledges that there are wrong actions and that the possibility of wrongdoing applies in this case. Furthermore, if the law requires citizens to report possible crimes and if she has no quarrel with the law, then the mother should report the alleged rape. Her questioning of her son and her willingness to report the charge honor the neighbor's sense that this case involves a serious charge requiring a reasoned response. At the same time, by insisting that her son have a chance to contest the charge, the boy's mother creates an environment encouraging thoughtfulness. Her response may encourage the other mother to similarly question her daughter carefully and thoughtfully.

The son may deny any wrongdoing even when confronted with physical evidence suggesting that he did rape the young girl. If there is substantial physical evidence contradicting his version of the event, then further conversation with the son may be pointless. To the extent he feels himself under no obligation to account for the contradicting evidence, he reveals that he is not unconditionally committed to avoiding wrong. That is, he fails to adhere to P2, a condition for ongoing thoughtful conversation. With the breakdown of conversation, the only option may be to let the case wind its way through the criminal justice system. Alternatively, the son may admit to wrongdoing and plead guilty to the charge of rape. In the interest of continued thoughtfulness, the mother and authorities should ask the son what punishment he thinks he deserves for his wrongdoing. If the son proposes what the law mandates, then the conversation may end there. But if the son accuses the law of imposing an unjust punishment, then the conversation must continue. If the law does not allow him to argue against the punishment it seeks to impose, then his charge of injustice would be warranted because the dialogical ethic makes such an opportunity a precondition of the law's legitimacy. Determining what is just requires thoughtfulness, and procedures that preclude thoughtfulness (e.g. the refusal to give the accused a chance to protest sentences) are intrinsically opposed to justice.

The son's criticism of his punishment may be just. This possibility must be recognized if injustice is to be avoided. But how exactly should this charge be met? The case is not as neat as it may seem at first glance. When I discussed this case with a female colleague who subscribes to the care ethic, she contended that the demands of care and justice could be easily reconciled because they are one and the same in this case. On her view, the mother should empathically listen to her son's account, but she should also turn her son in to stand trial. By doing so, she would show that she cared enough about the girl to want to protect her from future attacks. The action would also demonstrate caring for her son because it would be in his long-term interest to take responsibility for the harm he did to the girl when he raped her.[16]

The dialogical ethicist, however, will be less sanguine about the perfect coincidence between empathic care and justice. A dialogical ethic obligates the mother and authorities to do more for the convicted son than merely encourage him to take responsibility for his action. Recall that the dialogical ethic stipulates that the legal system must not only allow the accused a chance to protest his sentence but must also provide him with a viable right of exit from the community in the event his attempt to persuade the authorities fails. Truly caring for the son means caring for justice, and caring for justice requires that the mother fight to insure her son a right of exit.

What would a right of exit look like in this case? It is difficult to say. Perhaps the laws could give the son the option to leave the country for a specified number of years. The son would need money to get settled abroad. Some provision would have to be made for the son to leave with his own assets or to receive help from family members. Maybe the government could give him the option of going to some community the government has established for the express purpose of taking in accused criminals who have chosen a right of exit. The government might pay him some portion of the net present value of the dollars it would spend incarcerating him for the length of his sentence. (NB: The options posed to the convicted party must be minimally viable. They do not, however, have to be the best of all possible options. We often have to choose between options which are not optimal in the abstract. The son is no exception.)

By challenging the mother and community to admit that the punishments meted out by the *status quo* may be unjust, the dialogical ethic pushes the frontier regarding what qualifies as an ethical response when we are dealing with persons who have been deemed a threat to their fellow citizens. While the options mentioned above would have to be vetted publicly and discussed by the persons actually facing the prospect of exile, the dialogical ethic's response is superior to current versions of female ethics in three ways. First, the mother's willingness to give her son a chance to speak to the law's possible injustice acknowledges that he may be right in his criticism of the law, even though he was wrong to attack the girl. The mother does not presume to know for certain what is in his best interest. She is not locked, in the name of caring, into a stance which unjustly crushes her son. Nor is she forced into distrusting her son. Her response creates the possibility for the two of them to share trust in dialogue with each other.

Second, the mother does not grant herself a right to unilaterally and privately determine what qualifies as the best response to the accusations against her son, even if her judgment subverts the rule of law. The type of response I am defending supports the rule of law understood as the community's requirement that individuals answer to the law in the event their actions seem to violate communal rules. The son may be right in his critique of the law; he also may be wrong. We will not know until the affected parties discuss the issue and do so in accordance with the principles of the dialogical ethic, principles designed to encourage maximal thoughtfulness on the part of the conversants.

Third, by arguing for a right of exit, the mother suggests a nonviolent solution to the problem. Some female ethics, by contrast, would permit violence by the state (e.g. execution of those convicted of certain crimes against persons) if this violence aims at limiting or containing oppression (e.g. rape). Bell argues, for example, that "it is important to choose violence against violence" in those cases where a failure to strongly resist reinforces oppression.[17] A dialogical ethic would suspect this argument because it presumes that the agent can, with "forethought, clarity and caution,"[18] infallibly identify cases where violence is the only option.

As this example illustrates, we may have other options (e.g. a right of exit), options we will discover only if we commit to never doing wrong instead of assuming that we can unerringly judge when we should resort to violence.

A provisional ending

Throughout this book, I have intentionally refrained from "solving" ethical dilemmas. While the dialogical ethic I have been defending enables particular people to responsibly and jointly address the crises they are confronting, it cannot legitimately be used to resolve the crisis for them. In fact, the dialogical ethicist distrusts the extremely sketchy descriptions of case studies often cited by traditional and female ethics to illustrate or support their claims regarding the character of right action. Use of such cases presumes an abstract point of view or framework that: (1) thinks a given case can be decided on the strength of a few salient features;[19] and (2) presumes to know for certain what these salient features are in advance of any thoughtful discussion with agents involved in the cases. The dialogical ethic disputes both of these claims for reasons given in the prior section.

Furthermore, the dialogical ethic forces the issue of point of view. These cases are always "given" by a somebody with a point of view to someone with a point of view. Who exactly are these people? By attaching particular persons to positions— to their own voiced positions—the dialogical ethic resists any attempt to abstract away from the relevance of persons' life experiences in arriving at a description of the problem at hand.[20]

Instead of attempting to decide a variety of cases, I have used examples to advance our understanding of the type of important insights we might achieve if we shift our perspectives away from interpersonal care and trust toward caring for and trusting in principled dialogue. In the language of Chapter 4, I have treated the cases as though they have *critical dialogical value*. By now it should be apparent why I have done so. To analyze examples as case studies for applied ethics is, paradoxically, to deprive them of their ethical value. Such an attempt presupposes a rule-bound or algorithm-driven mode of analysis, a mode antithetical to the consistent thoughtfulness with which we should approach all of our inherited opinions. This is not to say that all persons' reasoning regarding practical problems is equally good. Nor is it to say that, as outsiders, we are bound to keep silent about other persons' choices and actions. It *is* to say that we should try to ask questions designed to foster thoughtfulness on our part and theirs.

No doubt some ethicists will be dissatisfied with my refusal to decide the cases discussed above. The analysis will be dismissed as too "soft." To these critics, I would respond that it is, as Aristotle says, the mark of the educated person not to demand more precision than the subject matter admits of.[21] I have been arguing that the most defensible ethical stance is one of continuing thoughtfulness. While I have identified certain principles of an ethic of thoughtfulness, I also suspect that thinking "is equally dangerous to all creeds and by itself does not bring forth any new creed."[22] To demand a creed when none is possible is, at best, a form of arrogance, at worst a dodge. I am inclined to agree with David Wiggins that those who

> want a scientific theory [of ethics make this demand] not so much from a passion for science, even where there can be no science, but because they hope and desire, by some conceptual alchemy, to turn such a theory into a regulative or normative discipline, or into a system of rules by which to spare themselves some of the agony of thinking and all the torment of feeling and understanding that is actually involved in reasoned deliberation.[23]

Other critics will find the dialogical ethic too lacking in a feminist orientation. These critics demand a point of view devoted to identifying and refuting perspectives hostile to the thriving of women. To these critics I would respond as follows: while feminist perspectives unquestionably have shed light on subtle, corrupt and dangerously repressive power dynamics, a raging commitment to women's liberation—what Tong has called the "Third Eye of Nemesis"[24]—may prove every bit as oppressive and corrupt as the male viewpoint it wants to challenge. Rage is never especially thoughtful.[25] Tong's own argument for why she favors feminist ethics paradoxically provides us with good reason to be cautious in our embrace of them.

Tong relates a disagreement with a male colleague over Akira Kurasawa's film *Rashomon*. The film portrays an attack by a bandit on a nobleman and his wife. During the course of the film, various accounts are given by the bandit, the nobleman, the noblewoman and a peasant witness. Tong's male colleague used the movie in his class to illustrate the relativity of truth. For him, the movie could have been about *any* event told from various perspectives. Tong, by contrast, is certain the movie is an account of a rape, a violation which is viewed quite differently by the female victim and the male witnesses and perpetrator. The fact that her male colleague "apparently did not see [the rape] the other observers actually *saw*" shows this professor, "[e]namored with the beauty of the myriad nature of abstract truth, . . . was oblivious to the horror of the concrete event of the young woman's rape."[26] His blindness convinces Tong of the necessity of having feminist approaches to ethics.[27]

At one level, I do not disagree with Tong. Intellectual game-playing and a fascination with differing accounts of an event can result in our becoming divorced from the evil of concrete events, an evil in which we may be complicitous. However, I do not share Tong's conviction that the feminist perspective is necessarily liberating. It puts all imagination, perception and thought in the service of discovering oppression of women. Our perceptions may be deadened as a result. Tong herself completely forgets that the movie is also about a murder-suicide and the abandonment of an infant, perhaps by the nobleman and noblewomen whom the bandit attacks. *These events, too, are part of the concrete situation.* If we are not to lose sight of the concrete situation, we need a dialogical ethic capable of cultivating thoughtful attentiveness to the world as a whole, not only to unjust power dynamics affecting women. Without this dialogical thinking, we will indeed find ourselves viewing events with the mind-narrowing *blind* eye of nemesis.

Or—to return to a central metaphor in female ethics—we will find ourselves deaf to the many different voices in the human community. An individual does not become a just and respectful listener simply because, in her eyes, she has cared for, trusted in and empathized with her fellow human beings. As we have repeatedly seen, what is meant by "care" or "trust" or "empathy" is contestable. Furthermore, these activities can be quite manipulative and disrespectful. If we are to honor the distinctive perspectives of individuals, we need principles that enable us to thoughtfully entertain the possible truth in another's claims without requiring that we endorse every statement or self-justifying assertion this person makes. We need a public space in which persons are maximally free to contest each other's descriptions of practical problems of mutual concern and to do so with a view to jointly progressing toward the truth regarding the best description of the problem and best response to it. The principles of the dialogical ethic provide for such a public space. The ethic is thus appropriately seen as an extension of, or complement to, female ethics. It equips us with the different ear we need to respectfully and fairly hear those who speak in a different voice and to critically assess the truth of their claims.

NOTES

INTRODUCTION

1 See, e.g., Carol Gilligan, *In A Different Voice*, Cambridge, MA: Harvard University Press, 1982: 22–3; Nel Noddings, *Caring: A Feminine Approach to Ethics and Moral Education*, Berkeley, CA: University of California Press, 1984: 40–43. Noddings refers to Ceres, the Latin name for the goddess the Greeks knew as Demeter.

2 Walker documents the connection between a desire to be scientific and ethical systems of rules in Margaret Urban Walker, "Feminism, Ethics, and the Question of Theory," *Hypatia* 7(3), Summer, 1992: 23–38.

3 Rights are discussed in Gilligan, *Voice*, 1982: 19, 21–2, 54, 57, 100, 132, 136–8, 147–9, 164–6, 173–4. For a discussion of hierarchies see p.101.

4 Women see "in the dilemma not a math problem with human beings but a narrative of relationships that extends over time." Gilligan, *Voice*, 1982: 28. She goes on to argue that women strive to find solutions to problems that will preserve connections. Gilligan, *Voice*, 1982: 19. The idea that women are more inclusive in their problem-solving has been picked up and developed by other women writers. For example, Helgesen claims to have found that women leaders do not rely on hierarchical pyramid top-down methods but instead reach out to form a matrix or web of inclusion and information sharing. Sally Helgesen, *The Female Advantage*, New York: Doubleday Currency, 1995.

5 Gilligan, for example, contends that developmental theory as developed by male psychologists "rules out from consideration the differences in the feminine voice." Gilligan, *Voice*, 1982: 105. She develops this point about a systematic silencing of women's voices in Carol Gilligan, "Reply by Carol Gilligan," *Signs* 11(2), Winter, 1986: 324–33.

6 It is true, as Rita Manning has claimed, that "microdiversity" is the order of the day among women who are doing ethical theorizing. Yet even Manning thinks that there are certain ideas that recur in these women's writing. For her list, see Rita Manning, "Review of Mary Jeanne Larrabee, *An Ethic of Care*; Virginia Held, *Feminist Morality*; Joan C. Tronto, *Moral Boundaries: A Political Argument for an Ethic of Care*," *American Philosophical Association Newsletter on Feminism and Philosophy* 94(1), Fall, 1994: 68–71.

7 Rosemarie Tong, *Feminine and Feminist Ethics*, Belmont, CA: Wadsworth, 1993. See note 14.

8 Margaret Urban Walker, "Moral Understandings," *Hypatia* 4(2), Summer, 1989: 16. Walker correctly notes that this charge has been raised in a variety of forms by Jean Grimshaw, Claudia Card, Jeffner Allen, Lorraine Code, and Barbara Houston. Linda Bell also warns against seeing caring or mothering as unconditional love because " . . .

the traditional role of self-sacrifice is still generally expected of women. Feminists must be careful in any endorsement of love, lest they inadvertently strengthen the ways men's dominance of women is embedded in the status quo." She goes on to argue that given "the power imbalance in even the most enlightened parent/child relationship, however, this hierarchical relationship simply cannot be taken as a model for relationships between individuals who are both responsible adults, whatever their existing differences in wisdom, strength, foresight, or other abilities." Linda A. Bell, *Rethinking Ethics in the Midst of Violence: A Feminist Approach to Freedom*, Lanham, MD: Rowman & Littlefield, 1993: 200–01. See, too, Sarah Hoagland who criticizes Noddings for limiting female agency to caring for the other. Sarah Lucia Hoagland, "Some Thoughts About 'Caring'," in Claudia Card (ed.), *Feminist Ethics*, Lawrence, KS: University of Kansas Press, 1991: 246–63. Tong summarizes various dangers of associating women with caring in Tong, *Feminist Ethics*, 1993: 5–6.

9 Tong, *Feminist Ethics*, 1993: 6–11. "What makes an ethic feminist, as opposed to feminine or maternal, then, is . . . its utter opposition to structures of oppression . . . ." Tong, *Feminist Ethics*, 1993: 224.

10 Lawrence Blum might qualify as an exception. He has spent the last decade expanding and refining some of Gilligan's insights. He has tried to speak to women's experience of oppression, arguing that ethical action includes acting with a consciousness of gender group identity. Lawrence A. Blum, *Moral Perception and Particularity*, Cambridge: Cambridge University Press, 1994: 252. I think, however, that Gilligan would be rightly suspicious of Blum's argument. Women should be allowed to speak in their own individual voices precisely because no one, including Blum, is entitled to proclaim what constitutes "woman's consciousness."

11 "Many feminists characteristically see persons as at least partly constituted by their relations to other persons and social groups." Virginia Held, "Rights and the Ethics of Care," *American Philosophical Association Newsletter* 94(2), Spring, 1995: 41. "Though the truth of separation is recognized in most developmental texts, the reality of continuing connection is lost or relegated to the background where figures of women appear." Gilligan, *Voice*, 1982: 155. Also see Noddings, *Caring*, 1984: 3–5. Feminist ethics equally emphasize relationality insofar as they are concerned to create and preserve community among women. See Claudia Card, "The Feistiness of Feminism," and Hoagland, "Some Thoughts About 'Caring'," in Card, *Feminist Ethics*, 1991: 3–31 and 246–63 respectively.

12 Noddings claims, "It is not just that I as a preformed continuous individual enter into relations; rather, the I of which we speak so easily is itself a relational entity. I really am defined by the set of relations into which my physical self has been thrown." Nel Noddings, *Women and Evil*, Berkeley, CA: University of California Press, 1989: 237.

13 "Let us consider men . . . as if but even now sprung out of earth, and suddenly, like mushrooms, come to full maturity, without all kind of engagement to each other." Thomas Hobbes quoted in Seyla Benhabib, "The Generalized and The Concrete Other: The Kohlberg–Gilligan Controversy and Feminist Theory," *Praxis International* 5(4), January, 1986: 408.

14 Claudia Card, "Lesbian Ethics," in Lawrence C. Becker and Charlotte B. Becker (eds), *Encyclopedia of Ethics*, II, New York: Garland, 1992: 694.

15 Baier hints at as much in her quarrel with Thomas Scanlon's contractualism. See Annette Baier, "Sustaining Trust," in *The Tanner Lectures on Human Values*, Lecture II, vol. 13, Salt Lake City, UT: University of Utah Press, 1992: 136–74. I have also discussed this possibility at length in Daryl Koehn, *The Ground of Professional Ethics*, London: Routledge, 1994.

16 Noddings contends we have a duty to those we can help, those whom she calls "proximate others." While some caring is not onerous, other caring must be described as an

obligation because it is felt to be burdensome. See Noddings, *Caring*, 1984: 32, 112–13. Ethicists who are more explicitly feminist equally reject the minimal duties of the sort one gets in Kantian (or, at least, some versions of Kantian) ethics. See Onora O'Neill, "Kantian Approaches to Some Famine Problems," in Tom L. Beauchamp and Terry P. Pinkard (eds), *Ethics and Public Policy*, Englewood Cliffs, NJ: Prentice-Hall, 1983: 208–09, 219. Bell goes so far as to argue that we are each responsible for starving people in Africa. Bell, *Rethinking Ethics*, 1993: 36, 140–44.

17 Virginia Held, "The Obligation of Mothers and Fathers," in Joyce Trebilcot (ed.), *Mothering: Essays in Feminist Theory*, Totowa, NJ: Rowman & Allanheld, 1984: 7.

18 This line of argument is developed in Mary Ann Glendon, *Rights Talk*, New York: Free Press, 1991. I would also note that, insofar as the law, largely written by men, sanctions male power and prerogatives, the law may support violence against women and children. Another relevant text is Catherine A. MacKinnon, *Feminism Unmodified: Discourses on Life and Law*, Cambridge, MA: Harvard University Press, 1987.

19 For a non-rights-based account of parenting, see Noddings, *Caring*, 1984: *passim*; Sara Ruddick, *Maternal Thinking: Towards a Politics of Peace*, Boston, MA: Beacon Press, 1995.

20 Badhwar discusses problems with a Kantian or duty-based view of love in Neera Kapur Badhwar, "Friendship, Justice, and Supererogation," *American Philosophical Quarterly* 22(2), April, 1985: 123–9.

21 Gilligan characterizes Kohlberg as appealing to a rational person model in Gilligan, *Voice*, 1982: 22.

22 Marilyn Friedman, "Beyond Caring: The De-Moralization of Gender," in Mary Jeanne Larrabee (ed.), *An Ethic of Care*, New York: Routledge, 1993: 270.

23 Benhabib, "Concrete Other," 1986: 413.

24 Noddings, e.g., argues that ethics requires us to avoid violence, to ask: "Is there not some other way?," and to explore and choose among the other options we can imaginatively uncover. Noddings, *Caring*, 1984: 44.

25 Meyers is thus led to emphasize empathy, a practice that allegedly enables us to enter into other people's worlds, in Diana Tietjens Meyers, *Subjection and Subjectivity: Psychoanalytic Feminism and Moral Philosophy*, New York: Routledge, 1994: 31–2.

26 Benhabib, "Concrete Other," 1986: *passim*. See also Gilligan's emphasis on conversation in *Voice*, 1982: 29, 54. Noddings ends her book praising dialogue. Noddings, *Caring*, 1984: 182–7.

27 Gilligan, *Voice*, 1982: 58–9. See also Noddings, *Caring*, 1984: 93, where she argues that we must see "the act itself in full context."

28 This focus on formal conditions for the interaction is very apparent in Noddings and Meyers. See Noddings, *Caring*, 1984: especially Chapters 2–4; Meyers, *Subjection*, 1994: Chapters 1 and 2 . Benhabib, too, has worked out these conditions in some detail in Seyla Benhabib, *Situating the Self: Gender, Community and Postmodernism in Contemporary Ethics*, Cambridge: Polity Press, 1992. Benhabib is aware that her analysis does not in and of itself constitute a freestanding ethic. She describes herself as offering a critical perspective because, having a formally equal, mutually reciprocal dialogue is, she thinks, only a necessary but insufficient condition for arriving at the right course of action. For this point, see Benhabib, *Situating the Self*, 1992: 54–5.

29 See, e.g., the authors' insistence that care must be situated in the context of prevalent power dynamics in Larry Blum, Marcia Horniak, Judy Housman and Naomi Scheman, "Altruism and Women's Oppression," in M. Bishop and M. Weinzweig (eds), *Philosophy and Women*, Belmont, CA: Wadsworth, 1979: 190–200. See also Cheshire Calhoun, "Justice, Care, Gender Bias," *The Journal of Philosophy* 85(9), September, 1988: 455–7.

30 It is this problem that drives Bell to situate ethics within a context of widespread violence. Bell, *Rethinking Ethics*, 1993: *passim*.

31 The term is from Benhabib, *Situating the Self*, 1992: 11. Manning, too, contends that beginning with the "situated self" rather than the "unencumbered self" of traditional liberal ethics makes it easier to identify oppression. Rita C. Manning, *Speaking from the Heart: A Feminist Perspective on Ethics*, Lanham, MD: Rowman & Littlefield, 1992: 2–3.

32 Claudia Card comments on the existential quality of the ethics offered by Linda Bell and Sarah Lucia Hoagland in Card's foreword to Bell, *Rethinking Ethics*, 1993: xii–xiii.

33 I have discussed this point at some length in Daryl Koehn, "A Role for Virtue Ethics in the Analysis of Business Practice," *Business Ethics Quarterly* 5(3), July, 1995: 533–40

34 See, e.g., John Stuart Mill, *On Liberty*, Indianapolis, IN: The Liberal Arts Press, 1956.

35 For a particularly lucid treatment of this point, see Wolfgang Kersting, "Politics, Freedom and Order: Kant's Political Philosophy," in Paul Guyer (ed.), *The Cambridge Companion to Kant*, Cambridge: Cambridge University Press, 1992: 342–66.

36 Koehn, *Professional Ethics*, 1994: *passim*.

37 This point has been made by a number of authors. See, e.g., Brison who quotes a number of women who have argued for the primacy of accounts rendered in one's own voice and for the desirability of concrete, first-person narratives. Susan Brison, "On the Personal as Philosophical," in *American Philosophical Association Newsletter on Feminism and Philosophy* 95(1), Fall, 1995: 37–40.

38 Virginia Held, *Feminist Morality: Transforming Culture, Society, and Politics*, Chicago, IL: University of Chicago Press, 1993: 88.

39 See bibliography for references to these three thinkers.

40 Work on the dynamics of exclusion is not confined to philosophers. A number of literary critics and historians have analyzed this dynamic at length. These writers, however, tend to assume an ethical perspective—namely, that more inclusionary narratives are better than exclusionary ones; that neglected perspectives offer us valuable insights we ought not to neglect. Female ethicists are trying to provide the justification for these and other normative claims. Since it is this justification that I am interested in here, I have confined my analysis to their arguments.

41 Meyers, *Subjection*, 1994: 165; Virginia Held, "Feminism and Moral Theory," in Eva Kittay and Diana T. Meyers (eds), *Women and Moral Theory*, Totowa, NJ: Rowman & Littlefield, 1987: 112.

42 Some philosophers have argued that Rawlsian and Kantian theories can accommodate the concerns of a concrete other who is shaped by his or her history and ethnic commitments. See Amy Gutmann, "Communitarian Critics of Liberalism," *Philosophy and Public Affairs* 14, Summer, 1985: 308–22. Herman contends that Kantianism can accommodate sensitivity to the particular because the categorical imperative is not a rule but rather a formal principle for testing our maxims of action. Since these maxims are inevitably subjective, they contain "as much of the particulars of precision and circumstance as the agent judges . . . necessary to describe and account for his proposed action." Barbara Herman, "The Practice of Moral Judgment," *The Journal of Philosophy* 82, 1985: 416. However, to mount these arguments is to concede that there may be a logical difficulty with the idea of totally interchangeable individuals who have no interest apart from that of acting justly.

43 Or perhaps it is more accurate to say that the individuals get re-made in the theorist's image. Rawls' analysis illustrates the problem well. Let us grant that it makes sense to speak of individuals who have no interest apart from one of being treated fairly or

justly. We will need some proxy for justice, some common measure to which all individuals would agree, if we are to show that a particular individual's allocation of
benefits and costs is just. Rawls appeals to economic criteria as this common measure.
But there is no god's eye point of view from which to judge the individual's allocation. If we follow Rawls and say that the allocation is just when the welfare of the
worst off person has been maximized, we are still left with the issue of how to understand the idea of being "worst off." Rawls appeals to economic standards as a proxy
for being well off. See John Rawls, *A Theory of Justice*, Oxford: Oxford University
Press, 1971: 65–75. But the level of income does not necessarily measure whether a
person is doing well. Jesus, Socrates, and Buddha all voluntarily chose lives of relative
poverty, so it is hard to see how the mere fact of their poverty shows that they have
been treated unjustly. Before making that claim, we would need to consider the coun-
terarguments a Buddha or Jesus would advance, including the different visions of the
good life and of the role material possessions play in such a life. However, insofar as
traditional theorists (e.g. Rawls) claims to know what justice is and how to ascertain
the justice or injustice of some act, their theories foreclose these conversations. They
project a view of the self onto others and do not give these others a chance to contest
this projected view. Everyone is to be reconceived in the image of the theorist's own
vision or fantasy of what a self is. We all become identical selves molded in the same
image. So once again our individuality disappears.

44 For a good discussion of this point, see John Kleinig, *The Ethics of Policing*,
Cambridge: Cambridge University Press, 1996: 50–51.

45 As MacKinnon has observed, the distinction of the public versus private is itself a
political distinction historically drawn by largely male judges and legislators. She
contends that this distinction is systematically biased against women's interests.
Catherine A. MacKinnon, *Feminism Unmodified*, 1987: 100, and her article,
"Feminism, Marxism, Method, and the State: Toward Feminist Jurisprudence," in
Sandra Harding (ed.), *Feminism and Methodology*, Bloomington, IN: Indiana
University Press, 1987: 148.

46 Bell argues that, if we are concerned to guarantee respect for women, then "[n]o
longer would any social institutions or practices [be labeled as private and] be
excluded a priori from public discussion and expression." Bell, *Rethinking Ethics*,
1993: 180.

47 Bell discusses in detail the case of a battered woman who is driven to make a false
promise. According to Bell, Kant would condemn the woman for making a false
promise rather than defending her honor to the death. Bell, however, thinks that the
battered woman is entitled to escape, even if this requires making a lying promise.
Bell, *Rethinking Ethics*, 1993: 134–40.

48 Benhabib, "Concrete Other," 1986: 414. The problem of perspective is also at the
heart of Baier's quarrel with Scanlon in Baier, *Tanner Lectures*, Lecture II, 1992:
136–74.

49 Virginia Held argues for this strategy in Held, *Feminist Morality*, 1993. It seems likely
that Noddings and Gilligan would second her proposal given the centrality of needs
in their ethics. In my view, Dancy is correct in his observation that, for the care ethicist, needs are central. Jonathan Dancy, "Caring about Justice," *Philosophy* 67,
October, 1992: 448.

50 Stanley Rosen, *Plato's Statesman*, New Haven, CT: Yale University Press, 1995: 38.

51 The idea of mimetic desire is developed at length by René Girard, *Things Hidden
Since the Foundation of the World*, trans. Stephen Bann and Michael Metteer,
Stanford, CA: Stanford University Press, 1987.

52 Michael L. Westmoreland-White, "Setting the Record Straight: Christian Faith,
Human Rights, and the Enlightenment," in Harlan Beckley (ed.), *Annual of the*

Society of Christian Ethics, Baltimore, MD: Georgetown University Press, 1995: 75–96.

53 Gilligan's appeal to principles and ideals is discussed by John M. Broughton, "Women's Rationality and Men's Virtues: A Critique of Gender Dualism in Gilligan's Theory of Moral Development," *Social Research* 50(3), Autumn, 1983: 597–642.

54 This insensitivity to particular goods is apparent, for example, in Noddings' suggestion that we simply abandon professionalism. Noddings, *Caring*, 1984: 184. Since the professionalism of doctors and lawyers is tied to and derives constraints from particular goods (health and legal justice, respectively), professionalism does tend to fall by the wayside once the theorist has thrown out particular goods.

55 Noddings claims that whenever a caring person thinks a law involves her in uncaring and hence unethical behavior, she has no responsibility to abide by the law. Noddings, *Caring*, 1984: 55.

56 Noddings does discuss a case of competing objects of care. A woman must choose between staying at home to nurse her sick child or going out with her husband who has been greatly looking forward to the outing. Noddings simply dissolves away the dilemma by positing that the child is really sick while her husband is merely whining. Noddings, *Caring*, 1984: 53. What is the woman to do if the two cases are more evenly balanced? And what check is there on this woman's decision? Isn't it possible that she did not really want to go out to the theater and now unfairly maligns her husband in order to rationalize her own decision? It is both very striking and typical that this "caring" woman simply unilaterally decides what to do without much discussion with the affected parties. Although Noddings praises dialogue, her own descriptions are consistently visual—the woman "sees" her husband's real condition and then opts to stay home—rather than descriptions of voice and hearing.

1 AN ETHIC OF CARE

1 J.L. Borges quoted in E. Monegal and A. Reid (eds), *Borges: A Reader*, New York: E.P. Dutton, 1981: 243.

2 While my main focus is on Noddings and Gilligan, I will also draw upon the works of several philosophers (e.g. Lawrence Blum; Diana Meyers) who have taken up the idea of an ethic of care and attempted to further elaborate it and to defend various of Gilligan's and Noddings' ideas against objections raised by other philosophers. See bibliography for works of Blum and Meyers.

3 I have some doubts as to whether Kant would agree with all of the claims female ethicists have imputed to him. However, since my purpose here is not to produce a commentary on Kant but rather to assess which features of female ethics are defensible, I will let this imputation stand.

4 Gilligan initially discusses this druggist example in *Voice*, 1982: 25–31.

5 Gilligan, *Voice*, 1982: 32.

6 Ibid.

7 Noddings, *Caring*, 1984: 37.

8 This description of Gilligan's position on moral judgment appears in Benhabib, "Concrete Other," 1986: 78.

9 By and large, female ethicists think both Kantians and utilitarians treat the rule as the highest concept of the moral life. This claim certainly could and would be contested, particularly by those Kantians who do not think the categorical imperative is properly understood as a rule. It is also doubtful whether a utilitarian would subscribe to all of the claims female ethicists attribute to the traditional, male "justice perspective." See Dancy, "Caring About Justice," 1992: 342–4. Nevertheless, the female ethicists' claim that utilitarian and Kantian ethics do not require agents to actively and routinely

consult with others seems plausible. In none of Kant's four examples of moral reasoning does Kant show the agent consulting with others affected by his actions or being persuaded by them. Immanuel Kant, *Groundwork of the Metaphysic of Morals*, trans. H.J. Paton, New York: Harper & Row, 1964: 89–91.

10 "At bottom, all caring involves engrossment." Noddings, *Caring*, 1984: 10, 16, 17, 161. She goes on to argue that, in true caring, the other "fills the firmament." Noddings, *Caring*, 1984: 74, 114. The other person becomes the interest of the caregiver. In Noddings' terms, there is a "motivational displacement" of the caregiver's interests. Noddings, *Caring*, 1984: 161. It is not clear whether Gilligan would identify caring with such a complete "motivational displacement" because Gilligan is so intent on having women reclaim a voice of their own. Nevertheless, even in Gilligan, there is, as Michele Moody-Adams has noted, a marked tendency to discuss only the sorts of cases where the language of care would tend to come up. Michele M. Moody-Adams, "Gender and the Complexity of Moral Voices," in Card (ed.), *Feminist Ethics*, 1991: 202–03. This role by definition is other-oriented. So I would argue that Gilligan and Noddings are closer than they may initially appear.

11 Noddings, *Caring*, 1984: 30–35. David B. Annis, too, argues that caring involves "a shift from how I would feel to how the other person feels. The attention is on the other person, his or her wants, needs, beliefs, and what that person may be feeling." David B. Annis, "The Meaning, Value, and Duties of Friendship," *American Philosophical Quarterly* 24(4), October, 1987: 349.

12 Gilligan emphasizes "affective qualities of sympathy, caring and tolerance of ambiguity which ground an ethical focus on responsibility and nonviolence." John M. Broughton, "Women's Rationality and Men's Virtues: A Critique of Gender Dualism in Gilligan's Theory of Moral Development," *Social Research* 50(3), Autumn, 1983: 601.

13 Noddings, *Caring*, 1984: 43–4.

14 Noddings, *Caring*, 1984: 11, 25. The point is picked up by Graham who contends that "[the] 'daily grind' of caring cannot be defined in the abstract." Hilary Graham, "Caring: A Labour of Love," in Janet Finch and Dulcie Groves (eds), *A Labour of Love: Women, Work and Caring*, London: Routledge & Kegan Paul, 1983: 26.

15 Noddings, *Caring*, 1984: 1. Noddings is not entirely consistent on this point. At other places she argues that there is a "fundamental and natural desire to be and to remain related." Noddings, *Caring*, 1984: 83. Also see p. 206. So it is unclear whether it is the socially acquired memory of having been cared for or the allegedly natural feeling that motivates caring.

16 Or so Gilligan and Noddings claim. In fact, Gilligan claims that the practice of self-sacrifice is itself a consequence of failing to take responsibility for one's own actions. Gilligan, *Voice*, 1982: 67–8. Also see Noddings, *Caring*, 1984: 99–100. Hoagland argues that Noddings' ethic is agapeistic and may very well demand self-sacrifice. Hoagland, "Some Thoughts About 'Caring'," 1991: *passim*. I am inclined to agree with Hoagland's assessment of Noddings, particularly since Noddings defines the self as a relation. See my critique on pp. 38–40. Gilligan may escape the charge of being agapeistic. She could be read, for example, as arguing less for an ethic of care and more for an ethic of voice in which each agent is bound to acquire her own voice. For this interpretation, see Daryl Koehn, "With A Different Ear: Hearing Gilligan Anew," *Southwest Philosophy Review* 10(1), January, 1994: 77–86. But even Gilligan's analysis might be said to be agapeistic insofar as it does approve of actions "that . . . go in the direction of self-sacrifice . . . . Here there is no natural limit set to the requirements of care, and so the demand for self-sacrifice is there in the nature of the system . . . ." Dancy, "Caring about Justice," 1992: 451–2.

17 This phrase is from Larry Blum *et al.*, "Altruism and Women's Oppression," 1979:
191. All of these authors are concerned to articulate what it means to care in a way
which is not destructive of the self. The idea of "caring with autonomy" nicely
captures Noddings' and Gilligan's concern that caring not degenerate into self-
sacrifice.

18 For a "generic" analysis of care of the sort care ethicists would suspect, see Werner
Marx, *Towards a Phenomenological Ethics* with a foreword by Thomas Nenon, New
York: State University of New York Press, 1992. Gilligan understands her own
method of interviewing particular women to reflect an ethical commitment to letting
people speak in their own voices. Gilligan, *Voice*, 1982: 2.

19 Kathryn Pyne Addelson characterizes female theorists as claiming that "women are
creative agents generating a world through nurturance and love." She adds that the
caring approach paradoxically offers an "ideal of the nurturing woman [that] belongs
to the same individualistic framework" female ethicists criticize. Kathryn Pyne
Addelson, *Moral Passages: Toward a Collectivist Moral Theory*, London: Routledge,
1994: xii. I concur with this assessment. Female ethicists fall into this trap because
they offer ethics of feelings and think of these feelings as belonging to some private,
core self. In Chapter 4, I offer an argument for thinking that the self is more intrinsically political than many female ethicists have been willing to acknowledge to date.

20 See Noddings, *Caring*, 1984: 30–35, where she argues that the one caring must
examine whether she truly becomes engrossed in the other.

21 Noddings, *Caring*, 1984: 47–8.

22 Noddings, *Caring*, 1984: 5.

23 Gilligan would associate such demonization with a tendency toward separation that,
in turn, leads to violence. Gilligan, *Voice*, 1982: 45.

24 Hoagland correctly observes that Noddings treats all withdrawals from relations as
diminishments of the ethical self and as a loss of an opportunity to care for the other.
Hoagland counters that "[w]ithdrawal may be the only way one can help another."
Hoagland, "Some Thoughts About 'Caring'," 1991: 256.

25 While Noddings argues that there are no action criteria for caring, she clearly thinks of
the concern as an active receiving of the other, a displacement of energy from the one
caring toward the cared-for. Noddings, *Caring*, 1984: 30–58.

26 Tronto makes an argument along this line in Joan C. Tronto, *Moral Boundaries:
A Political Argument for an Ethic of Care*, New York: Routledge, 1993. Noddings
almost certainly would agree with it, given that she widens the scope of caring at the
end of her book. See Chapter 7, "Caring for Animals, Plants, Things and Ideas," in
Noddings, *Caring*, 1984: 148–70. Gilligan, too, seems to want to expand caring to
include the earth as a whole because she takes Demeter, the goddess of agriculture, to
be an exemplary caregiver. Gilligan, *Voice*, 1982: 22–3.

27 "By and large, we do not say with any conviction that a person cares if that person acts
routinely according to some fixed rule." Noddings, *Caring*, 1984: 13.

28 Noddings, *Caring*, 1984: 17.

29 Lawrence Blum is, as far as I know, the only other theorist to recognize this problem
with the care ethics. He seems to concede that care must have a principled dimension.
But he then goes on to worry, like Noddings, that the principled care of professionals
will not minister to the total person. Lawrence A. Blum, "Vocation, Friendship, and
Community: Limitations of the Personal–Impersonal Framework," in Owen
Flanagan and Amélie Oksenberg Rorty (eds), *Identity, Character, and Morality*,
Cambridge, MA: MIT Press, 1990: 173–97.

30 "There is a general antipathy to moral principles in the care perspective." Dancy,
"Caring About Justice," 1992: 449.

31 Graham, "Caring: A Labour of Love," 1983: 27.

32 Stocker discusses the moral insensitivity of deontological and utilitarian theories in this case and others in Michael Stocker, "The Schizophrenia of Modern Ethical Theories," *The Journal of Philosophy* 73(14), 12 August 1976: 453–66.

33 Blum has offered the most sustained defense of the legitimacy of caring acts that are not motivated by a commitment to an impartial duty of benevolence but that are rooted rather in the particularity of the relation between the caregiver and cared-for. Blum argues that

> membership in certain groups can imply a trust and confidence in the appropriateness and ability of one's helping the others, a trust and confidence that ground the caring response to the other person and make it not a preferential caring (or not a morally suspect one) but simply a specific form of caring.

Blum also argues that even when our care is mediated by specific commitments we have by virtue of our role, the care still will have an intrinsic partiality to it. Different students will need to be cared for by the same teacher in different ways. The teacher needs to "have a clear sense of the value of her pupils as individuals in their own right." Blum, "Vocation, Friendship, and Community," 1990: 190 and 183 respectively.

34 Gilligan and Noddings both are aware of the element of risk involved in the creation of a shared self. However, the dimension of risk is more thoroughly explored in Annette Baier, "Caring about Caring: A Reply to Frankfurt," *Synthèse* 53, November, 1982: 273–90. I critique Baier's views on risk in Chapter 3.

35 Simon Gray, *Otherwise Engaged and Other Plays*, Harmondsworth: Penguin, 1975: 57.

36 Meyers discusses and rejects many forms of sympathy in Meyers, *Subjection*, 1994: 31–3.

37 We generally do not sympathize with others' joys or pleasures but rather with their distressing plights, pains, grief and other feelings or states typically thought to be undesirable and hence unwelcome.

38 I have drawn this definition of sympathy from the analysis in Meyers, *Subjection*, 1994: 31–3.

39 William Blake, "The Human Abstract," in *The Complete Poetry and Selected Prose of John Donne and The Complete Poetry of William Blake* with an introduction by Robert Silliman Hillyer, New York: Random House, 1941: 558. Arendt makes a similar point when she argues that an emotion like pity entails that there be weak people to be pitied. We should not be surprised that the reign of terror in post-revolutionary France co-existed quite comfortably with romantic expressions of pity. Hannah Arendt, *On Revolution*, New York: Viking Press, 1965: 80–90. She also contends that pity-inspired politics historically have played havoc with the rule of law and that true compassion is never elicited by sufferings of large groups of people or by world hunger.

40 I owe this phrase to Robert C. Solomon, *About Love: Reinventing Romance For Our Times*, Lanham, MD: Rowman & Littlefield, 1994: 260.

41 Lawrence A. Blum, "Care," in Lawrence C. Becker and Charlotte B. Becker (eds), *Encyclopedia of Ethics*, New York: Garland, 1992: 260. Gilligan and Noddings both see caring as an active movement toward another person and so would agree with Blum's characterization of care as an active "feeling with" and concern for other people.

42 The self risks its self in non interpersonal ways as well—e.g. in devotion to dangerous sports like spelunking or skiing. In the last half of the book, I argue that caring does involve risk to the self but that the self may put itself into play in a very profound way through care for argument, even more than through interpersonal care, empathy or trust.

43 Both Kant, *Groundwork*, 1964: 90–99, and W.D. Ross, *The Right and the Good*, Indianapolis, IN: Hackett Publishing, 1988: 160–73, argue for duties of benevolence. These duties might be thought to be akin to female ethicists' caring. However, the relational self does not merely have duties. It discovers the joys of caring and creates for itself further obligations to care through concrete acts of reaching out to others. To speak metaphorically: The male ethics make the self into a sort of point; female ethics treat the self as an ever-expanding set of circles.

44 Kohlberg, whose theories of moral development Gilligan attacks, initially rejected Gilligan's analysis because Gilligan did not speak to the "specifically moral dimension in reasoning" but rather studied ego development. Lawrence Kohlberg, "A Reply to Owen Flanagan and Some Comments on the Puka–Goodpaster Exchange," *Ethics* 92(3), April, 1982: 514.

45 This claim could undoubtedly be further refined. Defending it would require looking at a whole array of various ethical theories. However, that project would require a book in itself. Since my interest here lies both in what female ethics have to contribute to our thinking about ethical matters and what problems there are with these ethics, I will let this claim stand as a rough and ready approximation of the subject matter of ethics.

46 It might be objected that the care ethic claims we *are* in relation and not that we *should desire* to be in them. To this I would respond that Gilligan herself constantly equivocates between descriptive and normative claims. See Broughton, "Women's Rationality," 1983: 607. Furthermore, if the ethic is to have normative force, it must provide an argument to the effect that we should want to be in relations since it is clear that agents can and do refuse to be in some relations. That problem is precisely what motivates Noddings' entire discussion of what, if anything, we owe to the beggar who shows up on our doorstep.

47 Bill Puka, "The Liberation of Caring: A Different Voice for Gilligan's 'Different Voice'," in Mary Jeanne Larrabee (ed.), *An Ethic of Care*, New York: Routledge, 1993: 215–39.

48 Noddings, *Caring*, 1984: 1–8. While Gilligan contends that the care perspective should be thought of as complementary to the justice perspective, other parts of her analysis certainly suggest that she thinks the care perspective is superior.

> Gilligan's alternative moral vision carries with it the clear implication that men harbor an illusory reality. She sees men as guilty of what Hampshire has called "false individuation," the illegitimate reduction of the complex ongoing flow of everyday moral situations and behavior to a definite grid of discrete actions and fixed elements which fail to reflect the true difficulties and nuances of the ethical life.
>
> (Broughton, "Women's Rationality," 1983: 603)

Certainly much of the current literature on care does privilege the care perspective over other ones.

49 Noddings, *Caring*, 1984: 5–6.

50 According to Noddings, we should feed the cat with which we have a relation. But killing a rat that has come to our door is permissible as long as we do not torture it.

Killing the rat is allowed because the agent has not, and never will, develop a relation with it. Noddings, *Caring*, 1984: 156–7. The stance is odd because I am in relation with the rat that I kill. I am the killer of the rat; the rat is killed by me. Granted, the relation is somewhat accidental; I did not choose to have the rat come into my house. But Noddings grants the possibility of accidental relations. It is also odd because Noddings oscillates between making relations good because they meet needs; and making the meeting of needs good because it creates a relation.

51 Again and again meeting physical needs is taken as paradigmatic by proponents of interpersonal caring. See Graham, "Caring: A Labour of Love," 1983: 26–7.

52 Jung, for example, discusses the devastation of the loneliness that "does not come from having no people about one, but from being unable to communicate the things that seem important to oneself, or from holding certain views which others find inadmissible." C.G. Jung, *Memories, Dreams, Reflections*, ed. Aniela Jaffé, New York: Vintage Books, 1989: 356.

53 Gilligan and her subjects seem to presuppose something like "the right of all to respect as a person," "the right to be treated sympathetically and as an equal," and "the duty to respect and not to hurt others." See Broughton, "Women's Rationality," 1983: 612.

54 Consider the following story reported in *The New York Times*:

> At the Lincoln Plaza Cinema, I try to find the perfect seat way before the film begins. The other day a woman tapped me on the shoulder as I was about to sit. "Excuse me," she said, "but I want to let you know I cough a lot." I said thank you and moved back several rows. The woman who coughs proceeded to do so, also making a series of other infectious sounds. Patrons began moving away from the poor woman, but eventually an elderly couple entered and unwittingly sat just one seat away from her. "Excuse me, but I want you to know that I cough a lot," the woman told them. The elderly woman stared straight into her eyes. "Well maybe you'll stop," she said. And she did.
> (Renee W. Chaifetz, "Entry 2," in Metropolitan Diary section of *The New York Times*, 20 August 1995, sect. 1: 17)

55 Annis notes, but does not explore, the possible connection between being someone who truly cares and being trustworthy in the eyes of the cared-for party. If someone lies to me in the name of caring for me, have they really cared for *me* if I oppose such paternalism? Annis, "Duties of Friendship," 1987: 350.

56 Noddings, *Caring*, 1984: 21, 148–69. Tronto seems to want to argue for a wider vision of care as including everything we do to maintain our world and environment. She sees, for example, an affinity between Gilligan's care ethic and Native American morality. Joan C. Tronto, "Beyond Gender Difference to a Theory of Care," *Signs* 12(4), 1987: 650. This definition, though, with its heavy emphasis on nurturance remains subject to most of the objections discussed in this chapter. In addition, it seems too wide. The lawyer's care is collapsed into the doctor's care, yet there surely are relevant ethical differences. My defense attorney may legitimately ask me a host of questions about my activities which a doctor probably should not ask. We allow the questioning on a need to know basis. What doctors need to know varies from what lawyers need to know because of specific differences in their practices, differences glossed over by this definition of care.

57 Moody-Adams severely criticizes the care ethic's privileging of intimate relations. Moody-Adams, "Complexity of Moral Voices," 1991: 195–212.

58 See Noddings, *Caring*, 1984: 176. "Clearly, in professions where encounter is frequent and where the ethical ideal of the other is necessarily involved, I am first and foremost one-caring and, second, enactor of specialized functions." This tendency to completely neglect the ends specific to particular practices or professions is quite apparent in recent attempts to apply female ethics to business. We are told, for example, that a corporation is nothing but a relation: "[t]he corporation is constituted by the network of relationships which it is involved in with the employees, customers, suppliers, communities, businesses and other groups who interact with and give meaning and definition to the corporation." See Andrew C. Wicks *et al.*, "A Feminist Reinterpretation of the Stakeholder Concept," *Business Ethics Quarterly* 4(4), October, 1994: 483.

59 I concur with both Boatright, Goodpaster and Holloran that management is widely thought of as having a special relation with shareholders. John R. Boatright, "Fiduciary Duties and the Shareholder–Management Relation: Or, What's So Special About Shareholders?," and Kenneth E. Goodpaster and Thomas E. Holloran, "In Defense of a Paradox," *Business Ethics Quarterly* 4(4), October, 1994: 393–408, 423–30.

60 It is the goodness of the end that leads the client to form the relation with the professional in the first place. Koehn, *Ground*, 1994: *passim*.

61 Strictly speaking, it is not the pledge alone which grounds this obligation. The pledge must be public, accepted by the professionals, etc. For a full discussion of the ground of professional responsibilities and authority, see Koehn, *Ground*, 1994: *passim*.

62 Judy Auerbach *et al.*, "Commentary on Gilligan's *In A Different Voice*," *Feminist Studies* 11(1), Spring, 1985: 160.

63 Meyers favors a variant of this approach in her attempt to apply care ethics to the realm of the law. Meyers, *Subjectivity*, 1994: 152–69.

64 Virginia Held, *Feminist Morality*, 1993: 202.

65 The same point is made by Beverly Kracher, "Rights and Care in Business," unpublished manuscript, Creighton University, 1994.

66 See Books 1–4 of the *Republic* and Socrates' speech in which he tells Glaucon that Glaucon will not be able to follow his discussion of dialectic in Book 7, *Republic*, trans. Allan Bloom, New York: Basic Books, 1968: 533a1–5.

67 Noddings clearly appeals to the idea of a biologically-based or "natural" caring. Noddings, *Caring*, 1984: 43, 83. Gilligan sometimes talks as if caring is a biologically programmed activity of women. But then she appeals to Chodorow's analysis of relations. Since Chodorow is arguing against an essentialistic view of women's caring, Gilligan's stance is somewhat confusing. In later work, Gilligan contends that men, too, adopt a caring perspective. Carol Gilligan, "Moral Orientation and Moral Development," in Kittay and Meyers, *Women and Moral Theory*, 1987: 19–33.

68 I say more about care ethics' inability to handle cases of violence in Chapter 4.

69 Gilligan, *Voice*, 1982: 33.

70 Noddings, *Caring*, 1984: 5, 99.

71 Noddings, *Caring*, 1984: 107.

72 The care ethic is "grounded in assumptions about the mutual interdependence of persons, in responsiveness rather than in reciprocity, in relationships rather than in selves." Mary Ellen Waithe, "Twenty-three Hundred Years of Women Philosophers: Toward a Gender Undifferentiated Moral Theory," in Mary M. Brabeck, *Who Cares? Theory, Research, and Educational Implications of the Ethic of Care*, New York: Praeger, 1989: 4.

73 Noddings takes the mother–child case as a paradigm for caring and contends that for ethics the relation is ontologically basic. Noddings, *Caring*, 1984: 4.

74 Noddings says the child should never be forced to do anything the child finds repugnant. Noddings, *Caring,* 1984: 63.

75 Even those who argue that "mother" and/or sexual identity are socially constructed concede the point. For example, the "mothers" in the gay street gangs profiled in Jennie Livingston's *Paris is Burning* see themselves as persons who warn their "daughters" about dangers on the street, etc. In other words, they don't *qua* mothers simply ratify every desire of their daughters. They try to modify these desires in a direction more consistent with human thriving. Sara Ruddick sees that there is a problem here and offers an extended account of the ends of mothering. Ruddick, *Maternal Thinking,* 1995: *passim.*

76 Solomon uses the criterion of a "merging" to describe the truly loving, caring relation. Solomon, *About Love,* 1994: 24. Noddings clearly would accept Solomon's central idea that "love is the experience of conceiving of oneself with and through another." But this idea obviously would apply to Bonnie and Clyde as well, and it is unclear whether we would want to term their relation either loving or caring. If the self is reconceived through the other in such a way as to exclude appreciation of those outside the relation, then this form of caring degenerates into a narrow parochialism or cronyism.

77 More explicitly feminist versions of care ethics suffer from the same problem. Benhabib, for example, argues for an ethic in which all parties have formally equal rights in conversations. Benhabib, *Situating the Self,* 1992: *passim.* But as I show in Chapter 4, mutually manipulative relations will meet her formal requirements.

78 Noddings, *Caring,* 1984: 111–12.

79 "Dialogue, practice, attribution of the best possible motive: All these are essential in nurturing the ethical ideal." Noddings, *Caring,* 1984: 124.

80 Noddings, *Caring,* 1984: 116.

81 See note 24.

82 John 8: 1–11, The NIV Study Bible.

83 Other women philosophers have registered their concern as well. See Sarah Hoagland, "Some Thoughts About 'Caring'," 1991: 246–63, and Barbara Houston, "Prolegomena to Future Caring," in Brabeck, *Who Cares,* 1989: 90–91.

84 Noddings contends that even when caring is not reciprocated or when the one caring is not acting in a truly loving fashion, the cared-for should act as a "potential cared-for" by responding with a magnanimous receptivity—i.e. to act in a way that maintains the relation so that caring will be possible in the future. Noddings, *Caring,* 1984: especially 74–8.

85 Noddings, *Caring,* 1984: 34.

86 Noddings refuses to specify any such criteria because every act of caring is unique. It is tailored "with special regard for the particular person in a concrete situation," and "the one-caring displays a characteristic variability in her actions—she acts in a non-rule-bound fashion in behalf of the cared-for." Noddings, *Caring,* 1984: 25.

87 For a good discussion of issues involved in "caring" for the "disabled" see Anita Silvers, "Reconciling Equality to Difference: Caring (F)or Justice For People With Disabilities," *Hypatia* 10(1), Winter, 1995: 30–55.

88 Onora O'Neill argues that this dependence plays an important role in the Kantian understanding of duties and that there is a general duty to help others (although the precise form this help will take will vary from case to case). Onora O'Neill, *Constructions of Reason,* Cambridge: Cambridge University Press, 1989: 100–01.

89 Gewirth derives our duties from the notion of prospective agency as such. Alan Gewirth, *Human Rights: Essays on Justification and Applications,* Chicago, IL: University of Chicago Press, 1982.

90 Noddings, *Caring,* 1984: 6.

91 Noddings, *Caring*, 1984: 75–6.

92 Kenneth D. Alpern, *The Ethics of Reproduction*, New York: Oxford University Press, 1992.

93 In Chapter 4, I defend a principled critical dialogue in which the personal is political. However, this identity is the result of adopting a critical perspective which is essentially pluralistic. So the counterweight of the other is available in this dialogical ethic in a way it simply isn't in the care ethic.

94 Noddings, *Caring*, 1984: 74.

95 Norma Haan, "Hypothetical and Actual Moral Reasoning in a Situation of Civil Disobedience," *Journal of Personality and Social Psychology* 32(2), 1975: 262.

96 See the review of Alison Lurie's book *Don't Tell the Grownups* in Kelly Bulkeley, "Psychological and Spiritual Development in Childhood," *Religious Studies Review* 21(2), April, 1995: 86–90.

97 Solomon goes on to argue: "Caring is essential to love, and it is no small virtue in a relationship that, *no matter how bad things may be*, two people continue to care for and about each other." Solomon, *About Love*, 1994: 260; emphasis mine. Opting out too quickly is no virtue; but submitting to abuse is not a happy alternative. While this quote comes from Solomon's ethic of care, Tong points out a similar problem in Noddings and asks whether Jews on the way to the gas chambers truly were morally obligated, as Noddings seems to think, to try to form a caring relation with the Nazi guards. Tong contends that it was the oppressors, not the victims, who had a duty to care. Tong implies, although she does not argue for, a right of the victims to break off relations with their oppressors. Rosemarie Tong, *Feminine and Feminist Ethics*, 1993: 122.

98 Gilligan seems to me to be far more sensitive to this problem than Noddings. I have argued elsewhere that Gilligan could be reinterpreted as arguing for an ethic of responsiveness instead of an ethic of care because she puts more emphasis on the desirability and obligation to acquire one's own voice in order to contribute to a self-defining conversation with one's intimates and friends. See Koehn, "With a Different Ear," 1994: 77–86.

99 Solomon, *About Love*, 1994: 331.

100 Nel Noddings, "Feminist Fears in Ethics," *Journal of Social Philosophy* 21(2 and 3), Fall/Winter, 1990: 29–31. The conflict is also noted by Blum *et al.*, "Altruism and Women's Oppression," 1979: 191.

101 Noddings, "Feminist Fears," 1990: 29–32.

102 There is a very real danger that this "female" duty to care will be used against women who have been slotted into the role of caretaker.

> Often accusations of failure to care are directed at women in a way which serves to divert attention from the issues of women's subordination to men, or from certain injustices women suffer. For example, women who seek some time, privacy, or increased control over their lives are often accused by their husband or families of not caring; women are accused of man-hating if they propose women's studies programs or the need for women-only space; women who lobby for equal pay for work of equal value are bizarrely accused of lesbianism or denying men sexual access to them.
>
> (Houston in Brabeck, *Who Cares*, 1989: 93)

103 Marilyn Frye, "Some Thoughts on Separation and Power," *Sinister Wisdom* 6, Summer, 1978: 35.

104 It may be objected that this point loses its force if the care ethic should become so successful that men begin to act as caregivers as well. However, given current power structures, there is little danger of this happening any time soon. Lesbian ethicists are acutely aware of some of the ways in which care can be corrupted by these power structures. See, e.g., Sarah Lucia Hoagland, "Lesbian Ethics and Female Agency," in Eve Browning Cole and Susan Coultrap-McQuin (eds), *Explorations in Feminist Ethics: Theory and Practice*, Bloomington, IN: Indiana University Press, 1992: 156–64.

105 John Fowles, *The Collector*, New York: Dell Publishing, 1963.

106 Kaminer also notes feminists' desire for a totally safe classroom. Wendy Kaminer, "Feminism's Third Wave," in *The New York Times Book Review* 4 June 1995: 3, 22–3.

107 I am also concerned that the care ethic will be used to channel women into corporate personnel positions and to deny them the higher profile and better paying jobs. Some women may enjoy being on the trading floor and prefer it to more nurturing activities in business. Their perspective gets short shrift in care ethics which consistently privilege relational activities of a certain sort—namely, needs-meeting nurturance.

108 Noddings attacks human striving on the ground that "[w]hen we pursue projects that challenge some strong inclination in ourselves we create a formidable opponent in our own shadow side" and can become evil by indulging our imagination. More generally, Noddings condemns striving because it interferes with our human "relatedness." Noddings, *Women and Evil*, 1989: 199ff.

109 "Sunday in the Park with George", music and lyrics by Stephen Sondheim, directed by James Lapine, RCA Records, 1984.

110 Hoagland also worries about the tendency of female ethics to reinforce sacrificial tendencies. Sarah Lucia Hoagland, "Why Lesbian Ethics?," *Hypatia* 7(4), Fall, 1992: 198. The fear seems justified. Solomon, e.g., argues that a wife or husband might sacrifice having sex with other parties, bestowing this refusal as a "gift" on her or his spouse. Solomon, *About Love*, 1994: 325. I would argue that this gift may well prove to be a source of resentment. The spouse may reject this "gift." And the strategy does not in any way help the person with erotic longings to understand what these longings are about. They are merely repressed by the giftgiver.

111 Mary Frances Berry, *The Politics of Parenthood: Child Care, Women's Rights, and the Myth of the Good Mother*, New York: Penguin, 1993: *passim*.

112 Gunneman offers an excellent analysis of how a naive desire to nurture everyone (what he calls an "alchemic temptation") and refusal to do the hard thinking regarding limits must lead to a brutal, somewhat arbitrary, Machiavellian approach to the imposing of boundaries. Jon P. Gunneman, "Alchemic Temptations," in *The Annual of the Society of Christian Ethics*, Boston, MA: Society of Christian Ethics, 1995: 3–18.

113 Noddings repeatedly refers to inclusion. Noddings, *Caring*, 1984: 38, 67, 70. Others, too, have interpreted feminist versions of ethics as driving in the direction of ever greater inclusivity. See Linda Fisher, "Feminist Theory and the Politics of Inclusion," *Journal of Social Philosophy* 21(2 and 3), Fall/Winter, 1990: 174–83.

114 See note 53.

115 M. Carmela Epright, "Impartialism, Care and the Self," unpublished manuscript.

116 For this important point, see Baier's discussion of Harry Frankfurt's idea that we need to care about caring. Baier, "Caring about Caring," 1982.

2 AN ETHIC OF BROAD EMPATHY

1 Diana Tietjens Meyers, *Subjection and Subjectivity: Psychoanalytic Feminism and Moral Philosophy*, New York: Routledge, 1994: 91, 93–118.

2 Meyers, *Subjection*, 1994: 91.

3 Meyers, *Subjection*, 1994: 92.

4 Meyers, *Subjection*, 1994: 155.

5 Meyers, *Subjection*, 1994: 22–6.

6 For an alternative view of what Kantian ethics require, see Onora O'Neill, *Constructions of Reason*, 1989: 100–01, 116, 228–33. O'Neill argues that Kantian ethics impose substantial duties to offer help to persons which is tailored to their individual interests and needs. I have my doubts, therefore, whether Meyers' attack on Kantian universalism is totally fair. However, it is interesting to note that, by and large, it has been the *women* commentators who have accepted that caring is a vital part of a moral response and have sought to clear Kant of the charge that he did not pay sufficient attention to our positive duties toward others.

7 Meyers, *Subjection*, 1994: 26.

8 Example from Andrew Weil, *Spontaneous Healing*, New York: Alfred A. Knopf, 1995: 64.

9 Meyers' discussion of the engineering professor case appears in Meyers, *Subjection*, 1994: 29–38.

10 John Le Carré, *The Little Drummer Girl*, New York: Alfred A. Knopf, 1983: 143.

11 Meyers, *Subjection*, 1994: 3–8, 42–56.

12 Meyers, *Subjection*, 1994: 25.

13 Meyers, *Subjection*, 1994: 25–6.

14 Meyers, *Subjection*, 1994: 30.

15 Ibid.

16 Ibid.

17 Meyers, *Subjection*, 1994: 31.

18 Meyers, *Subjection*, 1994: 31–4.

19 Ibid.

20 Meyers, *Subjection*, 1994: 29.

21 This thought seems to be the key one behind Meyers' discussion of rights and justice. Meyers, *Subjection*, 1994: 152–69.

22 Meyers, *Subjection*, 1994: 32.

23 Meyers, *Subjection*, 1994: 31.

24 Meyers takes this metaphor from Maria Lugones. Meyers, *Subjection*, 1994: 14.

25 Meyers does not herself actually refer to the fecundity of the images themselves, although she does say that she has found some of the imagery employed by psychoanalytic feminists incredibly suggestive. I think though that my stress on this fecundity is consistent with what she is saying about images. To say that images possess a fecundity of their own is another way of saying that, when we construct images for our experience, we introduce some otherness, some distance into our experience. However, I think Meyers pays too little attention to the importance of *mediated* engagement with other people. In the last half of this book, I explore in detail the form ethically good mediation must assume.

26 Meyers, *Subjection*, 1994: 33.

27 Meyers, *Subjection*, 1994: 72–8.

28 Meyers' reference to apprenticing is from Elizabeth V. Spelman. Meyers, *Subjection*, 1994: 152.

29 For a good discussion of Jaspars' views on schizophrenia and empathy, see Louis A. Sass, *Madness and Modernism*, New York: Basic Books, 1992: 16–19.

30 Meyers, *Subjection*, 1994: 35–6.

31 To some extent, the incompleteness of empathy is due simply to the fact that each of us is different from every other person. Indeed, this difference is exactly what makes empathy partial. However, empathy may also appear partial because of the power of

empathy to feel its way into a person-in-the-making. Margulies argues that sometimes the therapist has stepped "into a possible self's shoe, a self that perhaps now (with us) can bear the unbearable, a self we know is there but squelched, cut off in misery or fear. It is as if that person almost exists—but not yet. We are beyond the person into a potential person." Margulies is well aware that there are dangers of paternalism and control in thinking one's self into another's potential self. But he may be right: the healing process may require empathy to function this way in cases of denial. If so, the party being empathized with may very well be confused by the therapist's focus and questions. Alfred Margulies, *The Empathic Imagination*, New York: Norton, 1989: 128–32.

32 "Stories can 'say something' to us only when we already know what is going on and what we might expect to hear." Rebecca Redwood French, *The Golden Yoke*, Ithaca, NY: Cornell University Press, 1995: 346.

33 Meyers, *Subjection*, 1994: 7, 73, 82.

34 Diana T. Meyers, "Work and Self-Respect," in Tom L. Beauchamp and Norman E. Bowie (eds), *Ethical Theory and Business*, Englewood Cliffs, NJ: Prentice-Hall, 1988: 275–9.

35 Meyers, *Subjection*, 1994: 179.

36 Wayne C. Booth, *The Company We Keep: An Ethics of Fiction*, Berkeley, CA: University of California Press, 1988: 255–60.

37 Meyers, *Subjection*, 1994: 164–5.

38 Meyers, *Subjection*, 1994: 165. I would also note that Meyers' conception of trust tends toward cronyism. The only people we can trust are those whom we know to share the same moral ideals as we do. I argue against this understanding of trust in the next two chapters.

39 Meyers, *Subjection*, 1994: 167.

40 Meyers herself concedes that moral ideals and injunctions apply only in the realm of the possible. Meyers, *Subjection*, 1994: 130.

41 It might be objected that the ethic of empathy does not require that we empathize with others all the time, but only that when we do encounter them, we take care to empathize with them. This response is somewhat disingenuous because the empathy ethicist does not think it is acceptable for us to choose, for example, a life of non-interaction with others. Respecting difference in interactions is the privileged value in this ethic. It provides little guidance regarding how to integrate a variety of activities into a thriving life.

42 Even Kant seems to concede this point. He addresses his moral arguments only to those who have a "sound natural understanding." Such talk certainly implies that some agents have an "unsound" or "unnatural" understanding. Immanuel Kant, *Groundwork of the Metaphysic of Morals*, New York: Harper & Row, 1964: 64.

43 Jane Austen, *Persuasion*, New York: Bantam Books, 1984: 141.

44 Austen, *Persuasion*, 1984: 141.

45 Meyers, *Subjection*, 1994: 153.

46 Austen, *Persuasion*, 1984: 141.

47 Austen, *Persuasion*, 1984: 218–19.

48 Austen, *Persuasion*, 1984: 135.

49 See, e.g. Father Brown's praise of his adversary in G.K. Chesterton, "The Dagger With Wings," in *The Incredulity of Father Brown*, *The Father Brown Omnibus*, New York: Dodd, Mead & Co., 1935: 579.

50 G.K. Chesterton, "The Secret of Flambeau," in *The Secret of Father Brown*, *The Father Brown Omnibus*, New York: Dodd, Mead & Co., 1935: 809.

51 Thornton Wilder, *The Alcestiad*, New York: Avon Books, 1979: 37.

52 Norman Brown quoted in Margulies, *Empathic Imagination*, 1989: 107.

53 Leo Steinberg quoted in Jorunn Jacobsen Buckley, "Sex, Suffering and Incarnation," in Robert A. Segal *et al.* (eds), *The Allure of Gnosticism*, Chicago, IL: Open Court, 1995: 104.

54 Wilder, *Alcestiad*, 1979: 132.

55 Meyers, *Subjection*, 1994: 162–6.

56 Meyers, *Subjection*, 1994: 163–4.

57 Meyers, *Subjection*, 1994: 152.

58 I would also note that a professional ethic imposes a certain distance between professional and client. Lawyers can and do keep confidences for their clients. Yet, as the old adage goes, if it is a question of whether the lawyer or the client should go to jail, the client is the one to be incarcerated. In general, the lawyer should not be so over-involved with the client that he can no longer distinguish his cause from the client's. Nor is the client entitled to manipulate the ethics of the professional in such a way that the professional instead of the client winds up being on trial. This distanced tension is healthy and appropriate because it reminds professionals of their own desire to thrive and of the need to be cautious in caring and to observe some strictures.

In short, ethical agents do not and should not apprentice themselves to anyone. Historically, apprentices took their orders from masters and were little more than indentured servants. The autonomous lawyer or professional does not forfeit her ability or responsibility to judge. Furthermore, while there are clearly masters of technique, it is not clear that anyone is a master when it comes to making ethical decisions. In fact, the metaphor of apprenticeship is a curious one for Meyers to choose, given that her whole argument hinges on the partiality and non-expertness of all agents.

59 Hannah Arendt, *Eichmann in Jerusalem*, New York: Penguin Books, 1976: 265.

60 It might be objected that hubris is not a natural human trait but rather the consequence of a lack of interpersonal empathy. While there is no denying that hubris may become a settled character trait as a result of an unempathic past, this answer ignores the profound selfishness and egoism apparent in small children. Socializing this egoism is a necessary part of maturation and may require that the individual grapple with the demons of frustration and rage that arise as his or her egoism is opposed and challenged. To the extent Meyers' analysis ignores the need for psychic work on our individual demons, it relies upon an overly sanguine view of the human psyche.

61 We might also consider the case of Julien, the protagonist in Stendhal, *The Red and the Black*, trans. C.K. Scott Moncrieff, New York: Modern Library, 1926. Julien becomes increasingly skilled in taking on others' perspectives and in assessing the value or disvalue these others assign to actions as the book progresses. However, since every bit of his empathy ultimately is directed toward ascertaining whether or not he has failed in his own eyes and those of others to live up to his Napoleonic ideal, his empathy is rather skewed. The narrative is wonderfully ironic because Julien and others have a number of fundamental beliefs they never critically assess. The irony arises as the critical audience comes to perceive a massive disjunction between what the character thinks to be real and what this audience takes to be real. The audience, of course, may also be misled. Nevertheless, the existence of irony is important because it points to the need for the self to be on guard against being deluded and to scrutinize beliefs that might lead the self to illusions of the sort Julien suffers. The ethic of empathy, like the other female ethics, errs in totally ignoring the phenomenon and implied value of irony. We are told instead to try on the others' perspective and to look at matters in terms of their values without ever making an effort to judge whether or not this other point of view reflects reality. If we remain totally deluded, in what sense is empathy "enriching"?

62 Gayatri Chakravorty Spivak, *The Post-Colonial Critic: Interviews, Strategies, Dialogues*, Sarah Harasym (ed.), New York: Routledge, 1990: 51. Spivak goes on to argue that in

> deconstructive critical practice, you have to be aware that you are going to essentialize anyway. So then strategically you can look at essentialisms, not as descriptions of the way things are, but as something that one must adopt to produce a critique of anything.

Notice that Spivak has appealed to an essential "you" and "one." I find Spivak's strategic essentialism more persuasive than Trinh's assertion that

> there is no real me to return to, no whole self that synthesizes the woman, the woman of color and the writer; there are instead, diverse recognitions of self through difference, and unfinished, contingent, arbitrary closures that make possible both politics and identity.
> (T. Minh-ha Trinh, *Framer Framed*, New York: Routledge, 1992: 157)

Even for Trinh, discourse has an essence and there really is a discursive "me." If so, this fact is a non-contingent truth of discourse that we are driven to admit if we are going to engage in critique. I argue in Chapter 4 that what individuates the discursive "me" we think and talk about is not radical difference but rather something that has a generic dimension. It is this generic quality that makes politics and the rule of law possible.

63 Arendt notes that the idea of law presupposes an idea of an essential humanity. Arendt, *Eichmann*, 1976: 272ff.

3 AN ETHIC OF TRUST

1 Virginia Held, "On the Meaning of Trust," *Ethics* 78, January, 1968: 156–9.
2 Held, "Meaning," 1968: 156–9.
3 Fukuyama makes this claim. See Daryl Koehn, "Book Review: Francis Fukuyama's *Trust*," *Journal of OnLine Ethics* 1(2): website http://www.depaul.edu/ethics.
4 Annette C. Baier, "Trust and Anti-Trust," *Ethics* 96, January, 1986: 231–60; Trudy Govier, "Distrust as a Practical Problem," *Journal of Social Philosophy* 23(1), Spring, 1992: 52–63. Henceforth, I will abbreviate this Baier article as "Trust" and this Govier article as "Distrust."
5 Baier, "Trust," 1986: 231–8; Govier, "Distrust," 1992: *passim*.
6 Baier, "Trust," 1986: 235.
7 Govier, "Distrust," 1992: 54.
8 Ibid.
9 Baier, "Trust," 1986: 241.
10 Baier, "Trust," 1986: 241–2.
11 Baier, "Trust," 1986: 248.
12 Annette C. Baier, "What Do Women Want in a Moral Theory?," *Nous* 19(1), March, 1985: 55.
13 Baier, "Trust," 1986: 249.
14 Baier, "Women," 1985: 59.
15 Govier, "Distrust," 1992: 52. She develops the importance of self-trust further in Trudy Govier, "Self-Trust, Autonomy, and Self-Esteem," *Hypatia* 8(1), Winter, 1993: 99–120.

16 Govier, "Distrust," 1992: 55.

17 Govier, "Distrust," 1992: 53–7.

18 I have chosen to use Baier's definition of trust because it is more precise than Govier's. Govier defines trust loosely as "fundamentally an attitude, an attitude based on beliefs and feelings and implying expectations and dispositions." Govier, "Self-Trust," 1993: 104. Two counter-examples suffice to show the inadequacy of Govier's definition. My friend expects her eye doctor to cause her pain when he examines her. She suspects him of a sadistic streak because she has had far less painful examinations. Although Dr Pain routinely fulfills her expectations, she is becoming less and less trusting of this doctor because she is not certain of his good will. To qualify as trust, the trustor must not merely think (or be disposed to believe) that another will meet expectations. Baier correctly notes that she must hope as well *for a benefit* from the trusted party (or at least for no harm).

In addition, it matters that the expectation fulfilled is the trustor's, and not someone else's. Members of the French underground may trust a fellow member who works for the Nazis but does so as a spy. Although their fellow member may be working in a Nazi deportation unit, the underground has every reason to believe that this member is actually subverting the deportation process. So, in a case like this, one trustor (underground) trusts the trustee (their spy) precisely because the trustor is confident that the trustee will betray Nazi expectations. As long as the trustor's (the underground) expectation of good will (i.e. help from this spy) from the trustee is fulfilled, it does not matter whether the trustee is failing to meet others' (e.g. Nazis') expectations. Baier's definition of trust as the trustor's expectation of the trusted party's good will toward the trustor is more precise than Govier's and is to be preferred.

19 Baier argues for sowing "seeds of distrust in the established ways." Annette C. Baier, "Some Thoughts on How We Moral Philosophers Live Now," *Monist* 67, October, 1984: 496.

20 Govier, "Distrust," 1992: 53.

21 Mike W. Martin, "Rationalization and Responsibility: A Reply to Whisner," *Journal of Social Philosophy* 23(2), Fall, 1992: 176–84.

22 Baier, "Trust," 1986: 236.

23 Baier, "Trust," 1986: 239. Baier puts a heavy emphasis on trusting in persons based upon our role-based expectations regarding what they will do for us, the nature of their expertise, etc.

24 Stendhal is quoted in Solomon, *About Love*, 1994: 45.

25 Baier repeatedly refers to the trustor's need to forgive. Baier, "Trust," 1986: 239, 255. It is intriguing the extent to which the trustee's perspective drops out of her account.

26 Or so she implies. She sees the contractual view as reflecting self-assertive individualism and such individualism is "adolescent." Baier, "Trust," 1986: 242.

27 James Hillman, *Loose Ends*, Dallas, TX: Spring Publications, 1975: 64.

28 Santayana quoted in Hillman, *Loose Ends*, 1975: 64.

29 See Aurel Kolnai, "Forgiveness," in Proceedings of the Aristotellian Society, 1974: 91–106.

30 Kolnai, "Forgiveness," 1974: 91–106.

31 See, for example, the teaching tapes produced by "experts" who offer techniques to teachers for gaining others' trust. Video recordings by *Association for Supervision and Curriculum Development*, "Another Set of Eyes: Techniques for Classroom Observation" in series for 1992–93, Alexandria, VA.

32 Annette C. Baier, "Sustaining Trust," *The Tanner Lectures on Human Values, Lecture II*, 13, Salt Lake City, UT: University of Utah Press, 1992: 136–74.

33 Govier, "Distrust," 1992: 59–60.
34 M.K. Gandhi, *Collected Works of Mahatma Gandhi*, Publications Division, Ministry of Broadcasting, Government of India, vol. L, 382, n.d.
35 Govier, "Distrust," 1992: 58.
36 Baier, "Trust," 1986: 235.
37 Fisher and Brown, quoted in Govier, "Distrust," 1992: 61.
38 H.J.N. Horsburgh, a leading interpreter of Gandhi's thought, develops this line of reasoning in his article "The Ethics of Trust," *Philosophical Quarterly* 10, 1960: 343–54.
39 This point echoes my concern in Chapter 2 that empathy not degenerate into a voyeuristic attitude toward those with whom we are empathizing. See pp. 69–70.
40 Richard Wright, *Native Son*, New York: Harper & Row, 1940.
41 Wright, *Native Son*, 1940: vii–xxxiv.
42 For a discussion of Hannah Arendt's and Martin Heidegger's existential understanding of the political realm, see Einar Øverenget, "Heidegger and Arendt: Against the Imperialism of Privacy," *Philosophy Today* 39(4), Winter, 1995: 430–44.
43 Annette C. Baier, "Sustaining Trust," *The Tanner Lectures on Human Values, Lecture II*, 13, Salt Lake City, UT: University of Utah Press, 1992: 146.

4 A DIALOGICAL ETHIC

1 Benhabib argues that even people promoting a racist or sexist agenda will try to persuade others. "Inegalitarian arguments usually also require that others 'see' the validity of these principles." Benhabib, *Situating the Self*, 1992: 33.
2 I concur with Marilyn Friedman that

> [k]eeping open the possibility of deep-level moral change seems to require that one sustain an uneasy, although vital, balance between commitments to one's abstract moral values and principles, on the one hand, and on the other, commitments to persons such as our friends in their unique, whole particularity.
>
> (Friedman, *What Are Friends For?*, 1993: 205)

However, as will become clear, I go much further than Friedman in arguing for specific principles. What is more, I think thought is essentially pluralistic, while Friedman relies on values of openness and trust as the basis of pluralism.
3 Hannah Arendt, *The Life of the Mind*, New York: Harcourt Brace Jovanovich, 1978: Part 1: 5.
4 Henceforth, when I speak of "Socrates," I should be understood to refer to the Socrates we know through Plato's dialogues. Even when this Socrates is represented as the historical Socrates (as he is in the *Apology, Crito*, etc.), he remains a character in a highly artificial dialogue. I will say more about this artificiality a bit later in this chapter.
5 Plato, *Crito*, 1971: 43a–b.
6 Plato, *Crito*, 1971: 44b–45c.
7 Both Robert Audi and John Rawls argue for excluding certain forms of religious and secular speech from public discourse. For a good discussion of their positions, see Philip L. Quinn, "Political Liberalisms and Their Exclusions of the Religious," *Proceedings and Addresses of the American Philosophical Association* 69(2) November 1995: 35–56. Rawls seeks

to charge us an admission ticket, as it were, before we may participate in political conversation. We can only join the dialogue if we can manage to speak in the accents of the approved transcendent being without falsifying our primary moral commitments. If this is the price of admission, it is perfectly reasonable to refuse to pay it . . .

(Bruce Ackerman, "Why Dialogue?" *The Journal of Philosophy* 86(1), January, 1989: 15)

8 Plato, *Crito*, 1971: 48b, 50b–c.
9 Benhabib argues for these privileges more explicitly than other female ethicists. Benhabib, *Situating the Self*, 1992: 23–33, 37–8, 105, 159–61. But it is clear that other female ethicists like Noddings and Meyers are committed to them as well. For example, insofar as caring and empathizing involve apprenticing oneself to someone else's point of view, the caregiver/empathizer obviously must allow the other person to articulate and clarify his position.
10 Plato, *Crito*, 1971: 45c–d, 54a–b.
11 Plato, *Crito*, 1971: 45a–46a.
12 Plato, *Crito*, 1971: 43a.
13 Plato, *Crito*, 1971: 43b.
14 Plato, *Crito*, 1971: 43a.
15 Liedtka discusses this needs-orientation in Jeanne M. Liedtka, "Feminist Morality and Competitive Reality: A Role for an Ethic of Care?," *Business Ethics Quarterly* 6(2), April, 1996: 179–200; especially p. 196 where she contends that the "focus of care is . . . upon needs, rather than interests."
16 Plato, *Crito*, 1971: 44b–46b.
17 See note 9.
18 In other words, this listening resists the "estheticizing" of experience where estheticizing means, in Henri Cartier-Bresson's terms, sensitizing ourselves to encounter others and their works "as if we're surfing on a wave. We must be open, open to what [a work] gives us." Bresson quoted in Michael Kimmelman, "With Henri Cartier-Bresson, Surrounded by his Peers," *The New York Times*, sect. 2, 20 August 1995: 28. Such openness accords equal value to everything. In so doing, it models practical thinking on sensation which does take in a series of sights, sounds, smells. Notice, too, the passivity implicit in such a view—we are "surfing a wave." Such passivity encourages a going with the flow of passions. Thomas Mann may, therefore, have been quite correct in his choice of a composer as the Nazi soul *par excellence*. For in his character, "the musicality of soul" produced a Germany in which "the esthetic had triumphed over the merely human." Alex Ross, "In Music, Though, There Were No Victories," *The New York Times*, sect. 1, 20 August 1995: 25. It is also interesting, in this connection, that Walter Benjamin described the Fascism of Mussolini "as the estheticization of the political." Benjamin quoted in Denis Donoghue, "The Politics of Homosexuality," *The New York Times Book Review*, 20 August 1995: 3. Female ethicists have, by and large, been insufficiently attentive to the ethical dangers of openness.
19 Plato, *Crito*, 1971: 44e–45b.
20 Plato, *Crito*, 1971: 45a.
21 Plato, *Crito*, 1971: 45b.
22 Plato, *Crito*, 1971: 45d.
23 Plato, *Crito*, 1971: 45b–c.
24 Plato, *Crito*, 1971: 45d.
25 Plato, *Crito*, 1971: 45a.
26 Plato, *Crito*, 1971: 46a.

27 Plato, *Crito*, 1971: 44d.

28 Plato, *Crito*, 1971: 53e–54a.

29 Plato, *Crito*, 1971: 44c–d, 45e.

30 Plato, *Crito*, 1971: 44e–46b.

31 Plato, *Crito*, 1971: 46a.

32 Liedtka, "Feminist Morality," 1996: 184.

33 Plato, *Crito*, 1971: 47a.

34 Plato, *Crito*, 1971: 47b.

35 Plato, *Crito*, 1971: 47c–d.

36 Plato, *Crito*, 1971: 47d.

37 I concur with Roochnik that the use of the analogy is "protreptic and therapeutic." It serves to establish the possibility of a knowing or thinking that is objective. David L. Roochnik, "Socrates' Use of the Techne-Analogy," in Hugh H. Benson (ed.), *Essays on the Philosophy of Socrates*, Oxford: Oxford University Press, 1992: 191.

38 Plato, *Crito*, 1971: 47b.

39 Or at least would not be able to answer *qua* doctor. A philosophic doctor might be able to address this problem by virtue of being philosophic.

40 Roochnik, "Socrates' Use of the Techne-Analogy," 1992: 191.

41 In technical language, the use of the expert analogy is epideictic. It shows forth the very point it is trying to persuade the audience to accept. As Brumbaugh says, the arts "become an onstage *testimony* (emphasis mine) for the possibility of some 'knowing' which is not purely subjective or relative." Robert Brumbaugh, "Plato's Relation to the Arts and Crafts," in W.H. Werkmeister (ed.), *Facets of Plato's Philosophy*, Amsterdam: van Gorcum, 1976: 46.

42 This definition of thought is equivalent to the one offered on p. 101. Thinking that is willing to consider any and all possible implications of an idea has no particular agenda nor is it focussed on any consequences in particular. It attends to any and all implications that occur to it.

43 Arendt makes this point repeatedly, approvingly quoting Heidegger's claim that "thinking does not produce usable practical wisdom." She also insists that thinking acts only for its own sake. Arendt, *Life of the Mind*, Part 1, 1978: 7, 56 and 176. I agree with Arendt's definition of thinking, but I disagree on the issue of the relation between thinking and practical judgment. She appears to believe that thinking affects judgment only insofar as we bring a habit of thinking to our practical judgments. I think that we can specify a number of principles of thoughtfulness that thinking must abide by in making its judgments. In other words, practical thinking can be "cashed out" in a much more substantive way than Arendt thinks.

44 Ruddick, *Maternal Thinking*, 1995: 18–22.

45 Ruddick, *Maternal Thinking* 1995: 90, 120–23.

46 Ruddick, *Maternal Thinking* 1995: 114–18, 122.

47 "Wars are sold by politicians and bought by citizens as wars of one nation against another, one ethnic group against another, or one religious sect against another. And women buy into these distinctions with all they entail, just as men do." Laura Duhan Kaplan, "Woman as Caretaker: An Archetype That Supports Patriarchal Militarism," *Hypatia* 9(2), Spring, 1994: 128–9.

48 Alison M. Jaggar, "Feminist Ethics: Projects, Problems, Prospects," in Card, *Feminist Ethics*, 1991: 78–104.

49 Ezekiel J. Emanuel, "Review of *Prescribing Our Future: Ethical Challenges in Genetic Counseling*," Dianne M. Bartels *et al.* (eds), *Ethics and Behavior*, 4(1), 1994: 71–2.

50 "Autonomy, properly understood, requires clearly formulating a life goal and a course of action to realize that goal." Emanuel, 1994: 72.

51 I mean that it does so insofar as the latter are not quacks. The fact that we distinguish between true doctors and trainers and quacks is yet another piece of evidence that we value relevant intelligence and therefore think it important to distinguish between those likely to exhibit it and those who lack it.

52 Plato, *Crito*, 1971: 49a–b.

53 Plato, *Crito*, 1971: 49d.

54 Plato, *Crito*, 1971: 49d.

55 Plato, *Crito*, 1971: 49b–d.

56 Plato, *Crito*, 1971: 49b–c.

57 This minimizing of distance between ourselves and others is crucial. As we have seen, if we empathize with others, believing all the while that they have done things we could never do, our empathy is likely to be voyeuristic and not especially ethically good. Empathy by itself cannot determine whether it will be voyeuristic or non-voyeuristic. We need an ethic such as the one I am defending to check our self-righteousness and to combat voyeurism.

58 I might note that this line of argument calls into question Isaiah Berlin's distinction between the fox and the hedgehog. The hedgehog is committed to "a single central vision . . . a single universal, organizing principle in terms of which alone all that they are and say has significance." Foxes, by contrast, "pursue many ends, often unrelated and often contradictory." Berlin mistrusts the hedgehog's moral absolutism and favors the fox's liberal commitment to a plurality of values and opinions about these values. I am suggesting that it may be a "hedgehogian" commitment to the absolute principle of never doing wrong that makes for "foxian" interlocutors who are willing to seek out and engage others in critical discussion. For a good discussion of Berlin's views, see Michael Walzer, "Are There Limits to Liberalism?," in *The New York Review of Books*, 42(16), 19 October 1995: 28–31.

59 Arendt, *The Life of the Mind*, Part 2, 1978: 35–6.

60 Plato, *Crito*, 1971: 48a–b.

61 The valorization of choice is readily discernible in Noddings' existential treatment of caring. Noddings, *Caring*, 1984: *passim*. See, also, Tong's approving explication of Ruddick's maternal ethics of care: "Eternal compliance with someone else's values is an inadequate substitute *for choosing one's own values and living in conformity to them*" (emphasis mine). Tong, *Feminine and Feminist Ethics*, 1993: 141.

62 See Plato's *Theatetus* and *Lysis* respectively.

63 Mary Midgley, *Can't We Make Moral Judgements?*, New York: St Martin's Press, 1993: 25–6.

64 In its absoluteness, the dialogical ethic resembles some lesbian/feminist ethics. Hoagland and Jaggar, for example, both argue for an absolute commitment to stop the exploitation of women and to celebrate women's relations with other women. Sarah Lucia Hoagland, *Lesbian Ethics*, Palo Alto, CA: The Institute of Lesbian Studies, 1988; Alison M. Jaggar, "Feminist Ethics: Projects, Problems, Prospects," in Card (ed.), *Feminist Ethics*, 1991. The difference lies in the way the absolutism functions. Principle 2's absoluteness is grounded in the realization that each of us might be wrong about the good life; the principle's worth lies in the way it binds us to a lifetime of thoughtfulness about this issue. The absolutism of much feminism, by contrast, proceeds from an alleged certainty that we know what constitutes exploitation; that it is wicked, maybe even supremely so; that the best way to fight such exploitation is through solidarity with other women who believe these same things; etc.

65 Plato, *Crito*, 1971: 48b–52a.

66 Plato, *Crito*, 1971: 48c.

67 Plato, *Crito*, 1971: 52a–54d.

68 Noddings is the only female ethicist I have found who seems at all concerned about the dangers of self-righteousness. In her discussion of marital difficulties, she contends both parties should try hard to work out differences, in part because she is aware that we often "commit wrongs supposing we are doing right" and wrongly attribute evil motives to other people. Noddings, *Caring*, 1984: 116. Although this argument comes dangerously close to requiring women to remain in abusive relations (see my discussion on p. 40), I am sympathetic to Noddings' concern about parties hubristically deciding the other party must be in the wrong. In my judgment, a principled dialogical ethic speaks to this concern much better than Noddings' care ethic because it does not require engagement with the other just for the sake of preserving a dubious relation.

69 Cocks adopts this position in Joan Cocks, "Worldless Emotions: Some Critical Reflections on Radical Feminism," *Politics and Society* 13(2), 1984: 37.

70 Plato, *Crito*, 1971: 49d.

71 See Noddings, *Caring*, 1984: 115, where she argues that the one-caring always must seek to preserve the possibility of future relations with the cared-for.

72 I put "opinion" in quotes because, as Young-Bruehl argues, the opinions of anti-Semites may be less beliefs and more ideological strategies designed to negate and suppress human differences and to silence those who are victims of the anti-Semites' hatred. Elisabeth Young-Bruehl, *The Anatomy of Prejudices*, Cambridge, MA: Harvard University Press, 1996: 457–68.

73 As I noted above, conversation appears to presuppose that there is a possibility of conversants persuading each other to alter their prior positions. If one person says, "I believe what I believe and I absolutely refuse to alter my beliefs on religious (or epistemological or political) grounds," there is little point in trying to converse with this party. He has effectively taken himself out of the conversation. I, therefore, disagree with Ackerman's assertion that dialogue must avoid requiring that any person or group ever condemn their own personal morality. Bruce Ackerman, "Why Dialogue?," *The Journal of Philosophy* 86(1), January, 1989: 12ff. For dialogue to truly be dialogue, the interlocutors may have to agree upon principles which make them able to be persuaded, in principle, by their exchange.

74 See my earlier discussion of Govier in chapter 3.

75 I have argued for this definition of conflict of interest in "Addressing Conflicts of Interest," unpublished manuscript.

76 Card worries that patriarchal culture creates women who are dependent and in need of caring relationships. Claudia Card, "Rape as a Terrorist Institution," in R.G. Frey and Christopher W. Morris (eds), *Violence, Terrorism, and Justice*, Cambridge: Cambridge University Press, 1991: 299. Sarah Lucia Hoagland, "Some Thoughts About 'Caring'," in Claudia Card (ed.), *Feminist Ethics*, 1991: 246–63.

77 Friedman, *What Are Friends For?*, 1993: 207–30.

78 I use the language of rights with some trepidation. Some versions of rights theory ground rights in a concept of autonomy I think is too thin (see p. 115). However, since some female ethics seem to be arguing for a right to speak in one's own voice, I have adopted the terminology for purposes of contrasting female ethics with a dialogical ethic.

79 Socrates refers to "that part of us, whatever it is, which is concerned with the right and wrong." Plato, *Crito*, 1971: 47e–48a. If this part is the soul, then failing to consider thoughtfully claims regarding the right and the wrong is a death blow to the soul.

80 For a case of principled silence, consider Plato's *Cleitophon*. Since Cleitophon clearly has already decided that Socrates must be either a fraud (Socrates possesses no knowledge at all about virtue and therefore should not go around praising its acquisition) or a cheat (Socrates knows the truth but refuses to share it with others). There may be a

middle ground. Socrates knows something about what we must believe if we are to have any chance of acquiring knowledge. The dialogical ethic is an articulation of these requisite principles. However, since Cleitophon has foreclosed entirely this middle option—the option which gives us a reason to talk with others—there is no reason to talk with him. Socrates therefore appropriately remains silent. I am indebted to Herman Sinaiko for calling the *Cleitophon* to my attention and suggesting that this dialogue may be an exploration of the minimal conditions for conversation.

81 Of course, the problem of judgment remains. The party who thinks non-participation is warranted may be in error. He may have harmed another by making this judgment. This possibility of error will always be with us and constitutes a good reason for guaranteeing people a right of exit.

82 Plato, *Crito*, 1971: 49e.

83 Plato, *Crito*, 1971: 50a.

84 Plato, *Crito*, 1971: 50a–e.

85 See Plato, *Phaedo*, 1971: 97c–100e.

86 Plato, *Crito*, 1971: 50d–e.

87 Plato, *Crito*, 1971: 50e.

88 Plato, *Crito*, 1971: 45c–d.

89 Plato, *Crito*, 1971: 45a–46a.

90 Plato, *Crito*, 1971: 45d.

91 Plato, *Crito*, 1971: 50e–51a.

92 Plato, *Crito*, 1971: 51c.

93 Plato, *Crito*, 1971: 51b.

94 MacKinnon argues that women are silenced in a variety of ways even though their right of "free speech" is constitutionally guaranteed. Catherine A. MacKinnon, *Feminism Unmodified: Discourses on Life and Law*, Cambridge, MA: Harvard University Press, 1987: 206–13.

95 Plato, *Crito*, 1971: 51d.

96 Bertrand de Jouvenel, *On Power*, Indianapolis, IN: Liberty Fund, 1993: 334.

97 Plato, *Crito*, 1971: 53a.

98 Plato, *Crito*, 1971: 51d.

99 Socrates understands that some support from others may be necessary if they are to have truly viable options. Indeed, it might be argued that he is far more sensitive to this issue than some female ethicists. Kathleen League, for example, chides Gilligan for condemning women who do not feel that they had a real choice between carrying a baby full term or having an abortion. Gilligan accuses such women of a moral backsliding in which they fail to take responsibility for their choice. League suggests that women who, unlike Gilligan, are not white and middle class and who are lacking in a support network or in funds for childrearing may have just cause to complain that they had little choice with respect to the abortion. Kathleen League, "Individualism, Class, and the Situation of Care: An Essay on Carol Gilligan," *Journal of Social Philosophy* 24(3), Winter, 1993: 69–79.

100 See Noddings' discussion of Abraham in Noddings, *Caring*, 1984: 43.

101 Plato, *Crito*, 1971: 50a.

102 "Mutually disinterested men might turn out to be uninterested men, men incapable of comprehending the meaning of interest." Benjamin Barber, "Justifying Justice: Problems of Psychology, Politics, and Measurement in Rawls," in Norman Daniels (ed.), *Reading Rawls*, Oxford: Blackwell, 1975: 295.

103 Those lesbian ethics, which make a woman's being dependent upon her being in relation with other women, are just as subject to this charge as those female ethics defining a woman as mothering, nurturing, etc.

104 Carol Gilligan, "Exit-Voice Dilemma in Adolescent Development," in Carol Gilligan *et al.* (eds), *Mapping the Moral Domain*, Cambridge, MA: Harvard Center for the Study of Gender, Education, and Human Development, 1988: 143, where Gilligan notes that the availability of exit may weaken incentives to develop voice. Hirschman is aware of this problem as well but insists upon exit as an option of last resort.

105 For a discussion of this type of veto, see Jouvenel, *On Power*, 1993: footnote on p. 228.

106 I concur with Midgley who argues that children need more than opportunities to play and to be self-expressive: "Children need to have people around them who care enough about them to mind what they do and to give them guidance about it. They need a world-picture from which to start . . . . If a child grew up surrounded by people who never expressed any views to it and never minded what it did . . . it could never orient itself in life at all." Midgley, *Moral Judgements*, 1993: 72–3. Midgley sees part of the parental role as including helping children to make moral judgments and to learn to be accountable for these judgments.

107 Robin S. Dillon, "Toward a Feminist Conception of Self-Respect," in *Hypatia* 7(1), Winter, 1992: 59.

108 While Gilligan does not explicitly argue for taking care of the law, she does suggest that we should define care not merely as not hurting but also as taking responsibility for discussions of issues. This point is consistent with my thesis that we need to care for the logos. Gilligan, *Voice*, 1982: 148.

109 One might respond by arguing that when one person dies, we will simply shift our object of care. However, this argument would be rejected by female ethicists because care is supposed to be grounded in our appreciation of the unique particularity and *non-interchangeability* of our objects of care. So the argument still stands.

110 Plato, *Crito*, 1971: 52a–b.

111 Plato, *Crito*, 1971: 50e, 52d, 53e.

112 Plato, *Crito*, 1971: 54d.

113 Plato, *Crito*, 1971: 53a.

114 Plato, *Crito*, 1971: 52b.

115 Plato, *Crito*, 1971: 52c.

116 Plato, *Crito*, 1971: 52b.

117 Plato, *Crito*, 1971: 52e, 53b.

118 Plato, *Crito*, 1971: 52c.

119 Socrates does go beyond the walls of the city in the *Phaedrus* and *Lysis*. We would need to consider what constitutes leaving the city.

120 It is true that not all forms of consistency are praiseworthy. There is nothing especially meritorious about continual stubbornness, perennial viciousness, and invariably indiscriminate openness. However, the existence of non-meritorious forms of consistency does not show, as some female ethicists appear to think, that our ethics can dispense with any concern about integrity and the consistency inevitably involved in creating an identity and "whole life" for ourselves.

121 Plato, *Apology*, 1971: 28e, 33a.

122 Davion has argued against the idea that integrity presupposes fixed commitments. She contends that human beings undergo radical shifts in perspective and that being will to change is more a mark of integrity than fixity. While she is surely right that a fixed attachment to just any principle or point of view cannot constitute integrity, Davion skirts the difficult logical question of who is undergoing these radical shifts. Identifying change in someone or something always presupposes a continuity as well. What is the basis for this continuity? She does not say. Victoria M. Davion, "Integrity and Radical Change," in Claudia Card (ed.), *Feminist Ethics*, 1991: 180–92. By contrast, the dialogical ethic allows for revisions in our commitments while preserving

continuity in the form of commitment to those principles that make thoughtful engagement with others possible.

123 I am indebted to John Cornell for this striking formulation of this issue.

124 It is noteworthy that Plato's Socrates defends a notion of courage as the recognition and acceptance of an incalculable risk. Naas contrasts this risk with other thinkers' idea of calculable risk. Michael Naas, "Philosophy Bound: The Fate of Promethean Socrates," *Research in Phenomenology* 25, 1995: 121–41.

CONCLUSION

1 Kenneth Inada, "A Buddhist Response to the Nature of Human Rights," in Claude E. Welch, Jr. and Virginia A. Leary (eds), *Asian Perspectives on Human Rights*, Boulder, CO: Westview Press, 1990: 91–103; and reproduced in *Journal of Buddhist Ethics* 1(1) on the Worldwide Web.

2 Gilligan, *Voice*, 1982: 25–30.

3 Gilligan, *Voice*, 1982: 54.

4 Gilligan, *Voice*, 1982: 54–5.

5 Ibid.

6 Manning, *Speaking from the Heart*, 1992: 108–10.

7 Manning, *Speaking from the Heart*, 1992: 109.

8 Margaret Urban Walker, "Feminism, Ethics, and the Question of Theory," *Hypatia* 7(3), Summer, 1992: 28.

9 Walker, "Question of Theory," 1992: 28–35.

10 Noddings, *Caring*, 1984: 176–9; Manning, *Speaking from the Heart*, 1992: 99.

11 Again one's professional commitment to promoting a specific good or end is relevant here. But it is precisely such professionalism that some care ethics assault. See Noddings, *Caring*, 1984: 179.

12 Quote is attributed to Augustine by James J. O'Donnell (ed.), *Confessions*, Oxford: Clarendon Press, 1992: xxiii.

13 Noddings contends that if a cared-for should initiate violence, the caring person would still act to minimize any physical harm that might come to such a once-cared-for from whom one would now be alienated. Moreover, she seems to sanction a form of denial. The caring person would say,"My cared-fors would not do this." Noddings, *Caring*, 1984: 111.

14 The law is abstraction, and the caring party never listens to the voice of abstraction. Noddings, *Caring*, 1984: 44.

15 See, e.g., Noddings' rather cavalier dismissal of the law: "we have no ethical responsibility to cooperate with law or government when it attempts to involve us in unethical procedures" that are anathema to one-caring. Noddings, *Caring*, 1984: 55.

16 My colleague's answer accords with Noddings' position. Noddings argues that we must receive each party we affect in a caring fashion. We cannot shirk responsibility for an act such as theft by claiming that our victim is a bad person. Even evil people must be received in a caring fashion. The care ethic, therefore, would insist that the boy take responsibility for having failed to care for his victim. Noddings, *Caring*, 1984: 93.

17 Bell, *Rethinking Ethics*, 1993: 267.

18 Bell, *Rethinking Ethics*, 1993: 270.

19 Gilligan seems to have this sketchy quality in mind when she defines care as taking the time and energy to consider everything and not to decide quickly on the basis of one or two factors. Gilligan, *Voice*, 1982: 147.

20 It should also be noted that the applied ethics model of presenting case descriptions and then "solving" them using some decision algorithm inevitably tacitly collapses

the two conceptually distinct issues of: (1) the conditions that make an act ethically legitimate; and (2) the question of whether these conditions have in fact been met in a particular case. See pp. 142–6 for an argument that these two issues are distinct.

21 Aristotle, *Nicomachean Ethics*, 1941: 1094b24–27.

22 Hannah Arendt, *The Life of the Mind*, 1978: 176.

23 David Wiggins, "Deliberation and Practical Reason," in Amélie Oksenberg Rorty (ed.), *Essays on Aristotle's Ethics*, Berkeley, CA: University of California Press, 1980: 237. While I agree with Wiggins' assessment of many of the analytic approaches to ethics, I disagree with him over the role of principles. I think we need principles to orient our discussion of facts. Merely aiming at a rich interpretation does not solve the problem of judgment. Even Aristotle recognizes a role for absoluteness. Wiggins ignores the passages in which Aristotle argues that adultery, theft and murder are never right under any circumstances.

24 Rosemary Tong, *Feminine and Feminist Ethics*, 1993: 227.

25 Mary Daly celebrates hate as well as love because both are "e-motions connecting one's psyche with others and with the external world." I disagree. There is no necessary connection between the object rage gives itself and the real world. Rage and hatred are perfectly capable of imagining aggressors and slights. The frequent lack of connection is all the more reason to be on guard against this emotion. Mary Daly, *Pure Lust: Elemental Feminist Philosophy*, Boston, MA: Beacon Press, 1984: 200.

26 Tong, *Feminine Ethics*, 1993: 228.

27 Ibid.

BIBLIOGRAPHY

Books

Addelson, Kathryn Pyne *Impure Thoughts: Essays on Philosophy, Feminism, and Ethics*,Philadelphia, PA: Temple University Press, 1991.
—— *Moral Passages: Toward a Collectivist Moral Theory*, London: Routledge, 1994.
Alpern, Kenneth D. *The Ethics of Reproduction*, New York: Oxford University Press, 1992.
Arendt, Hannah *Eichmann in Jerusalem*, New York: Penguin Books, 1976.
—— *On Revolution*, New York: Viking Press, 1965.
—— *The Life of the Mind*, New York: Harcourt Brace Jovanovich, 1978.
Aristotle *Nicomachean Ethics*, ed. Richard McKeon, *The Basic Works of Aristotle*, New York: Random House, 1941.
Augustine *Confessions*, ed. James J. O'Donnell, Oxford: Clarendon Press, 1992.
Austen, Jane *Persuasion*, New York: Bantam Books, 1984.
Baier, Annette *Postures of the Mind: Essays on Mind and Morality*, Minneapolis, MN: University of Minnesota Press, 1985.
Bailie, Gil *Violence Unveiled: Humanity at the Crossroads*, New York: Crossroad, 1995.
Barber, Bernard *The Logic and Limits of Trust*, New Brunswick, NJ: Rutgers University Press, 1983.
Belenky, Mary *et al.* (eds) *Women's Ways of Knowing: The Development of Self, Voice and Mind*, New York: Basic Books, 1986.
Bell, Linda A. *Rethinking Ethics in the Midst of Violence: A Feminist Approach to Freedom*, Lanham, MD: Rowman & Littlefield, 1993.
Benhabib, Seyla *Situating the Self: Gender, Community and Postmodernism in Contemporary Ethics*, Cambridge: Polity Press, 1992.
Benhabib, Seyla and Cornell, Drucilla *Feminism as Critique: On the Politics of Gender*, Minneapolis, MN: University of Minnesota Press, 1987.
Benjamin, Jessica *The Bonds of Love: Psychoanalysis, Feminism and the Problem of Domination*, New York: Pantheon, 1988.
Berry, Mary Frances *The Politics of Parenthood: Child Care, Women's Rights, and the Myth of the Good Mother*, New York: Penguin, 1993.
Bettelheim, Bruno and Janowitz, Morris *Social Change and Prejudice*, Glencoe, IL: Free Press, 1964.
Bloom, Allan *Love and Friendship*, New York: Simon & Schuster, 1993.
Blum, Lawrence A. *Friendship, Altruism, and Morality*, London: Routledge & Kegan Paul, 1980.

—— *Moral Perception and Particularity*, Cambridge: Cambridge University Press, 1994.

Blustein, Jeffrey *Care and Commitment*, New York: Oxford University Press, 1991.

Booth, Wayne C. *The Company We Keep: An Ethics of Fiction*, Berkeley, CA: University of California Press, 1988.

Brabeck, Mary *Who Cares? Theory, Research, and Educational Implications of the Ethic of Care*, New York: Praeger, 1989.

Brandt, Richard B. *A Theory of the Right and the Good*, Oxford: Clarendon Press, 1979.

Butler, Judith *Bodies That Matter*, New York: Routledge, 1989.

—— *Gender Trouble: Feminism and the Subversion of Identity*, New York: Routledge, 1990.

Card, Claudia (ed.) *Feminist Ethics*, Lawrence, KS: University of Kansas Press, 1991.

Cavell, Stanley *The Claim of Reason*, New York: Oxford University Press, 1979.

Chesterton, G.K. *The Father Brown Omnibus*, New York: Dodd, Mead & Co., 1935.

Chodorow, Nancy *The Reproduction of Mothering: Psychoanalysis and the Sociology of Gender*, Berkeley, CA: University of California Press, 1978.

Clough, Patricia Ticineto *Feminist Thought*, Oxford: Blackwell, 1994.

Cole, Eve Browning and Coultrap-McQuin, Susan *Explorations in Feminist Ethics*, Bloomington, IN: Indiana University Press, 1992.

Daly, Mary *Pure Lust: Elemental Feminist Philosophy*, Boston, MA: Beacon Press, 1984.

Dancy, Jonathan, Moravcsik, J.M.E. and Taylor, C.C.W. *Human Agency: Language, Duty, and Value*, Stanford, CA: Stanford University Press, 1988.

Diprose, Rosalyn *The Bodies of Women: Ethics, Embodiment and Sexual Difference*, London: Routledge, 1994.

Ehrenreich, Barbara *The Hearts of Men: American Dreams and the Flight from Commitment*, New York: Anchor Press/Doubleday, 1983.

Eisenstein, Hester and Jardine, Alice (eds) *The Future of Difference*, New Brunswick, NJ: Rutgers University Press, 1985.

Faludi, Susan *Backlash: The Undeclared War Against American Women*, New York: Crown, 1991.

Feldstein, Richard and Roof, Judith (eds) *Feminism and Psychoanalysis*, Ithaca, NY: Cornell University Press, 1989.

Ferguson, Ann *Blood at the Root: Motherhood, Sexuality, and Male Dominance*, London: Pandora, 1989.

Fowles, John *The Collector*, New York: Dell Publishing, 1963.

Fraser, Nancy and Bartky, Sandra Lee (eds) *Revaluing French Feminism: Critical Essays on Difference, Agency, and Culture*, Bloomington, IN: Indiana University Press, 1992.

French, Rebecca Redwood *The Golden Yoke*, Ithaca, NY: Cornell University Press, 1995.

Frey, R.G. and Morris, Christopher W. (eds) *Violence, Terrorism, and Justice*, Cambridge: Cambridge University Press, 1991.

Friedman, Marilyn *What Are Friends For? Feminist Perspectives on Personal Relationships and Moral Theory*, Ithaca, NY: Cornell University Press, 1993.

Frye, Marilyn *The Politics of Reality: Essays in Feminist Theory*, Trumansberg, NY: Crossing Press, 1983.

Gambetta, Diego (ed.) *Trust: Making and Breaking Co-operative Relations*, New York: Blackwell, 1988.

Gandhi, Mahatma K. *Collected Works of Mahatma Gandhi*, Publications Division, Ministry of Broadcasting, Government of India, n.d.

Garry, Ann and Pearsall, Marilyn *Women, Knowledge and Reality*, Boston, MA: Unwin Hyman, 1989.

Gauthier, David *Morals by Agreement*, Oxford: Oxford University Press, 1986.

Gaylin, Willard *Caring*, New York: Alfred A. Knopf, 1976.

Gewirth, Alan *Human Rights: Essays on Justifications and Applications*, Chicago, IL: University of Chicago Press, 1982.

Gilligan, Carol *In A Different Voice: Psychological Theory and Women's Development*, Cambridge, MA: Harvard University Press, 1982.

Gilligan, Carol, Ward, Janie Victoria, Taylor, Jill McLean and Bardige, Betty (eds) *Mapping the Moral Domain*, Cambridge, MA: Harvard Center for the Study of Gender, Education and Human Development, 1988.

Girard, René *Things Hidden Since the Foundation of the World*, trans. Stephen Bann and Michael Metteer, Stanford, CA: Stanford University Press, 1987.

Glendon, Mary Ann *Rights Talk*, New York: Free Press, 1991.

Goodin, Robert E. *Protecting the Vulnerable*, Chicago, IL: University of Chicago Press, 1985.

Graham, George and Lafollette, Hugh *Person to Person*, Philadelphia, PA: Temple University Press, 1989.

Gray, Simon *Otherwise Engaged and Other Plays*, Harmondsworth: Penguin Books, 1975.

Green, Karen *The Woman of Reason: Feminism, Humanism, and Political Thought*, New York: Continuum Publishing, 1995.

Guyer, Paul (ed.) *The Cambridge Companion to Kant*, Cambridge: Cambridge University Press, 1992.

Habermas, Jürgen *Knowledge and Human Interests*, Boston, MA: Beacon, 1971.

Hampshire, Stuart *Morality and Conflict*, Cambridge, MA: Harvard University Press, 1983.

Hanen, Marsha and Nielsen, Kai (eds) *Science, Morality and Feminist Theory*, Calgary, Alta.: University of Calgary Press, 1987.

Harding, Sandra (ed.) *Feminism and Methodology*, Bloomington, IN: Indiana University Press, 1987.

Hare, R.M. *Moral Thinking*, Oxford: Clarendon Press, 1981.

Hekman, Susan *Gender and Knowledge: Elements of a Postmodern Feminism*, Cambridge: Polity Press, 1989.

Held, Virginia *Feminist Morality: Transforming Culture, Society, and Politics*, Chicago, IL: University of Chicago Press, 1993.

—— *Rights and Goods: Justifying Social Action*, Chicago, IL: University of Chicago Press, 1989.

Helgesen, Sally *The Female Advantage: Women's Ways of Leadership*, New York: Doubleday Currency, 1995.

—— *The Web of Inclusion: A New Architecture for Building Great Organizations*, New York: Doubleday Currency, 1995.

Heller, Thomas C., Sosna, Morton and Welberry, David E. (eds) *Reconstructing Individualism*, Stanford, CA: Stanford University Press, 1986.

Hillman, James *Loose Ends*, Dallas, TX: Spring Publications, 1975.

Hirschman, Albert O. *Exit Voice and Loyalty*, Cambridge, MA: Harvard University Press, 1972.

Hoagland, Sarah Lucia *Lesbian Ethics*, Palo Alto, CA: Institute of Lesbian Studies, 1988.

Hooft, Stan van *Caring: An Essay in the Philosophy of Ethics*, Nivot, CO: University Press of Colorado, 1995.

Hutter, Horst *Politics as Friendship: The Origins of Classical Notions of Politics in the Theory and Practice of Friendship*, Waterloo, Ont.: Wilfrid Laurier University Press, 1978.

Irigaray, Luce *The Ethics of Sexual Difference*, trans. Carolyn Burke and Gillian C. Gill, Ithaca, NY: Cornell University Press, 1993.

——*Je, Tu, Nous*, trans. Alison Martin, New York: Routledge, 1993.

Johnson, Peter *Frames of Deceit: A Study of the Loss and Recovery of Public and Private Trust*, Cambridge: Cambridge University Press, 1993.

Jouvenel, Bertrand de *On Power*, Indianapolis, IN: Liberty Fund, 1993.

Jung, C.G. *Memories, Dreams, Reflections*, ed. Aniela Jaffé, New York: Vintage Books, 1989.

Kant, Immanuel *Groundwork of the Metaphysic of Morals*, trans. H.J. Paton, New York: Harper & Row, 1964.

Kaufman, Gershon *Shame: The Power of Caring*, Cambridge: Schenkman Publishing, 1980.

Kittay, Eva Feder and Meyers, Diana (eds) *Women and Moral Theory*, Totowa, NJ: Rowman & Littlefield, 1987.

Kleinig, John *The Ethics of Policing*, Cambridge: Cambridge University Press, 1996.

Koehn, Daryl *The Ground of Professional Ethics*, London: Routledge, 1994.

Kupperman, Joel *Character*, New York: Oxford University Press, 1991.

Kurtines, William M. and Gewirtz, Jacob L. (eds) *Morality, Moral Behavior, and Moral Development*, New York: Wiley, 1984.

Larrabee, Mary Jeanne (ed.) *An Ethic of Care*, New York: Routledge, 1993.

Le Carré, John *The Little Drummer Girl*, New York: Alfred A. Knopf, 1983.

Livingston, Jennie *Paris is Burning*, produced and directed by Jennie Livingston, Academy Entertainment Inc., 1992.

Lloyd, Genevieve *The Man of Reason: "Male" and "Female" in Western Philosophy*, Minneapolis, MN: University of Minnesota Press, 1984.

Long, Grace D. Cumming *Passion and Reason: Womenviews of Christian Life*, Louisville, KY: Westminster/John Knox Press, 1993.

MacKinnon, Catherine A. *Feminism Unmodified: Discourses on Life and Law*, Cambridge, MA: Harvard University Press, 1987.

—— *Toward a Feminist Theory of the State*, Cambridge, MA: Harvard University Press, 1989.

Manning, Rita C. *Speaking from the Heart: A Feminist Perspective on Ethics*, Lanham, MD: Rowman & Littlefield, 1992.

Margulies, Alfred *The Empathic Imagination*, New York: Norton, 1989.

Marx, Werner *Towards a Phenomenological Ethics: Ethos and the Life-World*, New York: State University of New York Press, 1992.

Mauss, Marcel *The Gift: The Form and Reason for Exchange in Archaic Societies*, trans. W.D. Halls, London: Norton, 1990.

Mayeroff, Milton *On Caring*, New York: Harper & Row, 1971.

McMillan, Carol *Women, Reason and Nature*, Princeton, NJ: Princeton University Press, 1982.

Meyers, Diana Tietjens *Self, Society and Personal Choice*, New York: Columbia University Press, 1989.

—— *Subjection and Subjectivity: Psychoanalytic Feminism and Moral Philosophy*, New York: Routledge, 1994.

Midgley, Mary *Can't We Make Moral Judgements?*, New York: St Martin's Press, 1993.

Mill, John Stuart *On Liberty*, Indianapolis, IN: The Liberal Arts Press, 1956.

Minow, Martha *Making All the Difference*, Ithaca, NY: Cornell University Press, 1990.

Monegal, E. and Reid, A. (eds) *Borges: A Reader*, New York: E.P. Dutton, 1981.

Mussen, Paul and Eisenberg-Berg, Nancy *Roots of Caring, Sharing, and Helping*, San Francisco, CA: W.H. Freeman, 1971.

Noddings, Nel *Caring: A Feminine Approach to Ethics and Moral Education*, Berkeley, CA: University of California Press, 1984.

—— *Women and Evil*, Berkeley, CA: University of California Press, 1989.

Okin, Susan Moller *Justice, Gender, and the Family*, New York: Basic Books, 1989.

O'Neill, Onora *Constructions of Reason: Explorations of Kant's Practical Philosophy*, Cambridge: Cambridge University Press, 1989.

Plato *Euthyphro, Apology, Crito, Phaedo, Phaedrus*, trans. Harold North Fowler, Cambridge, MA: Loeb Classical Library, Harvard University Press, 1971.

——*Republic*, trans. Allan Bloom, New York: Basic Books, 1968.

——*Theatetus, Sophist*, trans. Harold North Fowler, Cambridge, MA: Loeb Classical Library, Harvard University Press, 1967.

——*Timaeus, Critias, Cleitophon, Menexenus, Epistles*, trans. Rev. R.G. Bury, Cambridge, MA: Loeb Classical Library, Harvard University Press, 1975.

Rajchman, John *Truth and Eros: Foucault, Lacan and the Question of Ethics*, New York: Routledge, 1991.

Rawls, John *A Theory of Justice*, Oxford: Oxford University Press, 1971.

Rich, Adrienne *Blood, Bread, and Poetry*, New York: Norton, 1986.

Rosen, Stanley *Plato's Statesman: The Web of Politics*, New Haven, CT: Yale University Press, 1995.

Ross, W.D. *The Right and the Good*, Indianapolis, IN: Hackett Publishing, 1988.

Ruddick, Sara *Maternal Thinking: Towards a Politics of Peace*, Boston, MA: Beacon Press, 1995.

Ryder, Sandra L. "Feminist Ethics," Ph.D. dissertation, DePaul University, Chicago, IL, 1994.

Sass, Louis A. *Madness and Modernism*, New York: Basic Books, 1992.

Segal, Robert A., Singer, June and Stein, Murray *The Allure of Gnosticism: The Gnostic Experience in Jungian Psychology and Contemporary Culture*, Chicago, IL: Open Court, 1995.

Shklar, Judith N. *Ordinary Vices*, Cambridge: Belknap Press, 1984.

Smart, Carol *Feminism and the Power of Law*, London: Routledge, 1989.

Smiley, Marion *Moral Responsibility and the Boundaries of Community: Power and Accountability From a Pragmatic Point of View*, Chicago, IL: University of Chicago Press, 1992.

Solomon, Robert C. *About Love: Reinventing Romance For Our Times*, Lanham, MD: Rowman & Littlefield, 1994.

Sondheim, Stephen *Sunday in the Park with George*, written and directed by James Lapine, produced by Thomas Z. Shepherd, RCA Records, New York, 1984.

Spence, Donald P. *Narrative Truth and Historical Truth*, New York: Norton, 1982.

Spivak, Gayatri Chakravorty *The Post-Colonial Critic: Interviews, Strategies, Dialogues*, ed. Sarah Harasym, New York: Routledge, 1990.

Stein, Edith *On the Problem of Empathy*, trans. Waltraut Stein, The Hague: Martinus Nijhoff, 1970.

Stendhal *The Red and The Black*, trans. C.K. Scott Moncrieff, New York: Modern Library, 1926.

Taylor, Charles *The Ethics of Authenticity*, Cambridge, MA: Harvard University Press, 1991.

Tong, Rosemarie *Feminine and Feminist Ethics*, Belmont, CA: Wadsworth, 1993.

Trebilcot, Joyce (ed.) *Mothering: Essays in Feminist Theory*, Totowa, NJ: Rowman & Allanheld, 1984.

Trinh, T. Minh-ha *Woman, Native, Other*, Bloomington, IN: Indiana University Press, 1989.

—— *Framer Framed*, New York: Routledge, 1992.

Tronto, Joan C. *Moral Boundaries: A Political Argument for an Ethic of Care*, New York: Routledge, 1993.

Tuan, Yi-Fu *Morality and Imagination*, Madison, WI: University of Wisconsin Press, 1989.

Updike, John *Trust Me*, New York: Fawcett Books, 1988.

Vetlesen, Arne Johan *Perception, Empathy, and Judgment: An Inquiry into the Preconditions of Moral Performance*, University Park, PA: Pennsylvania State University Press, 1994.

Weil, Andrew, *Spontaneous Healing*, New York: Alfred A. Knopf, 1995.

Wilder, Thornton *The Alcestiad or A Life in the Sun*, New York: Avon Books, 1979.

Williams, Bernard *Moral Luck*, Cambridge: Cambridge University Press, 1981.

Wolheim, Richard *The Thread of Life*, Cambridge, MA: Harvard University Press, 1984.

Wright, Richard *Native Son*, New York: Harper & Row, 1940.

Young, Iris Marion *Justice and the Politics of Difference*, Princeton, NJ: Princeton University Press, 1990.

Young-Bruehl, Elisabeth *The Anatomy of Prejudices*, Cambridge, MA: Harvard University Press, 1996.

Articles

Ackerman, Bruce "Why Dialogue?," *The Journal of Philosophy* 86(1), January, 1989: 5–22.

Adams, William E., Jr "Rediscovering Trust: Towards an Alternative Psychotherapy," *Pastoral Psychology* 33, Fall, 1984: 5–14.

Addelson, Kathryn Pyne "Moral Passages," *Women and Moral Theory*, ed. Eva Feder Kittay and Diana T. Meyers, Totowa, NJ: Rowman & Littlefield, 1987, 87–110.

Adler, Jonathan E. "Particularity, Gilligan and the Two-Levels View: A Reply," *Ethics* 100, October, 1989: 149–56.

Amundson, Ron "Disability, Handicap, and the Environment," *Journal of Social Philosophy* 23(1), Spring, 1992: 105–19.

Annis, David B. "The Meaning, Value, and Duties of Friendship," *American Philosophical Quarterly* 24(4), October, 1987: 349–56.

Auerbach, Judy, Blum, Linda, Smith, Vicki and Williams, Christine "Commentary on Gilligan's *In A Different Voice*," *Feminist Studies* 11(1), Spring, 1985: 149–61.

Bachrach, Peter "Interest, Participation, and Democratic Theory," *Participation in Politics*, Nomos XVI, ed. J. Roland Pennock and John W. Chapman, New York: Lieber-Atherton, 1975, 39–55.

Badhwar, Neera Kapur "Friendship, Justice, and Supererogation," *American Philosophical Quarterly* 22(2), April, 1985: 123–31.

Baier, Annette "Caring about Caring: A Reply to Frankfurt," *Synthèse* 53, November, 1982: 273–90.

—— "Some Thoughts on How We Moral Philosophers Live Now," *Monist* 67, October, 1984: 490–7.

—— "Sustaining Trust," *Tanner Lectures on Human Values, Lecture II*, ed. Grethe B. Peterson, vol. 13, Salt Lake City, UT: University of Utah Press, 1992, 136–74.

—— "Trust," *Tanner Lectures on Human Values*, ed. Grethe B. Peterson, vol. 13, Salt Lake City, UT: University of Utah Press, 1992, 107–36.

—— "Trust and Anti-Trust," *Ethics* 96, January, 1986: 231–60.

—— "What Do Women Want in a Moral Theory?," *Nous* 19(1), March, 1985: 53–63.

—— "Why Honesty is a Hard Virtue," *Identity, Character, and Morality: Essays in Moral Psychology*, ed. Owen Flanagan and Amélie Oksenberg Rorty, Cambridge, MA: MIT Press, 1990, 259–82.

Baker, Judith "Trust and Rationality," *Pacific Philosophical Quarterly* 68, March, 1987: 1–13.

Barber, Benjamin "Justifying Justice: Problems of Psychology, Politics, and Measurement in Rawls," *Reading Rawls*, ed. Norman Daniels, Oxford: Blackwell, 1975, 292–318.

Baron, Marcia "Impartiality and Friendship," *Ethics* 101, July, 1991: 836–57.

Bartky, Sandra "Self, Sympathy, and Solidarity: Reflections on the Problem of Difference in Feminist Theory," *Feminists Rethink the Self*, ed. Diana Tietjens Meyers, Boulder, CO: Westview Press, 1997, 177–96.

Bebeau, Muriel J. and Brabeck, Mary M. "Integrating Care and Justice Issues in Professional Moral Education: A Gender Perspective," *Journal of Moral Education* 16(3), October, 1987: 189–203.

Becker, Lawrence C. "Impartiality and Ethical Theory," *Ethics* 101, July, 1991: 698–700.

Benhabib, Seyla "The Generalized and the Concrete Other: The Kohlberg–Gilligan Controversy and Feminist Theory," *Praxis International* 5(4), January, 1986: 402–24.

Blake, William "The Human Abstract," *The Complete Poetry and Selected Prose of John Donne and The Complete Poetry of William Blake*, intro. Robert Silliman Hillyer, New York: Random House, 1941, 558.

Blum, Lawrence A. "Care," *Encyclopedia of Ethics*, eds Lawrence C. Becker and Charlotte B. Becker, New York: Garland, 1992.

—— "Gilligan and Kohlberg: Implications for Moral Theory," *An Ethic of Care*, ed. Mary Jeanne Larrabee, New York: Routledge, 1993, 49–68.

—— "Kant's and Hegel's Moral Rationalism: A Feminist Perspective," *Canadian Journal of Philosophy* 12(2), June, 1982: 287–302.

—— "Moral Perception and Particularity," *Ethics* 101, July, 1991: 701–25.

—— "Philosophy and the Values of a Multicultural Community," *Teaching Philosophy* 14(2), June, 1991: 127–34.

—— "Vocation, Friendship, and Community: Limitations of the Personal–Impersonal Framework," *Identity, Character, and Morality: Essays in Moral Psychology*, ed. Owen Flanagan and Amélie Oksenberg Rorty, Cambridge, MA: MIT Press, 1990, 173–97.

Blum, Larry, Horniak, Marcia, Housman, Judy and Scheman, Naomi "Altruism and Women's Oppression," *Philosophy and Women*, eds M. Bishop and M. Weinzweig, Belmont, CA: Wadsworth, 1979, 190–200.

Boatright, John R. "Fiduciary Duties and the Shareholder–Management Relation: Or, What's So Special About Shareholders?," *Business Ethics Quarterly* 4(4), October, 1994: 393–408.

Boxer, Sarah "Derailing the Train of Thought," review of *Cracking Up* and *Being a Character* by Christopher Bollas, in *New York Times Book Review* 10 September 1995: 40.

Braybrooke, David "The Meaning of Participation and of Demands for It: A Preliminary Survey of the Conceptual Issues," *Participation in Politics*, Nomos XVI, eds J. Roland Pennock and John W. Chapman, New York: Lieber-Atherton, 1975, 56–88.

Brison, Susan "On the Personal as Philosophical," *American Philosophical Association Newsletter on Feminism and Philosophy* 95(1), Fall, 1995: 37–40.

Broughton, John M. "Women's Rationality and Men's Virtues: A Critique of Gender Dualism in Gilligan's Theory of Moral Development," *Social Research* 50(3), Autumn, 1983: 597–642.

Brumbaugh, Robert "Plato's Relation to the Arts and Crafts," *Facets of Plato's Philosophy*, ed. W.H. Werkmeister, Amsterdam: van Gorcum, 1976, 40–9.

Buckley, Jorunn Jacobsen "Sex, Suffering and Incarnation," *The Allure of Gnosticism*, eds Robert A. Segal, June Singer and Murray Stein, Chicago, IL: Open Court, 1995, 94–106.

Bulkeley, Kelly "Psychological and Spiritual Development in Childhood," *Religious Studies Review* 21(2), April, 1995: 86–90.

Calhoun, Cheshire "Justice, Care, Gender Bias," *The Journal of Philosophy* 85(9), September, 1988: 451–63.

—— "Responsibility and Reproach," *Ethics* 99, 1989: 389–406.

Card, Claudia "Caring and Evil," *Hypatia* 5(1), Spring, 1990: 101–08.

—— "Gender and Moral Luck," *Identity, Character, and Morality: Essays in Moral Psychology*, eds Owen Flanagan and Amélie Oksenberg Rorty, Cambridge, MA: MIT Press, 1990, 199–218.

—— "Lesbian Ethics," *Encyclopedia of Ethics*, eds Lawrence C. Becker and Charlotte B. Becker, New York: Garland, 1992, 694.

—— "Rape as a Terrorist Institution," *Violence, Terrorism, and Justice*, eds R.G. Frey and Christopher W. Morris, Cambridge: Cambridge University Press, 1991, 299.

—— "The Feistiness of Feminism," *Feminist Ethics*, ed. Claudia Card, Lawrence, KS: University of Kansas Press, 1991, 3–31.

Chaifetz, Renee W. "Entry 2: Metropolitan Diary," *The New York Times* 20 August 1995, sect. 1: 17.

Chodorow, Nancy "Gender, Relation, and Difference in Psychoanalytic Perspective," *The Future of Difference*, eds Hester Eisenstein and Alice Jardine, New Brunswick, NJ: Rutgers University Press, 1985, 3–19.

Cocks, Joan "Worldless Emotions: Some Critical Reflections on Radical Feminism," *Politics and Society* 13(2), 1984: 37.

Code, Lorraine "Experience, Knowledge, and Responsibility," *Feminist Perspectives in Philosophy*, eds Morwenna Griffiths and Margaret Whitford, Bloomington, IN: Indiana University Press, 1988, 187–204.

Cottingham, John "Ethics of Self-Concern," *Ethics* 101, 1991: 798–817.

Dancy, Jonathan "Caring about Justice," *Philosophy* 67, October, 1992: 447–66.

—— "Supererogation and Moral Realism," *Human Agency: Language, Duty, and Value*, eds Jonathan Dancy, J.M.E. Moravscik and C.C.W. Taylor, Stanford, CA: Stanford University Press, 1988, 170–88.

Dauenhauer, Bernard P. "Ricoeur and Political Identity," *Philosophy Today* 39(1), Spring, 1995: 47–55.

David, Marian "On the Roles of Trustworthiness and Acceptance," *Grazer Philosophische Studien* 40, 1991: 93–107.

Davion, Victoria M. "Pacifism and Care," *Hypatia* 5(1), Spring, 1990: 90–100.

—— "Integrity and Radical Change," *Feminist Ethics*, ed. Claudia Card, Lawrence, KS: University of Kansas Press, 1991, 180–92.

Dees, Richard H. "Trust and Tolerance," unpublished paper, St Louis University, 1995.

Deigh, John "Impartiality: A Closing Note," *Ethics* 101, 1991: 858–64.

—— "Morality and Personal Relations," *Person to Person*, eds George Graham and Hugh LaFollette, Philadelphia, PA: Temple University Press, 1989, 106–23.

Deutsch, Sarah "Dreams of Inclusion: Gender, Race, and Narratives of the Frontier," unpublished paper, Clark University, 1994.

Dhanda, Meena "Openness, Identity and Acknowledgement of Persons," *Knowing the Difference: Feminist Perspectives in Epistemology*, eds Kathleen Lennon and Margaret Whitford, London: Routledge, 1994, 249–64.

Dietz, Mary "Citizenship with a Feminist Face: The Problem with Maternal Thinking," *Political Theory* 13(1), February, 1985: 19–37.

Dillon, Robin S. "Care and Respect," *Explorations in Feminist Ethics: Theory and Practice*, eds Eve Browning Cole and Susan Coultrap-McQuin, Bloomington, IN: Indiana University Press, 1992, 69–81.

—— "Toward a Feminist Conception of Self-Respect," *Hypatia* 7(1), Winter, 1992: 52–69.

Donoghue, Denis "The Politics of Homosexuality," *The New York Times Book Review* 20 August 1995: 3, 26.

Dostal, Robert J. "The World Never Lost: The Hermeneutics of Trust," *Philosophical Phenomenological Research* 47, March, 1987: 413–34.

Eisenberg, Nancy and Lennon, Roger "Sex Differences in Empathy and Related Capacities," *Psychological Bulletin* 94(1), 1983: 100–31.

English, Jane "What Do Grown Children Owe Their Parents?," *Having Children*, eds Onora O'Neill and William Ruddick, New York: Oxford University Press, 1979, 351–6.

Emanuel, Ezekiel J. "Review of *Prescribing Our Future: Ethical Challenges in Genetic Counseling*," eds Dianne M. Bartels, Bonnie S. LeRoy and Arthur L. Caplan, *Ethics and Behavior* 4(1), 1994: 71–2.

Eugene, Toinette M. "Sometimes I Feel Like a Motherless Child: The Call and Response for a Liberational Ethic of Care by Black Feminists," *Who Cares? Theory, Research, and Educational Implications of the Ethic of Care*, ed. Mary Brabeck, New York: Praeger, 1989, 45–62.

Feinberg, Joel "Feminism and Political Theory," *Symposium in Ethics* 99, January, 1989: 219–406.

Ferguson, Ann "A Feminist Aspect Theory of the Self," *Women, Knowledge and Reality: Explorations in Feminist Philosophy*, eds Ann Garry and Marilyn Pearsall, Boston, MA: Unwin Hyman, 1989, 93–107.

Finifter, Ada W. "The Friendship Group as a Protective Environment for Political Deviants," *American Political Science Review* 68, June, 1974: 607–25.

Fisher, Linda "Feminist Theory and the Politics of Inclusion," *Journal of Social Philosophy* 21(2–3), Fall/Winter, 1990: 174–83.

Flanagan, Owen "A Reply to Lawrence Kohlberg," *Ethics* 92, April, 1982: 528–32.

—— "Virtue, Sex, and Gender: Some Philosophical Reflections on the Moral Psychology Debate," *Ethics* 92, April, 1982: 499–512.

Flanagan, Owen and Jackson, Kathryn "Justice, Care, and Gender: The Kohlberg–Gilligan Debate Revisited," *Ethics* 97(3), 1987: 622–37.

Flax, Jane "Postmodernism and Gender Relations in Feminist Theory," *Feminism/Postmodernism*, ed. Linda J. Nicholson, New York: Routledge, 1990, 39–62.

Ford, Maureen Rose and Lowrey, Carol Rotter "Gender Differences in Moral Reasoning: A Comparison of the Use of Justice and Care Orientations," *Journal of Personality and Social Psychology* 50(4), 1986: 777–83.

Fraser, Nancy "Talking about Needs: Interpretive Contests as Political Contests in Welfare-State Societies," *Ethics* 99, January, 1989: 291–313.

—— "The Abuses and Disabuses of French Discourse Theories for Feminist Politics," *Revaluing French Feminism*, eds Nancy Fraser and Sandra Bartky, Bloomington, IN: Indiana University Press, 1992, 177–94 .

Fraser, Nancy and Nicholson, Linda J. "Social Criticism without Philosophy: An Encounter between Feminism and Postmodernism," *Feminism/Postmodernism*, ed. Linda J. Nicholson, New York: Routledge, 1990, 19–38.

Friedman, Marilyn "Beyond Caring: The De-Moralization of Gender," *An Ethic of Care*, ed. Mary Jeanne Larrabee, New York: Routledge, 1993, 258–73.

—— "Care and Context in Moral Reasoning," *Women and Moral Theory*, eds Eva Feder Kittay and Diana T. Meyers, Totowa, NJ: Rowman & Littlefield, 1987, 190–204.

—— "Feminism and Modern Friendship: Dislocating the Community," *Ethics* 99, January, 1989: 275–90.

—— "The Practice of Partiality," *Ethics* 101, July, 1991: 818–35.

—— "The Social Self and the Partiality Debates," *Feminist Ethics*, ed. Claudia Card, Lawrence, KS: University of Kansas Press, 1991, 161–79.

—— "'They Lived Happily Ever After': Sommers on Women and Marriage," *Journal of Social Philosophy* 21(2–3), Fall/Winter, 1990: 57–65.

Frye, Marilyn "Some Reflections on Separatism and Power," *Sinister Wisdom* 6, Summer, 1978:30–9.

Gallop, Jane "The Monster in the Mirror: The Feminist Critic's Psychoanalysis," *Feminism and Psychoanalysis*, eds Richard Feldstein and Judith Roof, Ithaca, NY: Cornell University Press, 1989, 13–24.

Gauthier, Jeff "Sexist Agency, Morality, and Self-Ignorance," *Michigan Feminist Studies* 6, Fall, 1991: 109–18.

Gewirth, Alan "Ethical Universalism and Particularism," *Journal of Philosophy* 85(6), June, 1988: 283–302.

Gilligan, Carol "Exit-Voice Dilemmas in Adolescent Development," *Mapping the Moral Domain*, eds Carol Gilligan, Janie Victoria Ward and Jill McLean Taylor, with Betty Bardige, Cambridge, MA: Harvard Center for the Study of Gender, Education, and Human Development, 1988, 141–57.

League, Kathleen "Individualism, Class, and the Situation of Care: An Essay on Carol Gilligan," *Journal of Social Philosophy* 24(3), Winter, 1993: 69–79.

Liedtka, Jeanne M. "Feminist Morality and Competitive Reality: A Role for an Ethic of Care?," *Business Ethics Quarterly* 6(2), April, 1996: 179–200.

Lorber, Judith, Coser, Rose Laub, Rossi, Alice S. and Chodorow, Nancy "On *The Reproduction of Mothering*: A Methodological Debate," *Signs* 6(3), 1981: 482–514.

Lugones, Maria C. "Playfulness, 'World'-Travelling, and Loving Perception," *Hypatia* 2(2), 1987: 3–19.

Lyons, Nona Plessner "Two Perspectives: On Self, Relationships, and Morality," *Harvard Educational Review* 53(2), May, 1983: 125–45.

McDonald, Julie "Thin Examples of Moral Dilemmas," *Social Theory and Practice* 19(2), Summer, 1993: 225–37.

MacKinnon, Catherine A. "Feminism, Marxism, Method, and the State: Toward Feminist Jurisprudence," *Feminism and Methodology*, ed. Sandra Harding, Bloomington, IN: Indiana University Press, 1987.

—— "Sexuality, Pornography, and Method: Pleasure under Patriarchy," *Ethics* 99, January, 1989: 314–46.

Manning, Rita "Just Caring," *Explorations in Feminist Ethics: Theory and Practice*, eds Eve Browning Cole and Susan Coultrap-McQuin, Bloomington, IN: Indiana University Press, 1992: 45–54.

—— "Review of Mary Jeanne Larabee, *An Ethic of Care*; Virginia Held, *Feminist Morality*; Joan C. Tronto, *Moral Boundaries: A Political Argument for an Ethic of Care*," *American Philosophical Association Newsletter on Feminism and Philosophy* 94(1), Fall, 1994: 68–71.

Mansbridge, Jane "The Limits of Friendship," *Participation in Politics*, eds J. Roland Pennock and John W. Chapman, New York: Lieber-Atherton, 1975, 246–75.

Martin, Bill "Interpretation and Responsibility: Excavating Davidson's Ethical Theory," unpublished paper, DePaul University, 1995.

Martin, Mike W. "Rationalization and Responsibility: A Reply to Whisner," *Journal of Social Philosophy* 23(2), Fall, 1992: 176–84.

Mason, Andrew "Gilligan's Conception of Moral Morality," *Journal for the Theory of Social Behaviour* 20(2), 1990: 167–79.

Meyers, Diana Tietjens "Moral Reflection: Beyond Impartial Reason," *Hypatia* 8(3), Summer, 1993: 21–47.

—— "Personal Autonomy and the Paradox of Feminine Socialization," *The Journal of Philosophy* 84(11), 1987: 619–28.

—— "Personal Autonomy or the Deconstructed Subject? A Reply to Hekman," *Hypatia* 7(1), 1992: 124–32.

—— "Social Exclusion, Moral Reflection, and Rights," *Law and Philosophy* 12, 1993: 217–32.

—— "The Socialized Individual and Individual Autonomy: An Intersection Between Philosophy and Psychology," *Women and Moral Theory*, eds Eva Feder Kittay and Diana T. Meyers, Totowa, NJ: Rowman & Littlefield, 1987, 139–53.

—— "The Subversion of Women's Agency in Psychoanalytic Feminism: Chodorow, Flax, Kristeva," *Revaluing French Feminism*, eds Nancy Fraser and Sandra Bartky, Bloomington, IN: Indiana University Press, 1992, 136–61.

—— "In a Different Voice: Women's Conception of Self and of Morality," *The Future of Difference*, eds Hester Eisenstein and Alice Jardine, New Brunswick, NJ: Rutgers University Press, 1985, 274–317.

—— "Moral Orientation and Moral Development," *Women and Moral Theory*, eds Eva Feder Kittay and Diana T. Meyers, Totowa, NJ: Rowman & Littlefield, 1987, 19–33.

—— "Remapping the Moral Domain: New Images of the Self in Relationship," *Reconstructing Individualism*, eds Thomas C. Heller, Morton Sosna and David E. Wellbery, Stanford, CA: Stanford University Press, 1986, 237–52.

—— "Reply by Carol Gilligan," *Signs* 11(2), Winter, 1986: 324–33.

Godfrey, Joseph J. "Trust, the Heart of Religion: A Sketch," *American Catholic Philosophical Quarterly* 65, 1991: 157–67.

Goldman, Alvin I. "Empathy, Mind, and Morals," *Proceedings and Addresses of the American Philosophical Association* 66, 1992: 17–41.

Goodpaster, Kenneth E. and Holloran, Thomas E. "In Defense of a Paradox," *Business Ethics Quarterly* 4(4), October, 1994: 423–30.

Govier, Trudy "Distrust as a Practical Problem," *Journal of Social Philosophy* 23(1), Spring, 1992: 52–63.

—— "An Epistemology of Trust," *International Journal of Morality and Social Studies* 8, Summer, 1993: 155–74.

—— "Self-Trust, Autonomy, and Self-Esteem," *Hypatia* 8(1), Winter, 1993: 99–120.

—— "Tolerance and 'Dogmatism' in Morals," *Mind* 82, January, 1973: 108–10.

—— "Trust, Distrust, and Feminist Theory," *Hypatia* 7(1), Winter, 1992: 16–33.

Graham, Hilary "Caring: A Labour of Love," *A Labour of Love: Women, Work and Caring*, eds Janet Finch and Dulcie Groves, London: Routledge & Kegan Paul, 1983, 13–30.

Gunneman, Jon P. "Alchemic Temptations," *The Annual of the Society of Christian Ethics*, 1995: 3–18.

Gutmann, Amy "Communitarian Critics of Liberalism," *Philosophy and Public Affairs* 14, Summer, 1985: 308–22.

Haan, Norma "Hypothetical and Actual Moral Reasoning in a Situation of Civil Disobedience," *Journal of Personality and Social Psychology* 32(2), 1975: 255–70.

—— "Two Moralities in Action Contexts: Relationships to Thought, Ego Regulation, and Development," *Journal of Personality and Social Psychology* 36(3), 1978: 286–305.

Harding, Sandra "The Curious Coincidence of Feminine and African Moralities: Challenges for Feminist Theory," *Women and Moral Theory*, eds Eva Feder Kittay and Diana T. Meyers, Totowa, NJ: Rowman & Littlefield, 1987, 296–315.

Hardwig, John "In Search of an Ethics of Personal Relationships," *Person to Person*, eds George Graham and Hugh LaFollette, Philadelphia, PA: Temple University Press, 1989, 63–81.

—— "The Role of Trust in Knowledge," *Journal of Philosophy*, December, 1991: 693–708.

—— "Should Women Think in Terms of Rights?," *Ethics* 94, April, 1984: 441–55.

Held, Virginia "Birth and Death," *Ethics* 99, January, 1989: 362–88.

—— "Feminism and Moral Theory," *Women and Moral Theory*, eds Eva Kittay and Diana T. Meyers, Totowa, NJ: Rowman & Littlefield, 1987, 111–28.

—— "Non-Contractual Society: A Feminist View," *Science, Morality, and Feminist Theory*, eds Marsha Hanen and Kai Nielson, Calgary, Alta.: University of Calgary Press, 1987, 111–38.

—— "On the Meaning of Trust," *Ethics* 78, January, 1968: 156–9.

—— "Rights and the Ethics of Care," *American Philosophical Association Newsletter* 94(2), Spring, 1995: 41.

—— "The Obligation of Mothers and Fathers," *Mothering: Essays in Feminist Theory*, ed. Joyce Trebilcot, Totowa, NJ: Rowman & Allanheld, 1984, 7–20.

Herman, Barbara "Agency, Attachment, and Difference," *Ethics* 101, 1991: 775–97.

—— "Integrity and Impartiality," *The Monist* 66, 1983: 233–50.

—— "Obligation and Performance: A Kantian Account of Moral Conflict," *Identity, Character, and Morality: Essays in Moral Psychology*, eds Owen Flanagan and Amélie Oksenberg Rorty, Cambridge, MA: MIT Press, 1990, 311–37.

—— "The Practice of Moral Judgment," *The Journal of Philosophy* 82, 1985: 414–36.

Hill, Thomas, Jr "The Importance of Autonomy," *Women and Moral Theory*, eds Eva Feder Kittay and Diana T. Meyers, Totowa, NJ: Rowman & Littlefield, 1987, 129–38.

Hoagland, Sarah Lucia "Lesbian Ethics and Female Agency," *Explorations in Feminist Ethics: Theory and Practice*, eds Eve Browning Cole and Susan Coultrap-McQuin, Bloomington, IN: Indiana University Press, 1992, 156–64.

—— "Some Concerns About Nel Noddings' *Caring*," *Hypatia* 5(1), Winter, 1990: 109–26.

—— "Some Thoughts About 'Caring'," *Feminist Ethics*, ed. Claudia Card, Lawrence, KS: University of Kansas Press, 1991, 246–63.

—— "Some Thoughts About Heterosexualism," *Journal of Social Philosophy*, Fall/Winter, 1990: 98–107.

—— "Why Lesbian Ethics?," *Hypatia* 7(4), Fall, 1992: 195–206.

Hoffman, Martin "Empathy, Its Limitations and Its Role in Comprehensive Moral Theory," *Morality, Moral Behavior, and Moral Development*, eds William M. Kurtines and Jacob L. Gewirtz, New York: Wiley, 1984, 283–302.

Horsburgh, H.J.N. "The Ethics of Trust," *Philosophical Quarterly* 10, October, 1960: 343–54.

Houston, Barbara "Prolegomena to Future Caring," *Who Cares? Theory, Research, and Educational Implications of the Ethic of Care*, ed. Mary Brabeck, New York: Praeger, 1989, 84–100.

—— "Rescuing Womanly Virtues: Some Dangers of Moral Reclamation," *Science, Morality, and Feminist Theory*, eds Marsha Hanen and Kai Nielsen, Calgary, Alta.: University of Calgary Press, 1987, 237–62.

Hutter, Horst "Impartiality and Ethical Theory," *Symposium in Ethics* 101, 1991: 698–864.

Inada, Kenneth "A Buddhist Response to the Nature of Human Rights," eds Claude E. Welch, Jr and Virginia A. Leary, *Asian Perspectives on Human Rights*, Boulder, CO: Westview Press, 1990, 91–103; online version of *Journal of Buddhist Ethics* reproduced in 1(1) Worldwide Web.

Jackson, W.M. "Rules Versus Responsibility in Morality," *Public Affairs Quarterly* 3, April, 1989: 27–40.

Jaggar, Alison M. "Feminist Ethics: Projects, Problems, Prospects," *Feminist Ethics*, ed. Claudia Card, Lawrence, KS: University of Kansas Press, 1991, 78–104.

Kaminer, Wendy "Feminism's Third Wave: What Do Young Women Want?," *The New York Times Book Review* 4 June 1995: 3, 22–3.

Kaplan, Laura Duhan "Woman as Caretaker: An Archetype That Supports Patriarchal Militarism," *Hypatia* 9(2), Spring, 1994: 123–33.

Katzenstein, Mary Fainsod and Laitin, David D. "Politics, Feminism, and the Ethics of Caring," *Women and Moral Theory*, eds Eva Feder Kittay and Diana T. Meyers, Totowa, NJ: Rowman & Littlefield, 1987, 261–81.

Kekes, John "Morality and Impartiality," *American Philosophical Quarterly* 18(4), October, 1981: 295–303.

—— "Shame and Moral Progress," *Midwest Studies in Philosophy* 13, 1988: 282–96.

Kenny, Anthony "Aristotle on Moral Luck," *Human Agency: Language, Duty, and Value*, eds Jonathan Dancy, J.M.E. Moravscik and C.C.W. Taylor, Stanford, CA: Stanford University Press, 1988, 105–19.

Kerber, Linda *et al.* "On *In A Different Voice*: An Interdisciplinary Forum," *Signs* 11(2), 1986: 304–33.

Kersting, Wolfgang "Politics, Freedom and Order: Kant's Political Philosophy," *The Cambridge Companion to Kant*, ed. Paul Guyer, Cambridge: Cambridge University Press, 1992, 342–66.

Kidder, Paulette "Gadamer and the Platonic *Eidos*," *Philosophy Today* 39(1), Spring, 1995: 83–92.

Kimmelman, Michael "With Henri Cartier-Bresson, Surrounded by his Peers," *The New York Times*, sect. 2, 20 August 1995: 28.

King, Jonathan B. "Prisoner's Paradoxes," *Journal of Business Ethics* 7, 1988: 475–87.

Kittay, Eva Feder "In Whose Different Voice?," *The Journal of Philosophy* 88(11), 1991: 645–6.

Koehn, Daryl "A Role for Virtue Ethics in the Analysis of Business Practice," *Business Ethics Quarterly* 5(3), July, 1995: 533–40.

—— "Book Review: Francis Fukuyama's *Trust*," *Journal of Online Ethics* 1(2) at website http://www.depaul.edu/ethics.

—— "With a Different Ear: Hearing Gilligan Anew," *Southwest Philosophy Review* 10(1), January, 1994: 77–86.

Kohlberg, Lawrence "A Reply to Owen Flanagan and Some Comments on the Puka–Goodpaster Exchange," *Ethics* 92(3), April, 1982: 513–28.

Kohlberg, Lawrence and Gilligan, Carol "The Adolescent as a Philosopher: The Discovery of the Self in a Postconventional World," *Daedalus* 100, 1971: 1051–86.

Kolnai, Aurel "Forgiveness," *Proceedings of the Aristotelian Society* 1974: 91–106.

Kourany, Janet A. "Philosophy in a Different Voice," *The Journal of Philosophy* 88(10), 1991: 557–67.

Kracher, Beverly "Rights and Care in Business," unpublished manuscript, Creighton University, 1994.

Kroeger-Mappes, Joy "The Ethic of Care *vis-à-vis* the Ethic of Rights: A Problem for Contemporary Moral Theory," *Hypatia* 9(3), Summer, 1994: 108–31.

Kupperman, Joel "Ethics for Extraterrestrials," *American Philosophical Quarterly* 28(4), 1991: 311–20.

Kuykendall, Eleanor H. "Toward an Ethic of Nurturance: Luce Irigaray on Mothering and Power," *Mothering*, ed. Joyce Trebilcot, Totowa, NJ: Rowman & Allanheld, 1984, 263–74.

Ladd, John "The Ethics of Participation," *Participation in Politics*, Nomos XVI, eds J. Roland Pennock and John W. Chapman, New York: Lieber-Atherton, 1975, 98–125.

—— "Work and Self-Respect," *Ethical Theory and Business*, eds Tom L. Beauchamp and Norman E. Bowie, Englewood Cliffs, NJ: Prentice–Hall, 1988, 275–9.

Michalos, Alex C. "The Impact of Trust on Business, International Security and the Quality of Life," *Journal of Business Ethics* 9, 1990: 619–38.

Midgley, Mary "Homunculus Trouble, Or, What is Applied Philosophy?," *Journal of Social Philosophy* 21(1), Spring, 1990: 5–15.

Minow, Martha "Equalities," *The Journal of Philosophy* 88(11), 1991: 633–44.

Moody-Adams, Michele M. "Gender and the Complexity of Moral Voices," *Feminist Ethics*, ed. Claudia Card, Lawrence, KS: University of Kansas Press , 1991, 195–212.

Moravcsik, J.M.E. "The Perils of Friendship and Conceptions of the Self," *Human Agency: Language, Duty, and Value*, eds Jonathan Dancy, J.M.E. Moravcsik and C.C.W. Taylor, Stanford, CA: Stanford University Press, 1988, 133–51.

Murphy, Jeffrie G. "Forgiveness and Resentment," *Virtues and Values: An Introduction to Ethics*, ed. Joshua Halberstom, Englewood Cliffs, NJ: Prentice–Hall, 1988, 124–34.

Mussen, Paul and Eisenberg-Berg, Nancy "Cognition, Moral Judgment, Role-Taking, and Empathy," *Roots of Caring, Sharing, and Helping: The Development of Prosocial Behavior in Children*, San Francisco, CA: W.H. Freeman, 1977, 109–38.

Naas, Michael "Philosophy Bound: The Fate of Promethean Socrates," *Research in Phenomenology* 25, 1995: 121–41.

Noddings, Nel "Educating Moral People," *Who Cares? Theory, Research, and Educational Implications of the Ethic of Care*, ed. Mary Brabeck, New York: Praeger, 1989, 216–32.

—— "Feminist Fears in Ethics," *Journal of Social Philosophy* 21(2, 3), Fall/Winter, 1990: 29–32.

—— "A Response," *Hypatia* 5(1), Spring, 1990: 120–26.

Norris, Stephen P. "Trust and Deferential Belief," *Proceedings of the Forty-sixth Annual Meeting of the Philosophy of Education Society in 1990*, Normal, IL: Philosophy of Education Society, 1990: 235–8.

Nunner-Winkler, Gertrud "Two Moralities? A Critical Discussion of an Ethic of Care and Responsibility Versus an Ethic of Rights and Justice," *Morality, Moral Behavior and Moral Development*, eds William M. Kurtines and Jacob L. Gewirtz, New York: Wiley, 1984, 348–61.

Oakes, Guy "The Sales Process and the Paradoxes of Trust," *Journal of Business Ethics* 9, 1990: 671–9.

Okin, Susan Moller "Justice and Gender," *Philosophy and Public Affairs* 16, 1987: 42–72.

—— "Reason and Feeling in Thinking about Justice," *Ethics* 99, January, 1989: 229–49.

O'Neill, Onora "Kantian Approaches to Some Famine Problems," *Ethics and Public Policy*, eds Tom L. Beauchamp and Terry P. Pinkard, Englewood Cliffs, NJ: Prentice–Hall, 1983, 205–19.

Ostrom, Victor R. "Faithfulness," *Paraclete* 36, 1992: 20–3.

Øverenget, Einar "Heidegger and Arendt: Against the Imperialism of Privacy," *Philosophy Today* 39(4), Winter, 1995: 430–44.

Paterson, Katherine "Family Values," review of *The Moral Compass* and *The Book of Virtues for Young People*, by William J. Bennett, in *The New York Times Book Review* 15 October 1995: 32.

Paul, Jeffrey "Substantive Social Contracts and the Legitimate Basis of Political Authority," *Monist* 66(4), 1983: 517–28.

Piper, Adrian M.S. "Impartiality, Compassion, and Modal Imagination," *Ethics* 101, July, 1991: 726–57.

—— "Xenophobia and Kantian Rationalism," *The Philosophical Forum* 24(1–3), Fall–Spring, 1992–3: 188–232.

Puka, Bill "Ethical Caring and Development: Pros, Cons, and Possibilities," *Inquiries into Values: The Inaugural Session of the International Society for Value Inquiry*, ed. Sander H. Lee, Lewiston, NY: Edwin Meese Press, 1988, 99–113.

—— "The Liberation of Caring: A Different Voice for Gilligan's 'Different Voice'," *Hypatia* 5(1), Spring, 1990: 58–82; repr. in Mary Jeanne Larrabee (ed.), *An Ethic of Care*, New York: Routledge, 1993, 215–39.

Putnam, Daniel "Relational Ethics and Virtue Theory," *Metaphilosophy* 22(3), July, 1991: 231–8.

Quinn, Philip L. "Political Liberalisms and Their Exclusions of the Religious," *Proceedings and Addresses of the American Philosophical Association* 69(2) November, 1995: 35–56.

Raugust, Mary C. "Feminist Ethics and Workplace Values," *Explorations in Feminist Ethics: Theory and Practice*, ed. Eve Browning Cole and Susan Coultrap-McQuin, Bloomington, IN: Indiana University Press, 1992, 125–30.

Roochnik, David L. "Socrates' Use of the Techne-Analogy," *Essays on the Philosophy of Socrates*, ed. Hugh H. Benson, Oxford: Oxford University Press, 1992, 185–97.

Ross, Alex "In Music, Though, There Were No Victories," *The New York Times* sect. 2, 20 August 1995: 25.

Ruddick, Sara "Maternal Thinking," *Feminist Studies* 5(2), 1980: 342–67.

Scaltsas, Patricia Ward "Do Feminist Ethics Counter Feminist Aims?," *Explorations in Feminist Ethics*, eds Eve Browning Cole and Susan Coultrap-McQuin, Bloomington, IN: Indiana University Press, 1992, 15–26.

Sharpe, Virginia A. "Justice and Care: The Implications of the Kohlberg–Gilligan Debate for Medical Ethics," *Theoretical Medicine* 13(4), 1992: 295–318.

Shrage, Laurie "Should Feminists Oppose Prostitution?," *Ethics* 99, January, 1989: 347–61.

Sichel, Betty A. "Morality and Development: A Response to Gilligan's 'New Maps of Development'," *Proceedings of the Thirty-eighth Annual Meeting of the Philosophy of Education Society in 1982*, Normal, IL: Philosophy of Education Society, 1982: 70–4.

Silvers, Anita "Reconciling Equality to Difference: Caring (F)or Justice For People With Disabilities," *Hypatia* 10(1), Winter, 1995: 30–55.

Slote, Michael "Morality Not a System of Imperatives," *American Philosophical Quarterly* 19(4), October, 1982: 331–40.

Sommers, Christina "Do These Feminists Like Women?," *Journal of Social Philosophy* 21(2, 3), Fall/Winter, 1990: 66–74.

Spelman, Elizabeth V. "The Virtue of Feeling and the Feeling of Virtue," *Feminist Ethics*, ed. Claudia Card, Lawrence, KS: University of Kansas Press, 1991, 213–32.

Stocker, Michael "Duty and Friendship: A Synthesis of Gilligan's Contrastive Moral Concepts," *Women and Moral Theory*, eds Eva Feder Kittay and Diana T. Meyers, Totowa, NJ: Rowman & Littlefield, 1987, 56–68.

—— "Friendship and Duty: Some Difficult Relations," *Identity, Character, and Morality: Essays in Moral Psychology*, eds Owen Flanagan and Amélie Oksenberg Rorty, Cambridge, MA: MIT Press, 1990, 219–33.

—— "The Schizophrenia of Modern Ethical Theories," *The Journal of Philosophy* 73 (14), August, 1976: 453–66

—— "Values and Purposes: The Limits of Teleology and the Ends of Friendship," *The Journal of Philosophy* 78(12), December, 1981: 747–65.

Sunstein, Cass R. "Introduction: Notes on Feminist Political Thought," *Ethics* 99, January, 1989: 219–28.

Taylor, F. Kraü and Rey, J.H. "The Scapegoat Motif in Society and its Manifestations in a Therapeutic Group," *International Journal of Psychoanalysis* 34, 1953: 253–64.

Thomas, Laurence "Trust, Affirmation, and Moral Character: A Critique of Kantian Morality," *Identity, Character, and Morality: Essays in Moral Psychology*, eds Owen Flanagan and Amélie Oksenberg Rorty, Cambridge, MA: MIT Press, 1990, 235–57.

Tronto, Joan C. "Beyond Gender Difference to a Theory of Care," *Signs* 12(4), 1987: 644–63.

Ungerson, Clare "Why Do Women Care?," *A Labor of Love: Women, Work, and Caring*, eds Janet Finch and Dulcie Groves, London: Routledge & Kegan Paul, 1983, 31–49.

Verbrugge, Lois "The Structure of Adult Friendship Choices," *Social Forces* 56(2), 1977: 576–97.

Vermazen, Bruce "Aesthetic Satisfaction," *Human Agency: Language, Duty, and Value*, eds Jonathan Dancy, J.M.E. Moravcsik and C.C.W. Taylor, Stanford, CA: Stanford University Press, 1988, 201–18.

Vreeke, G.J. "Gilligan on Justice and Care: Two Interpretations," *Journal of Moral Education* 20(1), 1991: 33–46.

Waithe, Mary Ellen "Twenty-three Hundred Years of Women Philosophers: Toward a Gender Undifferentiated Moral Theory," *Who Cares? Theory, Research, and Educational Implications of the Ethic of Care*, ed. Mary Brabeck, New York: Praeger, 1989, 3–16.

Walker, James C. "In a Diffident Voice: Cryptoseparatist Analysis of Female Moral Development," *Social Research* 50(3), Autumn, 1983: 665–95.

Walker, Margaret Urban "Feminism, Ethics, and the Question of Theory," *Hypatia* 7(3), Summer, 1992: 23–38.

—— "Moral Particularity," *Metaphilosophy* 18(3–4), July/October, 1987: 171–85.

—— "Moral Understandings," *Hypatia* 4 (2), Summer, 1989: 15–28.

—— "Partial Consideration," *Ethics* 101, July, 1991: 758–74.

Walsh, W.H. "Pride, Shame, and Responsibility," *The Philosophical Quarterly* 20(78), January, 1970: 1–13.

Walzer, Michael "Are There Limits to Liberalism?," *The New York Review of Books* 42(16), 19 October 1995: 28–31.

Westmoreland-White, Michael L. "Setting the Record Straight: Christian Faith, Human Rights, and the Enlightenment," *Annual of the Society of Christian Ethics*, ed. Harlan Beckley, Baltimore, MD: Georgetown University Press, 1995, 75–96.

Whisner, William "Rationalization, Self-Deception, and the Demise of Practical Moral Reason," *Journal of Social Philosophy* 23(2), 1992: 157–75.

Wicks, Andrew C., Gilbert, Daniel R. Jr and Freeman, R. Edward "A Feminist Reinterpretation of the Stakeholder Concept," *Business Ethics Quarterly* 4(4), October, 1994: 475–98.

Wiggins, David "Deliberation and Practical Reason," *Essays on Aristotle's Ethics*, ed. Amélie Oksenberg Rorty, Berkeley, CA: University of California Press, 1980, 221–40.

Young, Iris Marion "Impartiality and the Civil Public: Some Implications of Feminist Critiques of Moral and Political Theory," *Feminism as Critique: On the Politics of Gender*, eds Seyla Benhabib and Drucilla Cornell, Minneapolis, MN: University of Minnesota Press, 1986, 56–76.

—— "Is Male Gender Identity the Cause of Male Domination?," *Mothering*, ed. Joyce Trebilcot, Totowa, NJ: Rowman & Allanheld, 1984, 129–46.

—— "Polity and Group Difference: A Critique of the Ideal of Universal Citizenship," *Ethics* 99, January, 1989: 250–74.

Zappone, Katherine E. "Is There a Feminist Ethic?," *Ethics and the Christian*, ed. Seán Freyne, Dublin: Columbia Press, 1991, 110–26.

NAME INDEX

Addelson, Kathryn Pyne, 171n19
Alcestis (literary character), 71, 72
Arendt, Hannah, 75, 101, 118, 172n39, 186n43
Aristotle, 9, 10, 36, 43, 62, 161
Augustine, 157
Austen, Jane, 67–9

Baier, Annette, 1, 2, 4, 10, 15, 122; on difference, 86–7; on mistrust, 83–5; and particularity, 98; on public/private realms, 97; on trust, 80–3, 88, 90, 183n18
Bell, Linda, 5
Benhabib, Seyla, 7–8, 101
Benjamin, Jessica, 53, 58
Berlin, Isaiah, 187n58
Blum, Lawrence, 165n10, 171n29, 172n33
Bok, Sissela, 83
Booth, Wayne, 63
Borges, J.L., 20
Buber, Martin, 43
Buckley, Jorunn, 72

Card, Claudia, 5, 127
Chesterton, G.K., 69
Cleitophon, 189n80
Cousin William (Persuasion), 68
Crito: and child rearing, 130–2; and consequences, 103; and consistency, 106–7; and differences of opinion, 109–12; and individuality, 142–7; and law, 129–32; and relativism, 121–2; and truth, 104–6; and unjust actions, 119

Daly, Mary, 192n25
Davion, Victoria M., 190n122
Dillon, Robin, 140

Elliot, Anne (Persuasion), 67–8
Elliot, William (Persuasion), 67–9

Fackenheim, Emil, 150
Father Brown (literary character), 69–70
Fowles, John, 48
Friedman, Marilyn, 7, 114, 127, 184n2
Frye, Marilyn, 48

Gandhi, Mahatma, 93
Gaylin, Willard, 10
Gewirth, Alan, 41–2
Gilligan, Carol, 1–4, 10, 14, 122; autonomy and the self, 47; on care and community, 28–30, 173n48; and child rearing, 139; definition of care, 23–6; and Demeter myth, 41–3, 49; on abstract reasoning, 164n4, 164n5; on ethics of trust, 80; example of Heinz and the druggist, 21, 151–4; and intimate relations, 25; on justice ethics, 37; and law, 34; on particular cases, 31–4; on right of exit, 138–9; on rights, 51–2, 73, 164n3; and selfishness, 22, 170n16; tenets of care ethics, 21–2; on violence, 36, 37
Goodin, Robert, 10
Govier, Trudy, 4, 15, 122; and conflict of interests, 126; on difference, 87; on mistrust, 83–5; and particularity, 98; and public/private realms, 97; role of institutions, 91–3; on trust, 80–3, 88, 183n18

SUBJECT INDEX

adolescent trust, 89-90
autonomy, 120, 140-1; ethics of care, 44-50; Gilligan on, 47; Kant on, 47; Noddings on, 45-7

broad empathy, 57-8
business ethics, 32-4

care, ethics of: autonomy and the self, 44-50; and community, 28-30; contrasted with particular
cases, 30; contrasted with professional and business ethics, 32-4; contrasted with virtue ethics, 37; definition of care, 23-6; and Demeter myth, 41-3; and dialogical ethics, 122-3, 149; and dimunition of responsibility, 44; expression in formal terms, 38-40; and intimate relations, 25; inadequate self-suspicion of, 40-1; and law, 34-8; principle tenets of, 21-3; and prioritization of needs, 30; problems with, 26-52; problems with particular cases, 30-4; and professionalism, 24; and projection, 30; respect for individualism, 22; and selfishness, 44-7; and sympathy, 26, and violence, 36
character, 66-70
child rearing: and dialogical ethics, 120, 141, 157-61; differences between female ethics and dialogical ethics, 157-61; Gilligan on, 139; and law, 129-32, 139-41; Noddings on, 139; Ruddick on, 127, 139; Socrates on, 120, 130-2, 139
children's literature, 45

community, 8-9, 11, 45, 50; and care ethics, 28-30, 125
criminality, 135
critical dialogical value, 110-12, 161; law and child rearing, 130, 140; and unjust actions, 117-19

dialogical ethics, 4, 16, 100-49; and autonomy, 120; basic tenets of, 109-49; and child rearing, 120, 141, 157-61; and closure, 107-8; and consequences, 103; and consistency, 106-7; contrasted to ethics of empathy, 147-8; contrasted to female ethics, 103-8, 151-63; and differences of opinion, 109-12, 123-4; example of Heinz and the druggist, 151-4; and the Holocaust, 125-6; improvements to female ethics, 120-8; and individuality, 126-7, 142-9; and law, 128, 129-36, 139-42; limits on interpersonal communication, 17-18, 124-6; and male ethics, 18; and motivation, 103-4; and practical deliberation, 121; prevention of violence, 136-8; and relativism, 120-2; similarities to female ethics, 101-2; student-professor relations, 156-7; and teleology, 112-16; and truth, 104-6; and unjust actions, 117-19, 128-9
Demeter myth, 1-3, 41-3, 49, 90, 127
difference, 7, 55-7, 86-8

empathy, ethic of, 53-79; and dialogical ethics, 147-8; disciplining children, 72-3; inadequate self-suspicion of, 77; and law, 72-4; and openness, 61-4;

214

portrayed in Austen's *Persuasion*, 67-9;
principle tenets of, 53-79; problem of
character, 66-70; problem of finitude,
65-6; problem of responsibility, 70-3;
problem of scope, 64-5; problems with,
59-75; and respect for others, 78; view
of self, 59-61
existentialism, 96

female ethics: central tenets of, 5-9; child-
parent relationship, 157-61; and
closure, 108; and community, 8-9, 11,
12-13; contrasted to dialogical ethics,
103-8; 151-63; contrasted to feminist
ethics, 4-5; contrasted to rights-based
ethics, 6-8; and ethics of care, 20-52;
example of Heinz and the druggist,
151-4; improvements offered through
dialogical ethics, 120-8; and judgment,
100; and needs, 13-14; and practical
deliberation, 121; prevention of
violence, 137; and principles, 100-1;
and public/private realms, 11-13;
reliance on imagination, 8; and rights,
14; similarities to dialogical ethics, 101-
2; student-professor relationship, 156-
7; teleological orientation of, 112-16
feminist ethics: contrasted to female ethics,
4-5
friendship, 46, 47; and dialogical ethics,
127; and ethics of trust, 87, 94

Holocaust, 90, 125-6

impartial reasoning, 54-9
infant trust, 88-9
individualism, 22; and dialogical ethics,
126-7; 142-9

justice ethics: contrasted to care ethics, 37

law: and care ethics, 34-8; and criminality,
139; and dialogical ethics, 128, 129-
36, 139-42; and ethics of empathy, 73-
5; and individuality, 142-7; revision of
and exit from, 133-6

male ethics: critiqued by Meyers, 54-6;
and dialogical ethics, 18; and ethics of
trust, 82; professional and business
ethics, 33

mature trust, 89-90
mother-child relationship, 38, 41-3 *see also*
Demeter myth
murder, 36
narcissism 90
needs: prioritization within ethic of care,
30

process-based teleology, 113-16
professional ethics, 9, 32-4, 141, 181n58
projection, 30, 41, 43

rationalization, 85-6
relativism, 120-2
Republic (Plato), 30
rights-based ethics, 6-8
right of exit, 133-6, 138-9, 160-1

selfishness, 44-7; Gilligan on, 22, 170n16
slavery, 143
substantive teleology, 113-16
sympathy, 26, 57

teleology, 112-16
theft, 36
trust, ethics of, 80-99; contrasted to ethics
of care and empathy, 97-9; and
dialogical ethics, 123, 148-9; and
existentialism, 96; and friendship, 87,
94; forms of trust, 88-91; and
judgment, 84; and law, 98; as matters
of policy, 93-6; and mistrust, 83-5;
principle tenets of, 81-3; problem of
difference, 86-8; problem of
rationalization, 85-6; and
public/private realms, 96-7; role of
institutions, 91-3; and self-suspicion,
94

utilitarianism, 55, 121, 169n9; private
determination of the good, 118

violence, 58-9, 71: prevention by
dialogical ethics, 136-8; Gilligan on,
36-7
virtue ethics, 9; compared to care ethics,
37; and Demeter myth, 42; and
openness, 62

willed trust, 94-5